DIFFICULT FREEDOM

Johns Hopkins Jewish Studies
Sander Gilman and Steven T. Katz, Series Editors

DIFFICULT FREEDOM

Essays on Judaism

Emmanuel Levinas

Translated by Seán Hand

Freedom on tablets of stone
(Tractate of Principles, 6.2)

The Johns Hopkins University Press · Baltimore

Originally published in France as *Difficile Liberté Essais sur le judaïsme*
© Editions Albin Michel, 1963 and 1976

English translation published 1990 by
The Johns Hopkins University Press
2715 North Charles Street
Baltimore, Maryland 21218-4319

Johns Hopkins Paperbacks edition, 1997
06 05 04 03 02 01 00 99 98 97   5 4 3 2 1

The Publishers wish to record their thanks to the French Ministry of
Culture for a grant towards the cost of translation.

Library of Congress Cataloging-in-Publication Data
Levinas, Emmanuel.
  [Difficile liberté. English]
  Difficult freedom: essays on Judaism / by Emmanuel Levinas:
  translated by Seán Hand.
     p.   cm. — (Johns Hopkins Jewish studies)
  Translation of: Difficile liberté.
  ISBN 0-8018-4074-0
  1. Judaism. 2. Judaism—20th century. I. Title. II. Series.
  BM45 L4213 1990
  296—dc20   90-31771
                                                          CIP

  ISBN 0-8018-5783-X (pbk.)

To
DOCTOR HENRI NERSON
A Friend
In memory of a teaching
which exalts that friendship

Contents

IV OPENINGS

V DISTANCES

VI HIC ET NUNC

VII SIGNATURE

Bibliographical Information

Publications in which the essays originally appeared:

First published in *Evidences*: Ethics and Spirit (27, 1952); The Diary of Léon Brunschvicg (2, 1949); Being a Westerner (17, 1951); Place and Utopia (10, 1950); Persons or Figures (11, 1950); A Voice on Israel (18, 1951); Simone Weil against the Bible (24, 1952); The State of Israel and the Religion of Israel (20, 1951).

First published in *Information Juive*: Religion and Tolerance (1960); The Meaning of History (1963); The Light and the Dark (1961); Heidegger, Gagarin and Us (1961); Assimilation Today (1954).

First published in *Les Nouveaux Cahiers*: Have You Reread Baruch? (7, 1966); Jacob Gordin (31, 1972–3).

First published in *L'Arche*: Jewish Thought Today (1961); Judaism and the Present (1969); How is Judaism Possible? (1959).

First published in *Les Cahiers de l'Alliance Israélite Universelle*: Reflections on Jewish Education (1951); For a Jewish Humanism (1956).

A Religion for Adults first published in *Tioumliline* (1957); Judaism in *Encyclopaedia Universalis*: Means of Identification in *Journées d'études sur l'identité juive*; A New Version of *Jesus Narrated by the Wandering Jew* in *La Terre Retrouvée* (1953); The Spinoza Case in *Trait d'Union* (1955–6); Poetry and the Impossible in *Bulletin de la société Paul Claudel* (1969); The Name of a Dog in *Celui qui ne peut pas se servir des mots*, a collection published in honour of Bram Van Velde (Montpellier, Fata Morgana, 1975); From the Rise of Nihilism to the Carnal Jew in a collective work, *From Auschwitz to Israel. Twenty years on*; Hegel and the Jew in *Bulletin of French*

Judaeo–Christian Friendship (1971); Antihumanism and Education in *Hamoré* (1973); Israel and Universalism in *Le Journal des Communeautés* (1958); Freedom of Speech in *Les Lettres Nouvelles* (51, 1957); Space is not One-dimensional in *Esprit* (1968).

Talks broadcast on 'Ecoute Israël': Loving the Torah more than God (29 April 1955); Judaeo–Christian Friendship (20 October 1961). Letter to *Le Monde*: The Struthof Case (17 July 1954). Monotheism and Language originated as a speech given at a meeting of the French Students' Union at the Mutualité, winter 1959; 'Between Two Worlds' as a paper given on 27 September 1959 to the second Colloquium of French-speaking Jewish Intellectuals, organized by the French section of the World Jewish Congress.

Judaism, Judaism and the Present, The State of Israel and the Religion of Israel, and Means of Identification are also published in *The Levinas Reader*. ed. Seán Hand (Oxford, Blackwell, 1989). Copyright © all the above translations Seán Hand 1989.

Translator's Note

Quotations from the Bible have been taken from the Collins
Revised Standard Version, and quotations from the Talmud come
from *The Babylonian Talmud*, under the editorship of Isidore
Epstein (London, Soncino Press, 1948).

French words have occasionally been retained in square brackets
in the English text, above all in order to show how Levinas is
elaborating a philosophical language that reveals the moral dimension present from the beginning in our physical being.

Foreword

The essays brought together in this volume were compiled over the years following the Liberation of France at the end of the Second World War. They bear witness to a Judaism that has been passed down by a living sense of tradition, one nourished by its reflections on stern texts that are more alive than life itself. These ancient texts, both biblical and rabbinic, not only attract the learned curiosity of philologists who, in looking into them, are already adopting a superior position. They respond to problems other than those of literary influence or dates. One must retain a keen ear: everything has perhaps been thought – before the Middle Ages covered the whole of Europe – by thinkers who were little concerned with developments, and who willingly hid, even from future historians, the sharp point of their real problems. Many of the pages you will read here attempt to uncover the difficult exegesis hidden beneath the apparent naivety of archaic commentaries, and to praise it in their own modest way.

In the aftermath of Hitler's exterminations, which were able to take place in a Europe that had been evangelized for fifteen centuries, Judaism turned inward towards its origins. Up to that point, Christianity had accustomed Western Judaism to thinking of these origins as having dried up or as having been submerged under more lively tides. To find oneself a Jew in the wake of the Nazi massacres therefore meant once more taking up a position with regard to Christianity, on another level again to the one sovereignly assumed by Jules Isaac.

But the return to origins immediately organized itself into a higher and less polemic theme. The experience of Hitler brought many Jews into fraternal contact with Christians who opened their hearts to them – which is to say, risked everything for their sake. In the face of the rise of the Third World, this memory remains precious – not because it allows one to revel in the emotions engendered, but because it reminds us of a neighbourly state which has lasted through history, the existence of a common language and of an action in which our antagonistic fates are shown to be complementary.

Thanks be to God, we are not going to offer up sermons on behalf of dubious crusades undertaken to 'link arms as believers' and unite 'as spiritualists' in the face of the rising tide of materialism. As if we should present a front against this Third World ravaged by hunger; as if the entire spirituality on earth did not reside in the act of nourishing; as if we need to salvage from a dilapidated world any other treasure than the gift of suffering through the hunger of the Other, a gift it none the less received. 'Of great importance is the mouthful of food' says Rabbi Johanan in the name of Rabbi Jose b. Kisma (Sanhedrin 103b). The Other's hunger – be it of the flesh, or of bread – is sacred; only the hunger of the third party limits its rights; there is no bad materialism other than our own. This first inequality perhaps defines Judaism. A difficult condition. An inversion of the apparent order. An inversion that is always on the point of recommencing. It is this which gives rise to the ritualism that leads the Jew to devote himself to service with no thought of reward, to accept a burden carried out at his own expense, a form of conduct involving both risks and perks. This is the original and incontestable meaning of the Greek word *liturgy*.

I
BEYOND
PATHOS

Let them not enter the Sanctuary drunk
(From Rachi's comment on Leviticus [10:2])

Ethics and Spirit

Boring Morality

Reading publications that define the social ideology of Christianity, or reviews such as *Esprit*, one could gain the impression that Christianity, even Catholicism, was moving towards a less realist interpretation of the dogma underlying the religious life of the faithful. Does not the authoritative exposé given recently by André Seigfried show that in certain Protestant churches religion has merged entirely with morality and social action?[1]

This impression is a complete illusion in the case of Catholicism. The recent promulgation of a new dogma shows the degree to which the Church remains faithful to a notion of the spirit that does not exclude the realist affirmation of irrational facts which draw their significance from some intimate and impenetrable experience. As a result we cannot discuss them. All the same, we should like to stress that for Catholics themselves other meanings can be attached to the spiritual. In fact, in a study on Catholicism, conducted with a rare nobility enlivened by the experience of all things modern, Professor Latreille, while showing the Church's vigilance in the discussions regarding the material and intellectual problems of the day, also recognizes the existence of 'two European types of Catholicism which are very different and sometimes vigorously opposed to one another'.[2] The one is Mediterranean, 'still close to the old ideal of *Christendom*, where a widespread popular practice, rooted in external, collective, traditional forms of devotion, maintains a horror of any religious dissidence, or concession to the liberalism and indifferentism of the State'. This first Catholicism 'would willingly reproach the second', the northern kind, 'for its temerity, suspecting it of sacrificing the integrity of doctrine by making concessions to an inadmissible modernism, in fact by being irenical and compromising in its dealings with other denominations who are ignorant of the characteristics and rights of the true Church'. And Latreille adds:

> In recent years, this move towards intransigence appears to have succeeded in bringing about a hardening of the Papacy's attitude towards those theologians suspected of favouring dreaded tendencies through their teaching or perhaps also through their presence in apostolic faculties considered too daring. (Encyclical humani generis, August 1950)[3]

Even in protestation, a similar movement of more rigorous orthodoxy appears to be taking shape. It is as if Christianity, having moved away from dogma and its realist interpretation, feels empty. Evidence of this can be seen in the book entitled *Protestantism*, published after the Liberation and bringing together several studies by Protestant theologians, professors and writers. Last winter a series of beautiful articles by M. R. Mehl, in *Le Monde*, confirmed the return to orthodoxy, or at least the nostalgia for such a return; the search for forms other than ethical to give to religious life and expression.

For a long time Jews thought that every situation in which humanity recognizes its religious progress finds in ethical relations its spiritual meaning – that is to say, its meaning for an adult. They consequently conceived of morality in a very vigorous way, feeling themselves attached to it as though to an inalienable heritage. Even in the nineteenth century, when Judaism entered the community of Western nations, it still claimed it as a *raison d'être*. It was convinced that it survived in order to preserve the teaching of the prophets in all its purity. In a world where, like material goods, spiritual values were offered to whoever wished to grow rich, morality meant it was worth remaining a poor Jew, even when one ceased to be a Jew who was poor.

And yet a long acquaintance with Western Christianity has created, even among Jews sincerely attached to Judaism, who have maintained through their family memories an emotional tie with the symbolism of Jewish life, a state of unease. Morality, social action, concern for justice – all that would be excellent. But it would be only morality! An earthly propaedeutic, too abstract to fill an inner life, too poor in figures of style to narrate the story of a Soul. Without the stuff of a literature or theatre. And, in fact, all that has ever given us is Psalms!

This Poor Nineteenth Century

This unease is not without cause, but it has nothing to do with Jewish morality.

Separated more and more from the rabbinical tradition and its exegeses, the morality offered in the Western temples no longer contained a message to justify the messenger. It more and more resembled the generous but general formulae of the European moral conscience. The European moral conscience did exist! It flourished in that happy period in which centuries of Christian and philosophical civilization had not yet revealed, in the Hitlerian adventure, the fragility of their works. Philosophical morality never seemed more conformist, or Israel's famous mission closer to its term.

And certainly the antiquity of the message, the existence of a Moses or an Isaiah in an age when Greece still wallowed in barbarism, sets the imagination racing. But historical worth cannot compensate for existing pointlessly. In the realm of the spirit, there are no automatic allowances to be claimed. Only a brilliant present can invoke its past merits without demeaning itself – or, if need be, can invent itself on the basis of them.

But did Jews at least continue to bring peoples a prophetic morality through the example of their lives? The virtues which, in the darkest periods of the Middle Ages, provoked the admiration of Christians of good faith, were shattered like the walls of the ghetto. Others replaced them but the Jews, in discovering certain freedoms, also took on much of the violence of the modern world. They joyfully espoused every form of nationalism, but equally burdened themselves with their quarrels and passions. Israel has not become worse than the surrounding world, whatever the anti-Semites say, but it has ceased to be better. The worst thing is that this was precisely one of its ambitions.

Perhaps, from that age on, the Jewish presence manifested itself more in the Israelites' participation in liberal and social movements – in the struggle for civil rights or true social justice – than in the sermons to be heard in emancipated synagogues. All these denigrators of tradition, all these atheists and rebels, unwittingly joined the divine tradition of intransigent justice which expiates blasphemy in advance. With these rebels, Judaism, which had scarcely been absorbed into the surrounding world, already opposed it on one level. But in this manifestation, it found itself deprived of its own language. Having nothing but will, it turned to a borrowed system of thought to understand itself. One cannot, in fact, be a Jew instinctively; one cannot be a Jew without knowing it. One must desire good with all one's heart and, at the same time, not simply desire it on the basis of a naive impulse of the heart. Both to maintain and to break this impulse is perhaps what constitutes the Jewish ritual. Passion mistrusts its pathos, and becomes and rebecomes *consci*ousness! Belonging to Judaism presupposes a ritual and a science. Justice is impossible to the ignorant man. Judaism is an extreme consciousness.

From this moment on, is it possible for a Jewish revival to operate under the sign of the Irrational, the Numinous, or the Sacramental? Here, in fact, are the religious categories we are looking for. We need a Saint Teresa of our own! Can one still be a Jew without Kierkegaard? Thankfully, we had Hassidism and the Kabbalah. Let us rest assured that one cannot be a Jew without having saints. Hassidism and Kabbalah are established in the Jewish soul only where that soul is full of talmudic science. This talmudic science is the continual unfolding of the ethical order, leading to the salvation of the individual soul. Ah! how the moralism of the nineteenth century, in spite of all its naivety, begins to shine anew in our dulled eyes. At least it had one thing to its credit: *it tried to interpret Judaism as a religion of the spirit*. This is an essential point, even if, in the eyes of a youth that has become familiar with the charm of myths and mysteries, this moralism seems anaemic and emptied of all specifically religious substance.

Spirit and Violence[4]

Nothing is more ambiguous than the term 'spiritual life'. Could we not make it more precise by excluding from it any relation to violence? But violence is not to be found only in the collision of one billiard ball with another, or the storm that destroys a harvest, or the master who mistreats his slave, or a totalitarian State that vilifies its citizens, or the conquest and subjection of men in war. Violence is to be found in any action in which one acts as if one were alone to act: as if the rest of the universe were there only to *receive* the action; violence is consequently also any action which we endure without at every point collaborating in it.

Nearly every causality is in this sense violent: the fabrication of a thing, the satisfaction of a need, the desire and even the knowledge of an object. Struggle and war are also violent, for the only element sought out in the Other is the weakness that betrays his person. But violence can also lie, in large part, in the poetic delirium and enthusiasm displayed when we merely offer our mouths to the muse who speaks through us; in our fear and trembling when the Sacred wrenches us out of ourselves; in the passion – call it love – that wounds our side with a perfidious arrow.

But is a cause without violence possible? Who welcomes without being shocked? Let mystics be reassured: nothing can shock reason. It collaborates with what it hears. Language acts without being subdued, even when it is the vehicle for an order. Reason and language are external to violence. They *are* the spiritual order. If morality must truly exclude violence, a profound link must join reason, language and morality. If religion is to coincide with spiritual life, it must be essentially ethical. Inevitably, a spiritualism of the Irrational is a contradiction. Adhering to the Sacred is infinitely more materialist than proclaiming the incontestable value of bread and meat in the lives of ordinary people.

The Jewish moralism of the nineteenth century based its negations on reason [*avait raison dans ses négations*]. In its naive respect for the scientism of the day, it excellently refused to confer any spiritual dignity on relations whose origins lay in magic and violence. For example, it perhaps threw suspicion on the idea of miracles solely in the name of scientific teaching. It is still the case that a miracle entails a degree of irrationality – not because it shocks reason, but because it makes no appeal to it. Spiritualizing a religion does not consist in judging one's experiences in the light of the scientific results of the day, but in understanding these very experiences as *links between intelligences*, links situated in the full light of consciousness and discourse. The intervention of the unconscious and, consequently, the horrors and ecstasies which it feeds – recourse to the magical action of the sacraments – all this is linked ultimately to violence.

Spirit and the Face

The banal fact of conversation, in one sense, quits the order of violence. This banal fact is the marvel of marvels.

To speak, at the same time as knowing the Other, is making oneself known to him. The Other is not only known, he is *greeted* [*salué*]. He is not only named, but also invoked. To put it in grammatical terms, the Other does not appear in the nominative, but in the vocative. I not only think of what he is for me, but also and simultaneously, and even before, I *am* for him. In applying a concept to him, in calling him this or that, I am already appealing to him. I do not only *know* something, I am also part of society. This *commerce* which the word implies is precisely action without violence: the agent, at the very moment of its action, has renounced all claims to domination or sovereignty, and is already exposed to the action of the Other in the way it waits for a response. Speaking and hearing become one rather than succeed one another. Speaking therefore institutes the moral relationship of equality and consequently recognizes justice. Even when one speaks to a slave, one speaks to an equal. What one says, the content communicated, is possible only thanks to this face-to-face relationship in which the Other counts as an interlocutor prior even to being known. One looks at a look. To look at a look is to look at something which cannot be abandoned or freed, but something which *aims* [*vise*] at you: it involves looking at the *face* [*visage*].

The face is not the mere assemblage of a nose, a forehead, eyes, etc.; it is all that, of course, but takes on the meaning of a face through the new dimension it opens up in the perception of a being. Through the face, the being is not only enclosed in its form and offered to the hand, it is also open, establishing itself in depth and, in this opening, presenting itself somehow in a personal way. The face is an irreducible mode in which being can present itself in its identity. A thing can never be presented personally and ultimately has no identity. Violence is applied to the thing, it seizes and disposes of the thing. Things *give*, they do not offer a face. They are beings without a face. Perhaps art seeks to give a face to things, and in this its greatness and its deceit simultaneously reside.

'You shall not kill'

Knowledge reveals, names and consequently classifies. Speech addresses itself to a face. Knowledge seizes hold of its object. It possesses it. Possession denies the independence of being, without destroying that being – it denies and maintains. The face, for its part, is inviolable; those eyes, which are absolutely without protection, the most naked part of the human body, none the less offer an absolute resistance to possession, an absolute resistance in which the temptation to murder is inscribed: the temptation of absolute negation. The Other is the only being that one can be tempted to kill. This temptation to murder and this impossibility of murder constitute the very vision of the face. To see a face is already to hear 'You shall not kill', and to hear 'You shall not kill' is to hear 'Social justice'. And everything I can hear [*entendre*] coming from God or going to God, Who is invisible, must have come to me via the one, unique voice.

'You shall not kill' is therefore not just a simple rule of conduct; it appears as the principle of discourse itself and of spiritual life. Henceforth, language is not only a system of signs in the service of a pre-existing system. Speech belongs to the order of morality before belonging to that of theory. Is it not therefore the condition for conscious thought?

Nothing, in fact, is more opposed to a relation with the face than 'contact' with the Irrational and mystery. The presence of the face is precisely the very possibility of understanding one another [*s'entendre*]. Inner life is defined, moves towards the single voice of the contract, and frees itself from the arbitrariness of our bad faith. The psychic fact receives from speech the power to be what it is. It is amputated from its unconscious prolongations which once transformed it into a mask and rendered its sincerity impossible. No more will thought be overrun by obscure and unconscious forces that subject it to a protean fate! We have entered the age of logic and reason!

In this way – and it, is after all, extraordinary – universality is established: a *self* [*moi*] can exist which is not a *myself* [*moi-même*]. This self, viewed face-on, is consciousness, existing by virtue of the fact that a sovereign self, invading the world naively – like 'a moving force', to use Victor Hugo's expression – perceives a face and the impossibility of killing. Consciousness is the impossibility of invading reality like a wild vegetation that absorbs or breaks or pushes back everything around it. The turning back on oneself of consciousness is the equivalent not of self-contemplation but of the fact of not existing violently and naturally, of speaking to the Other. Morality accomplishes human society. Can we ever gauge its miracle? It is something other than a coexistence of a multitude of humans, or a participation in new and complex laws imposed by the masses. Society is the miracle of moving out of oneself.

The violent man does not move out of himself. He takes, he possesses. Possession denies independent existence. To have is to refuse to be. Violence is a sovereignty, but also a solitude. To endure violence in enthusiasm and ecstasy and delirium is to be *possessed*. To know is to perceive, to seize an object – be it a man or a group of men – to *seize* a thing. Every experience of the world is at the same time an experience of self, possession and enjoyment of self [*jouissance de soi*]: it forms and nourishes me. The knowledge that makes us move out of ourselves is also like our slow absorption and digestion of reality. Reality's resistance to our acts itself turns into the *experience* of this resistance; as such, it is already absorbed by knowledge and leaves us alone with ourselves.

If 'know thyself' has become the fundamental precept of all Western philosophy, this is because ultimately the West discovers the universe within itself. As with Ulysses, its journey is merely the accident of a return. The *Odyssey*, in this sense, dominates literature. When a Gide recommends fullness of life and variety of experience as the fulfilment of freedom, he searches in freedom for the *experience* of freedom, not for the movement itself by which one moves out of oneself. It has to do with taking delight, experiencing oneself as a miraculous centre of radiance, and not with radiating.

Only the vision of the face in which the 'You shall not kill' is articulated does not allow itself to fall back into an ensuing complacency or become the experience of an insuperable obstacle, offering itself up to our power. For in reality, murder is possible, but it is possible only when one has not looked the Other in the face. The impossibility of killing is not real, but moral. The fact that the vision of the face is not an *experience*, but a moving out of oneself, a contact with another being and not simply a sensation of self, is attested to by the 'purely moral' character of this impossibility. A moral view [*regard*] measures, in the face, the uncrossable infinite in which all murderous intent is immersed and submerged. This is precisely why it leads us away from any experience or view [*regard*]. The infinite is given only to the moral view [*regard*]: it is not *known*, but is in *society* with us. The commerce with beings which begins with 'You shall not kill' does not conform to the scheme of our normal relations with the words, in which the subject knows or absorbs its object like a nourishment, the satisfaction of a need. It does not return to its point of departure to become self-contentment, self-enjoyment, or self-knowledge. It inaugurates the spiritual journey of man. A religion, for us, can follow no other path.

A Religion for Adults[1]

Common Language

When faced with Semites and Christians – who, according to Pius XI, are spiritually Semites – is it not superfluous to expound the thesis that places man above the natural order of things? They would learn nothing, if one wanted to teach them that man occupies an exceptional place in the world; that his situation is that of a dependent being; that this dependent being is sovereign in its very dependence, for it possesses not just any old dependence, but that of a creature; that this creaturely dependence does not exclude existing in the image of God; that education must maintain this society between man and God which has been instituted as a result of their resembling one another; and that, in a very large sense, education's goal is this society and is perhaps the very definition of man.

Like Jews, Christians and Muslims know that if the beings of this world are the results of something, man ceases to be just a result and receives 'a dignity of cause', to use Thomas Aquinas's phrase, to the extent that he endures the actions of the cause, which is external *par excellence*, divine action. We all in fact maintain that human autonomy rests on a supreme heteronomy and that the force which produces such marvellous effects, the force which institutes force, the civilizing force, is called God.

This common language which we rediscover spontaneously – and which here, at 1,600 metres, resonates in a particularly pure way – is not a source of uniquely academic satisfaction.

During the years when this language was confronted by the proud affirmation of energies at free play, and drowned out by the overflowing of purely natural forces, this common language has also been a common life. In front of the representatives of so many nations, some of whom have no Jews in their numbers, I should like to remind you of what the years 1933 to 1945 were like for the Jews of Europe. Among the millions of human beings who encountered misery and death, the Jews alone experienced a total dereliction.

11

They experienced a condition inferior to that of things, an experience of total passivity, an experience of Passion. Chapter 53 of Isaiah was drained of all meaning for them. Their suffering, common to them as to all the victims of the war, received its unique meaning from racial persecution which is absolute, since it paralyses, by virtue of its very intention, any flight, from the outset refuses any conversion, forbids any self-abandonment, any apostasy in the etymological sense of the term; and consequently touches the very innocence of the being recalled to its ultimate identity. Once again, Israel found itself at the heart of the religious history of the world, shattering the perspectives within which the constituted religions had enclosed themselves and re-establishing, in the most refined consciences, the link – which up until then had been incomprehensibly hidden – between present-day Israel and the Israel of the Bible. At the moment of this experience, whose religious range has for ever left its mark on the world, Catholics, whether secular, priests or monks, saved Jewish children and adults both in France and outside France, and on this very soil Jews menaced by racial laws heard the voice of a Muslim prince place them under his royal sovereignty.

I am reminded of a visit I once made, as part of a religious ceremony, to the church of Saint Augustine in Paris. It was at the beginning of the war, and my ears were still burning from the 'new morality' phraseology that for six years had been circulating in the press and in books. There, in a little corner of the church, I found myself placed beside a picture representing Hannah bringing Samuel to the Temple. I can still recall the feeling of momentarily returning to something human, to the very possiblity of speaking and being heard, which seized me at that moment. The emotion I experienced can be compared only with what I felt throughout the long months of fraternal detention spent in a Frontstalag in Brittany with the North African prisoners; or with my feelings in a Stalag in Germany when, over the grave of a Jewish comrade whom the Nazis had wanted to bury like a dog, a Catholic priest, Father Chesnet, recited prayers which were, in the absolute sense of the term, Semitic.

How can we hear the voice of Israel?

It is therefore useless within this precinct to recall the basic theses on man which unite us! The brief mention I made of them at the beginning would have been uncalled for if, by a sort of paradox of history, the philosophical anthropology of the most ancient of the monotheist religions did not seem outdated. It appears so because of its very ancientness. It appears so because of the Jewish people who teach it, but remains on the margins of the world political history, of which it has had the moral privilege to be the victim. In fact one generally thinks that the values of Judaism long ago entered into greater syntheses and that, in themselves, they represent mere stammerings set alongside the expression in spirit and in truth which they have received from the religions which Judaism engendered. One is subsequently allowed to present Judaism, stubbornly refusing to accept these new formulations, as a 'fossil', as a superstitious mode of thinking and living, proper to communities degraded by the miserable conditions of a victim, living in ghettos and mellahs.

Thus it is that the voice of Israel is at best heard in the world only as the voice of a precursor, as the voice of the Old Testament which – to use a phrase from Buber – the rest of us who are Jews have no reason to consider either a testament or old, or something to be situated in the perspective of the new. There is also another way to expose Judaism. For some time now, it has been revealed to the modern world in certain works which too easily retain the attention of Christians because they content themselves with generalities that are generous, seductive, declamatory, flattering and vague. They are too often greeted as the mystery and message of Israel. But that proves to what point this elementary generosity of the Jewish faith is unknown to the public at large.

Lest the union between men of goodwill which I desire to see be brought about only in a vague and abstract mode, I wish to insist here precisely on the *particular* routes open to Jewish monotheism. Their particularity does not compromise, but rather promotes universalism. For that reason, this monotheism must be sought in the Bible that is bathed by the sources in which, while being common to both Jewish and Christian tradition, it retains its specifically Jewish physiognomy. I have named the oral tradition of exegesis which crystallized in the Talmud and its commentaries. The *manner* which this tradition instituted constitutes rabbinic Judaism. Whatever the historical arguments in favour of its extreme ancientness – and they are weighty – the biblical canon, as received by the world, has been fixed by the upholders of this tradition. The Judaism with a historic reality – Judaism, neither more nor less – is rabbinic. The paths that lead to God in this Judaism do not cross the same landscapes as the Christian paths. If you had been shocked or amazed by that, you would have been shocked or amazed that we remain Jews before you.

Enthusiasm or Religious Majority?

For Judaism, the goal of education consists in instituting a link between man and the saintliness of God and in maintaining man in this relationship. But all its effort – from the Bible to the closure of the Talmud in the sixth century and throughout most of its commentators from the great era of rabbinical science – consists in understanding this saintliness of God in a sense that stands in sharp contrast to the numinous meaning of this term, as it appears in the primitive religions wherein the moderns have often wished to see the source of all religion. For these thinkers, man's possession by God, enthusiasm, would be consequent on the saintliness or the sacred character of God, the alpha and omega of spiritual life. Judaism has decharmed the world, contesting the notion that religions apparently evolved out of enthusiasm and the Sacred. Judaism remains foreign to any offensive return of these forms of human elevation. It denounces them as the essence of idolatry.

The numinous or the Sacred envelops and transports man beyond his powers and wishes, but a true liberty takes offence at this uncontrollable surplus. The numinous annuls the links between persons by making beings participate, albeit ecstatically, in a drama not brought about willingly by them, an order in which they founder. This somehow sacramental power of the Divine seems to Judaism to offend human freedom and to be contrary to the education of man, which remains *action on a free being*. Not that liberty is an end in itself, but it does remain the condition for any value man may attain. The Sacred that envelops and transports me is a form of violence.

Jewish monotheism does not exalt a sacred power, a *numen* triumphing over other numinous powers but still participating in their clandestine and mysterious life. The God of the Jews is not the survivor of mythical gods. Abraham, the father of believers, was the son of a seller of idols, according to one apologist. Profiting from the absence of Tereh, he apparently broke them all, saving the largest in order that it could assume, in the eyes of his father, responsibility for the massacre. But when Tereh came back he could not accept this incredible version, knowing that there is no idol in the world which can destroy the other idols. Monotheism marks a break with a certain conception of the Sacred. It neither unifies nor hierarchizes the numerous and numinous gods; instead it denies them. As regards the Divine which they incarnate, it is merely atheism.

Here, Judaism feels very close to the West, by which I mean philosophy. It is not by virtue of simple chance that the way towards the synthesis of the Jewish revelation and Greek thought was masterfully traced by Maimonides, who is claimed by both Jewish and Muslim philosophers; that a profound respect for Greek knowledge already fills the wise men of the Talmud; that education for the Jew merges with instruction and that the ignorant man can never really be pious! And one frequently encounters curious talmudic texts which try to present the nature of Israel's spirituality as something which lies in its intellectual excellence. They do this not through any Luciferian pride of reason, but because intellectual excellence is *internal* and the 'miracles' it makes possible do not at all wound, like thaumaturgy, the dignity of the responsible being; and above all because these 'miracles' do not ruin the conditions for action and effort. This is the reason, in the whole of Jewish religious life, for the importance of the exercise of intelligence – applied, of course, in the first instance, to the content of the Revelation, to the Torah. But the notion of the Revelation thereafter rapidly expands to include all essential knowledge.

One rabbinic apologue represents God teaching the angels and Israel. In this divine school the angels (intelligences that never falter but are devoid of malice) ask Israel, placed at the highest level, for the meaning of the divine word. Human existence, in spite of the inferiority of its onotological level – because of this inferiority, because of its torment, unease and self-criticism – is the true place in which the divine word encounters the intellect and loses the rest of its supposedly mystical virtues. But the apologue also wants to teach us that the truth of the angels is not of a different order to that of men, and that men accede to the divine word without ecstasy having to tear them away from their essence, their human nature.

The rigorous affirmation of human independence, of its intelligent presence to an intelligible reality, the destruction of the numinous concept of the Sacred, entail the risk of atheism. That risk must be run. Only through it can man be raised to the spiritual notion of the Transcendent. It is a great glory for the Creator to have set up a being who affirms Him after having contested and denied Him in the glamorous areas of myth and enthusiasm; it is a great glory for God to have created a being capable of seeking Him or hearing Him from afar, having experienced separation and atheism. A text from Tractate Taanith (page 5) provides a commentary to Jeremiah 2:13: 'for my people have committed two evils: they have forsaken me, the fountain of living waters, and hewed out cisterns for themselves, broken cisterns, that can hold no water'. It insists on the double transgression committed by idolatry. To ignore the true God is in fact only half an evil; atheism is worth more than the piety bestowed on mythical gods in which a Simone Weil can already distinguish the forms and symbols of the true religion. Monotheism surpasses and incorporates atheism, but it is impossible unless you attain the age of doubt, solitude and revolt.

The difficult path of monotheism rejoins the path of the West. One wonders, in fact, whether the Western spirit, philosophy, is not in the last analysis the position of a humanity that accepts the risk of atheism, if it must be held to ransom by its majority, but overcome it.

The Ethical Relation as a Religious Relation

From this point on, jealously guarding its independence but thirsting after God, how does Judaism conceive of humanity? How will it integrate the need for a virtually vertiginous freedom into its desire for transcendence? By experiencing the presence of God through one's relation to man. *The ethical relation* will appear to Judaism as an exceptional relation: in it, contact with an external being, instead of compromising human sovereignty, institutes and invests it.

Contrary to the philosophy that makes of *itself* the entry into the kingdom of the absolute and announces, in the words of Plotinus, that 'the soul will not go towards any other thing, but towards itself', and that 'it will therefore not be in any other thing, but in itself',[2] Judaism teaches us a *real* transcendence, a relation with Him Whom the soul cannot concern and without Whom the soul cannot, in some sense, hold itself together. All alone, the I finds itself rent and awry. This means that it discovers itself to be one who had already encroached on the Other, in an arbitrary and violent manner. Self-consciousness is not an inoffensive action in which the self takes note of its being; it is inseparable from a consciousness of justice and injustice. The consciousness of any natural injustice, of the harm caused to the Other, by my ego structure, is contemporaneous with my consciousness as a man. The two coincide.

The beginning of Genesis is, for a second-century commentator, less interested in what a man may expect than in what he must do. It is an object of astonishment: why does the Revelation begin with the account of Creation when God's commandments apply only to man? This astonishment is still to be found in the eleventh-century commentator Rachi, who for a thousand years now has been the way into the Bible for Jews throughout the world. And the ancient response that Rachi proposes consists in maintaining that, in order to possess the Promised Land, man must know that God created the earth. For without this knowledge, he will possess it only by usurpation. No rights can therefore ensue from the simple fact that a person needs *espace vital*. The consciousness of my I reveals no right to me. My freedom shows itself to be arbitrary. It appeals to an investiture. The 'normal' exercise of my ego, which transforms into 'mine' everything it can reach and touch, is put in question. To possess is always to receive. The Promised Land will never be in the Bible 'property' in the Latin sense of the term, and the farmer, at the moment of the first-born, will think not of his timeless link to the land but of the child of Aram, his ancestor, who was an *errant*.

It is not the legal status, however singular, of land property in the Old Testament that we need to invoke here, but the *self-consciousness* presiding over it, a consciousness in which the discovery of its powers is inseparable from the discovery of their illegitimacy. Self-consciousness inevitably surprises itself at the heart of a moral consciousness. The latter cannot be added to the former, but it provides its basic mode. To be oneself [*pour soi*] is already to know the fault I have committed with regard to the Other. But the fact that I do not quiz myself on the Other's rights paradoxically indicates that the Other is not a *new edition of myself*; in its Otherness it is situated in a dimension of height, in the ideal, the Divine, and through my relation to the Other, I am in touch with God.

The moral relation therefore reunites both self-consciousness and consciousness of God. Ethics is not the corollary of the vision of God, it is that very vision. Ethics is an optic, such that everything I know of God and everything I can hear of His word and reasonably say to Him must find an ethical expression. In the Holy Ark from which the voice of God is heard by Moses, there are only the tablets of the Law. The knowledge of God which we can have and which is expressed, according to Maimonides, in the form of negative attributes, receives a positive meaning from the moral 'God is merciful', which means: 'Be merciful like Him'. The attributes of God are given not in the indicative, but in the imperative. The knowledge of God comes to us like a commandment, like a *Mitzvah*. To know God is to know what must be done. Here education – obedience to the other will – is the supreme instruction: the knowledge of this Will which is itself the basis of all reality. In the ethical relation, the Other is presented at the same time as being absolutely other, but this radical alerity in relation to me does not destroy or deny my freedom, as philosophers believe. The ethical relation is anterior to the opposition of freedoms, the war which, in Hegel's view, inaugurates History. My neighbour's face has an alterity which is not allergic, but opens up the beyond. The God of heaven is accessible, without losing any of His Transcendence but without denying freedom to the believer. This intermediary sphere exists. The Talmud states it, in that apparently childish language that earns it, in the eyes of many who read it cursorily, the reputation of allying inextricable complications to a disarming naivety: 'God never came down from Sinai, Moses never ascended to heaven. But God folded back the heavens like a cover, covered Sinai with it, and so found Himself on earth without having even left heaven.' There is here a desacralization of the Sacred.

The Justice rendered to the Other, my neighbour, gives me an unsurpassable proximity to God. It is as intimate as the prayer and the liturgy which, without justice, are nothing. God can receive nothing from hands which have committed violence. The pious man is the just man. *Justice* is the term Judaism prefers to terms more evocative of sentiment. For love itself demands justice, and my relation with my neighbour cannot remain outside the lines which this neighbour maintains with various third parties. The third party is also my neighbour.

The ritual law of Judaism constitutes the austere discipline that strives to achieve this justice. Only this law can recognize the face of the Other which has managed to impose an austere role on its true nature. At no moment does the law acquire the value of a sacrament. In a remarkable passage in the Talmud, Rabbi Johanan Ben Zakkai is questioned by his pupils about the reasons for the rites concerning the lustral water in Numbers, and takes refuge behind the authority of the divine commandment. But he adds that, without this commandment, 'Contact with a dead person does not make one impure, nor does lustral water purify.' No intrinsic power is accorded to the ritual gesture, but without it the soul cannot be raised up to God.

The way that leads to God therefore leads *ipso facto* – and not in addition – to man; and the way that leads to man draws us back to ritual discipline and self-education. Its greatness lies in its daily regularity. Here is a passage in which three opinions are given: the second indicates the way in which the first is true, and the third indicates the practical conditions of the second. Ben Zoma said: 'I have found a verse that contains the whole of the Torah: "Listen O Israel, the Lord is our God, the Lord is One".' Ben Nanus said: 'I have found a verse that contains the whole of the Torah: "You will love your neighbour as yourself".' Ben Pazi said: 'I have found a verse that contains the whole of the Torah: "You will sacrifice a lamb in the morning and another at dusk".' And Rabbi, their master, stood up and decided: 'The law is according to Ben Pazi.'

The law is effort. The daily fidelity to the ritual gesture demands a courage that is calmer, nobler and greater than that of the warrior. We know the prophecy of Israel made by Balaam: 'See! this people rises up like a leopard, it stands up like a lion'. The talmudist does not hesitate to link this royal awakening to the sovereign power of a people capable of the daily ritual. The shudder of the leopard rising, but not rising under the yoke. The law for the Jew is never a yoke. It carries its own joy, which nourishes a religious life and the whole of Jewish mysticism.

In the Psalter in which the most nostalgic appeals so closely match the paternal presence of God, the plenitude of this consoling and saving presence which 'lacks nothing', and the glorification of His Kingdom, His Jurisdiction, His Legislation and His Law, Jews do not feel that they fall short of the horizons opened up by the Gospels. The harmony achieved between so much goodness and so much legalism constitutes the original note of Judaism. The Talmud measures with lucidity the height and apparent opposition, but also the real interdependence of the principles producing it. We cannot analyse here the ontological order that makes it possible, but nothing seems simpler or more authentic than the comingling of these principles within the same verse. The psalmist, in a striking way, associates the verse's profound human distress to a call made to the divine commandment, to the *Mitzvah*, to law: 'I am a sojourner on earth; hide not thy commandments from me' (Psalms 119:19) as he unites the intimate elation of the soul that thirsts after God with the austere vision of divine justice: 'My soul is consumed with longing for thy ordinances at all times' (Psalms 119:20).

Responsibility

The fact that the relationship with the Divine crosses the relationship with men and coincides with social justice is therefore what epitomizes the entire spirit of the Jewish Bible. Moses and the prophets preoccupied themselves not with the immorality of the soul but with the poor, the widow, the orphan and the stranger. The relationship with man in which contact with the Divine is established is not a kind of *spiritual friendship* but the sort that is manifested, tested and accomplished in a just economy and for which each man is fully responsible. 'Why does your God, who is the God of the poor, not feed the poor?' a Roman asks Rabbi Akiba. 'So we can escape damnation', replies Rabbi Akiba. One could not find a stronger statement of the impossible situation in which God finds himself, that of accepting the duties and responsibilities of man.

The personal responsibility of man with regard to man is such that God cannot annul it. This is why, in the dialogue between God and Cain – 'Am I my brother's keeper?' – rabbinical commentary does not regard the question as a case of simple insolence. Instead, it comes from someone who has not yet experienced human solidarity and who thinks (like many modern philosophers) that each exists for oneself and that everything is permitted. But God reveals to the murderer that his crime has disturbed the natural order, so the Bible puts a word of submission into the mouth of Cain: 'My punishment is greater than I can bear'. The rabbis pretend to read a new question in this response: 'Is my punishment too great to bear? Is it too heavy for the Creator who supports the heavens and the earth?'

Jewish wisdom teaches that He Who has created and Who supports the whole universe cannot support or pardon the crime that man commits against man. 'Is it possible? Did not the Eternal efface the sin of the golden calf?' This leads the master to reply: the fault committed with regard to God falls within the province of divine pardon, whereas the fault that offends man does not concern God. The text thus announces the value and the full autonomy of the human who is offended, as it affirms the responsibility incurred by whomsoever touches man. Evil is not a mystical principle that can be effaced by a ritual, it is an offence perpetrated on man by man. No one, not even God, can substitute himself for the victim. The world in which pardon is all-powerful becomes inhuman.

This austere doctrine in no way leads to the inhumanity of despair. God is patient – that is to say, lets time pass, awaits the return of man, his separation or regeneration. Judaism believes in this regeneration of man without the intervention of extrahuman factors other than the consciousness of Good, and the Law: 'Everything lies in the hands of God, except for the very fear of God.' Human effort has unlimited possibilities. There is finally the help given by a just society from which the unjust person may benefit.

But nothing in this help resembles the communication of the saints, the transitivity of the redemptive act is completely educative. We are familiar with the admirable passages from Ezekiel in which man's responsibility extends to the actions of his neighbour. Among men, each responds to the faults of the Other. We even respond to the just man who risks being corrupted. We cannot push the idea of solidarity any further. Therefore, the aspiration to a just society which we find in Judaism, beyond any individual piety, is an eminently religious action. A text from Tractate Tannith magnifies this salvation of the unjust by the just. The constitution of a just society – one which 'receives the rain' – is compared to the moments that mark, in all theology, the summit of religious life. Rabbi Abbahu said: 'The day of rain is greater than the resurrection of the dead, for the resurrection of the dead concerns only the just, while the rain concerns both the just and the unjust.' Rabbi Jehouda said: 'The day of rain is as great as the day when the Torah was given.' Rabbi Hamma b. Hanina said: 'The day of rain is as great as the day when the heavens and the earth were created.' There is a subordination of every possible relationship between God and man – redemption, revelation, creation – to the instruction of a society in which justice, instead of remaining an aspiration of individual piety, is strong enough to extend to all and be realized.

It is perhaps this state of mind that we normally call Jewish messianism.

Universalism

The role played by ethics in the religious relation allows us to understand the meaning of Jewish universalism.

A truth is universal when it applies to every reasonable being. A religion is universal when it is open to all. In this sense, the Judaism that links the Divine to the moral has always aspired to be universal. But the revelation of morality, which discovers a human society, also discovers the place of election, which, in this universal society, returns to the person who receives this revelation. This election is made up not of privileges but of responsibilities. It is a nobility based not on royalties [*droit d'auteur*] or a birthright [*droit d'aînesse*] conferred by a divine caprice, but on the position of each human I [*moi*]. Each one, as an 'I', is separate from all the others to whom the moral duty is due. The basic intuition of the majority perhaps consists in perceiving that I am not *the equal* of the Other. This applies in the very strict sense: I see myself *obligated* with respect to the Other; consequently I am infinitely more demanding of myself than of others. 'The more just I am, the more harshly I am judged', states one talmudic text.

From then on, there is no moral awareness that is not an awareness of this exceptional position, an awareness of being chosen. Reciprocity is a structure founded on an original inequality. For equality to make its entry into the world, beings must be able to demand more of themselves than of the Other, feel responsibilities on which the fate of humanity hangs, and in this sense pose themselves problems outside humanity. This 'position outside nations', of which the Pentateuch speaks, is realized in the concept of Israel and its particularism. It is a particularism that conditions universality, and it is a moral category rather than a historical fact to do with Israel, even if the historical Israel has in fact been faithful to the concept of Israel and, on the subject of morality, felt responsibilities and obligations which it demands from no one, but which sustain the world.

According to one apologue in the Talmud, only on the spot where a chosen society worships can the salvation of a humanity come about. The destruction of the Temple compromised the economy of the world. And Rabbi Meir, one of the chief Doctors of the Law, has ventured to say that a pagan who knows the Torah is the equal of the High Priest. This indicates the degree to which the notion of Israel can be separated, in the Talmud, from any historical, national, local or racial notion.

Citizens of Modern States

The first relation man has with being passes through his links with man.

The Jewish man discovers man before discovering landscapes and towns. He is at home in a society before being so in a house. He understands the world on the basis of the Other rather than the whole of being functioning in relation to the earth. He is in a sense exiled on this earth, as the psalmist says, and he finds a meaning to the earth on the basis of a human society. This is not an analysis of the contemporary Jewish soul; it is the literal teaching of the Bible in which the earth is not possessed individually, but belongs to God. Man begins in the desert where he dwells in tents, and adores God in a transportable temple.

From this existence – free with regard to landscapes and architectures, all those heavy and sedentary things that one is tempted to prefer to man – Judaism recalls, in the course of its whole history, that it is rooted in the countryside or in the town. The festival of 'the cabins' is the liturgical form of this memory and the prophet Zechariah announces, for the messianic age, the festival of cabins as though it were a festival of all the nations. Freedom with regard to the sedentary forms of existence is, perhaps, the human way to be in this world. For Judaism, the world becomes intelligible before a human face and not, as for a great contemporary philosopher who sums up an important aspect of the West, through houses, temples and bridges.

This freedom is not in the least bit pathological, or strained or heartrending. It relegates the values to do with roots and institutes other forms of fidelity and responsibility. Man, after all, is not a tree, and humanity is not a forest. It promotes more human forms, for they presuppose a conscious commitment; freer forms, for they allow us to glimpse a human society and horizons vaster than those of the village where we were born.

Is it not these consciously willed and freely accepted links – with all the traditions that freedoms entail – which constitute modern nations, defined by the decision to work in common much more than by the dark voices of heredity? Are these accepted links less solid than roots? In one circumstance they certainly are: when the groupings formed by them cease to correspond to the moral values in the name of which they were formed. But must we not accord to man the right to judge, in the name of moral conscience, the history to which on the one hand he belongs, rather than leave his right to judge to anonymous history? A freedom with regard to history in the name of morality, justice above culture (ancestral land, architecture, arts) – these are finally the terms that describe the way in which the Jew encountered God.

Old Hillel, the grand Doctor of the Law in the first century BC, exclaimed, on seeing a skull carried along by the current, 'You were killed for having killed, but those who killed you will be killed.' If the crimes of history do not always strike down the innocent, they are still not judgements. We wrongly conceive of a chain of violent events as the verdicts of history where history itself is the magistrate. Hillel knew that history does not judge and that, left to its fate, it echoes crimes. Nothing, no event in history, can judge a conscience. This is upheld by theological language, which measures the entire miracle of such a freedom, while stating that God alone can judge.

Judaism

In the present day the word 'Judaism' covers several quite distinct concepts. Above all it designates a religion, the system of beliefs, rituals and moral prescriptions founded on the Bible, the Talmud and rabbinic literature, and often combined with the mysticism or theosophy of the Kabbalah. The principal forms of this religion have scarcely varied for two thousand years and attest to a spirit that is fully conscious of itself and is reflected in a religious and moral literature, while still being open to new developments. 'Judaism' thus comes to signify a culture that is either the result or the foundation of the religion, but at all events has its own sense of evolution. Throughout the world, and even in the state of Israel, there are people who identify with Judaism but do not believe in God and are not practising Jews. For millions of Israelites who have been assimilated into the civilization around them, Judaism cannot even be called a culture: it is a vague sensibility made up of various ideas, memories, customs and emotions, together with a feeling of solidarity towards those Jews who were persecuted for being Jews.

This sensibility, this culture and this religion are none the less seen from the outside as aspects of a strongly characterized entity that cannot easily be classified. Is it a nationality or a religion, a fossilized civilization that somehow lives on, or the passionate desire for a better world? The mystery of Israel! This difficulty reflects a sense of presence to history that is unique of its kind. In fact, Judaism is the source of the great monotheistic religions, on which the modern world depends just as much as ancient religions, on which the modern world depends just as much as ancient Greece and Rome once did, and also belongs to the living present not only through the concepts and books it has supplied, but equally through real men and women who, as pioneers of various great ventures or as victims of great historical convulsions, form part of a direct and unbroken line of descent from the people of sacred History. The attempt to create a state in Palestine and to regain the creative

inspiration of old whose pronouncements were of universal significance cannot be understood without the Bible.

Judaism has a special essence: it is something that is laid down in
square letters and something that illuminates living faces; it is both
ancient doctrine and contemporary history. But this runs the risk of
favouring a mythical vision or a spirituality that can still none the
less be analysed. Objective science, such as sociology, history or
philology, tries to reduce the exception to the rule. Western Jews
promoted this kind of research. At the end of the seventeenth
century Spinoza's *Tractatus Theologico-Politicus* inaugurates a critical reading of the Scriptures. At the beginning of the nineteenth
century in Germany, the founders of the famous 'science of
Judaism' [*Wissenschaft des Judentums*] transformed the Holy Scriptures into pure documents. The paradoxes of an unequalled destiny
and an absolute teaching slot easily into the scientific categories
created for every spiritual reality and all other idiosyncrasies.
Everything can be explained by its causes; and by methodically
tracking down and logging every influence, many original features
dissolve. Judaism emerges, perhaps, more aware of what it has
received, but less and less sure of its own truth.

We may none the less ask whether the scientific categorization of
a spiritual movement can ever reveal its real contribution and
significance. Can wisdom ever bare its soul and reveal its secret
without displaying a power that imposes itself on us as a message or
appeals to us as a vocation? The Jewish conscience, in spite of its
different forms and levels, regains its unity and unicity in moments
of great crisis, when the strange combination of texts and men, who
often cannot speak the language of these texts, is renewed in
sacrifice and persecution. The memory of these crises sustains the
quiet intervals.

During these extraordinary moments, the lucid work of the
science of Judaism, which reduces the miracles of the Revelation or
the national genius to a series of influences, loses its spiritual
significance. In place of the miracle of the unique source, there
shines the marvel of confluence. The latter is understood as a voice
calling from the depths of converging texts and reverberating in a
sensibility and a form of thought that are already there to greet it.
What does the voice of Israel say, and how can it be translated into a
few propositions? Perhaps it announces nothing more than the
monotheism which the Jewish Bible brought to humanity. At first,
we might recoil from this hoary old truth or this somewhat dubious
claim. But the word denotes a set of significations based on which

the shadow of the Divine is cast beyond all theology and dogmatism over the deserts of Barbary. One must follow the Most High God and be faithful to Him alone. One must be wary of the myth that leads to the *fait accompli*, the constraints of customs or locale, and the Machiavellian State and its reasons of State. One follows the Most High God, above all by drawing near to one's fellow man, and showing concern for 'the widow, the orphan, the stranger and the beggar', an approach that must not be made 'with empty hands'. It is therefore on earth, amongst men, that the spirit's adventure unfolds.

The traumatic experience of my slavery in Egypt constitutes my very humanity, a fact that immediately allies me to the workers, the wretched, and the persecuted peoples of the world. My uniqueness lies in the responsibility I display for the Other. I cannot fail in my duty towards any man, any more than I can have someone else stand in for my death. This leads to the conception of a creature who can be saved without falling into the egotism of grace. Man is therefore indispensable to God's plan or, to be more exact, man is nothing other than the divine plans within being. This leads to the idea of being chosen, which can degenerate into that of pride but originally expresses the awareness of an indisputable assignation from which an ethics springs and through which the universality of the end being pursued involves the solitude and isolation of the individual responsible. Man is called before a form of judgement and justice which recognizes this responsibility, while the rigours of the Law are softened without being suspended by a sense of mercy. Man can do what he must do; he can master the hostile forces of history by helping to bring about a messianic reign, a reign of justice foretold by the prophets. The waiting for the Messiah marks the very duration of time.

This is the extreme humanism of a God who demands much of man – some would say He demands too much! It is perhaps in a ritualism regulating all the gestures of the complete Jew's day-to-day life, in the famous yoke of the Law, which the pious experience as something joyful, that we find the most characteristic aspects of Jewish existence. This ritualism has preserved Jewish existence for centuries. While itself remaining completely natural, it keeps this existence alive by maintaining a distance from nature. But perhaps, for that very reason, it maintains a presence to the Most High God.

The Pharisee is Absent

A spiral tries in vain to envelop its own movement. Is this a graphic representation of modern Jewish thought, in which the essence of Judaism appears like a tireless attempt to define that very essence? Of course, not everything is absurd in this line which forever recommences and can neither move forward nor rejoin its point of departure. The naivety of spontaneous movements, the rash reactions and the freshness of a cruel lack of conscience, are what make wild beasts and children charming. Nothing proves that human life owes them its human dignity. But not to be able to affirm anything – to renounce all axioms, not to risk any postulate, to stick to the definition – what a unique geometry!

How stunning it is for thought, therefore, when it enters the garden of Writing, even when that writing is translated. Shepherds of the East, nomadic tribes, peoples from two neighbouring kingdoms in dispute, are dear to our desiccated hearts. The wild adventure they ran matters to us, even if we firmly preserve the principles of the wisdom taught at school. The whole drama of the Revelation, the calling, the text, is repeated before our eyes and engages us. Henceforth, nothing is banal. There is no obscure existence, no anonymous fate. Life at the extreme point of life – religion! Kings, patriarchs and prophets, warriors, farmers, builders – these ancestors or contemporaries live innumerable lives in a life that has not yet been divided or has already been completely reunited, springing forth like a divine source, the Source. A source that springs up in us, as though the rod of Moses had struck our rock-like being. How happy one is to come from this world, to descend like the son of these men, in a straight line, without recourse to anyone's meditations! How good it feels to be a Jew!

But this life which wells up in each one of us carries within it declamatory forms. This famous prayer, spoken aloud – which, according to the wise men of Israel, is the very manifestation of false prophecy – already reverberates around the public square and at our meetings. Enthusiasm is born of shamelessness. In the intimate garden of Judaism to which a whole question of young Jews are now accustomed, there is still no sign of one person for whom the meaning of the divine can no longer be expressed by the image of the source that springs up in each of us.

The pharisee is absent. His features are no longer familiar to our young people and his stature no longer dominates our wretched debates. Instead of the image of the spring, he prefers the symbol of struggle, face-to-face war that opposes reason with reason, a war devoid of anger or envy in which authentic thought flourishes and brings down peace on the world. He know the daring of the idea developed fully to its end, even it if were to destroy the thick shades in which men had chosen to set up home. Nowhere else is so much certainty linked to so little naivety, so much daily obedience to so much sovereignty! In contrast to the idea of inspiring grace, he offers the labour of questions which spring up, more futile than evr, after each solution. He announces a paradise in which every joy is created from these eternal sufferings. Beyond the impatience of life – covering what living a life represents in intensity, fullness and truth – he knows. To know is the only method by which a spirit can touch a spirit outside it. The fact that Moses spoke face to face with God signifies that both disciple and Master relied on the same talmudic lesson, say the wise men. Enthusiasm is not the purest way in which to enter into a relationship with God.

The Pharisee has seen this in his life, and heard it from his masters. He cannot be easily dazzled. He smiles at the young men who want truth to be a monolith that squeezes, as he puts it, all the sons of the world into the one silk garment. His words are brief and incisive, his thought coalesces into examples that retain the possibilities lost in a concept. Only the sensitive can discern the subtlety concealed beneath the apparent platitude. From that point on, a dialogue is established between wise men, from master to pupil and from pupil to master, over the heads of the masses. How can one describe the austere tenderness of that pity of disciples, the despair of one who no longer has anyone to question, the tragic actor of death, reduced to an absence of replies?

This knowledge has been slandered. All those artists and hotheads! As if knowledge suffered from the gap between itself and beings.

As if a being who was truly outside things were not life's most prodigious adventure. As if the flame that burns this Bush without consuming it were not the light. As if the best way to receive the light consisted in burning in the fire it lights. The Pharisee experiences a Presence that overruns the limits of the inner life, indemnifies Presence at the heart of the thoughts that maintain it.

Rabbi Eliezer said:

> If all the seas were ink, reeds pens, the heavens parchment, and all men writers, they would not suffice to write down the Torah I have learned, and the Torah itself would be diminished only by the amount drawn out of it by the tip of a paintbrush dipped in the sea.

But Rabbi Aquiben takes fright at the audacity of his masters:

> They managed to extract their part from the Torah. For me, I have broached it surely like the man who breathes in the perfume of the cedar tree – his joy takes nothing away from the cedar. Or like the man who draws water from a spring. Or like the man who lights his flame from a flame.

The image of the source is still maintained. Generous and infinitely renewable, it continues to gush forth. But the Pharisee draws from it, he does not merge with it. He is not possessed by the forces that ravage and alter and dissolve self-presence. The liquid he drinks quenches his thirst without causing drunkenness. Everything remains in its place. God is outside and is God for that very reason. What is outside save Him? In this romantic age when spirit is confused with drama, when Jews understand only the Hassidic tales, what purity this represents in this world that in giving loses not even what the tip of a brush would take from the sea. To have an outside, to listen to what comes from outside – oh, miracle of exteriority! That is what is called knowledge or Torah. The sublime forms of the human are no longer full of pathos.

Judaism and the Feminine

The Jewish vision of the world is expressed in the Bible, but in the Bible as reflected by rabbinic literature, of which the Talmud and its commentators constitute the leading part. The Talmud, fixed in writing between the second and seventh centuries, goes back to a much older tradition than Christianity, a tradition already showing up clearly in the structure that Jewish life had acquired as early as the end of the First Exile. The biblical canon as we know it today was shaped and passed down under the authority of this tradition. Christianity itself, after all, had received the Old Testament from the hands of the Pharisees.

Whatever may be the case regarding the exegetical methods used by the Talmud, the meaning of the Old Testament is revealed to Jews through the talmudic tradition. It does not constitute the treasury of Israel's folklore, although it sometimes appears to. Its subtlety does not scorn forms without any embellishment. Nothing is less naive than these apologues. It is not easy to go through these fundamental texts, to survey them, or to make their acuteness felt again by a public that is ill-used to the language and methods in which this thought is worked through. Here is an esotericism that does not depend on the secrecy of the doctrine but on its rigour.

We may well ask whether ideas that cannot break through to the masses and cannot be transformed into techniques can still determine the progress of the world, and whether Christianity was not the last and only entry of Judaism into World History. But this would be to scorn in advance the intrinsic value of truth, which is not to acknowledge any universality in it other than what it receives from the consensus of all. This would, above all, be to think that the revealed idea lives exclusively in the history in which it was revealed. This would be to deny it a profound life and abrupt irruptions into history. This would involve misunderstanding the volcanic existence of spirit and, in short, the very possibility of the revolutionary phenomenon.

We must apologize for this declaration of principles presented in the guise of an introduction to the modest reflections that follow on woman in Jewish thought. But it explains why this thought is inseparable from the rabbinic sources and why we must speak of it while we have no penchant for archaeology, and why the analyses that we attempt are only an approach, both timid and rash, to this thought.

I

The characteristics of the Jewish woman can be fixed, thanks to charming feminine figures of the Old Testament. The wives of the patriarchs, Miriam and Deborah the prophetesses, Tamar the daughter-in-law of Judah, the daughters of Zelophehad, Naomi and Ruth the Moabite, Michal, daughter of Saul, Abigail, Bathsheba, the Shunammite, and a whole host of others, all play an active role in the attainment of the biblical purpose and are placed at the very pivot of Sacred History. We are far from the conditions prevailing in the Orient where, at the heart of a masculine civlization, woman finds herself completely subordinate to masculine whims or reduced to charming or lightening the harsh life of men. Isaac would have been schooled in the violent games and laughter of his brother but for the painful decision of Sarah; Esau would have triumphed over Israel but for Rebecca's ruse; Laban would have prevented the Return of Jacob but for the complicity of Leah and Rachel; Moses would not have been suckled by his mother if not for Miriam; David, and the Prince of Justice who one day was to be born of him, would not have been possible without Tamar's stubbornness, without Ruth the faithful, or the political genius of Bathsheba.

All the switches along this difficult path, on which the train of messianic history risked being derailed a thousand times, have been supervised and controlled by women. Biblical events would not have progressed as they did had it not been for their watchful lucidity, the firmness of their determination, and their cunning and spirit of sacrifice. But the world in which these events unfolded would not have been structured as it was – and as it still is and always will be – without the secret presence, on the edge of invisibility, of these mothers, wives and daughters; without their silent footsteps in the depths and opacity of reality, drawing the very dimensions of interiority and making the world precisely habitable.

'The house is woman', the Talmud tells us. Beyond the psychological and sociological obviousness of such an affirmation, the rabbinic tradition experiences this affirmation as a primordial truth. The last chapter of Proverbs, in which woman, without regard for 'beauty and grace', appears as the genius of the hearth and, precisely as such, makes the public life of man possible, can, if necessary, be read as a moral paradigm. But in Judaism the moral always has the weight of an onotological basis: the feminine figures among the categories of Being. The Doctors dare to place among the ten 'words' that served to create the universe the one that declares that 'it is not good for man to be alone'. Rabbi Menachem Bar Yossi, in order to include it in this number, excluded the 'word' which states that 'the breath of God hung over the face of the waters'. And when Rabbi Yossi (who is not necessarily, as the encyclopaedias claim, 'the father of the previous rabbi') meets the prophet Elijah, he merely asks what can be meant by the verse from Genesis on 'the woman lending aid to Adam'. But the good fortune of so marvellous an encounter, which happens from time to time in talmudic parables, is not above a question that seems so prosaic.

Continuing in the same tone in which the question was raised, the prophet's alleged reply fixes the role of woman: 'Man brings home corn – does he chew corn? He brings flax – can he clothe himself in flax? The woman is the light of his eyes. She puts him back on his feet.' Is it really just to ground the corn and spin the flax that woman exists? A slave would be good enough for such a task. One could certainly see in this text confirmation of the ancillary status of woman. Yet a more subtle interpretation is required once we recognize the converse nature of talmudic thought and the 'categorial' value of the examples it cites. This corn and flax are wrenched from nature by the work of man. They testify to the break with spontaneous life, to the ending of instinctive life buried in the immediacy of nature as given. They mark the beginning of what one can accurately call the life of spirit. But an insurmountable 'rawness' remains in the products of our conquering civilization.

The world in which reason becomes more and more self-conscious is not habitable. It is hard and cold, like those supply depots where merchandise which cannot satisfy is piled up: it can neither clothe those who are naked nor feed those who are hungry; it is impersonal, like factory hangars and industrial cities where manufactured things remain abstract, true with the truth of calculations and brought into the anonymous circuit of the economy that proceeds according to knowledgeable plans that cannot prevent, though they can prepare, disasters. This is spirit in all its masculine essence. It *lives outdoors*, exposed to the fiery sun which blinds and to the winds of the open sea which beat it and blow it down, in a world that offers it no inner refuge, in which it is disorientated, solitary and wandering, and even as such is already alienated by the products it had helped to create, which rise up untamed and hostile.

To add the work of servant to that of lord and master does not resolve the contradiction. To light eyes that are blind, to restore to equilibrium, and so overcome an alienation which ultimately results from the very virility of the universal and all-conquering *logos* that stalks the very shadows that could have sheltered it, should be the ontological function of the feminine, the vocation of the one 'who does not conquer'. Woman does not simply come to someone deprived of companionship to keep him company. She answers to a solitude inside this privation and – which is stranger – to a solitude that subsists in spite of the presence of God; to a solitude in the universal, to the inhuman which continues to well up even when the human has mastered nature and raised it to thought. For the inevitable uprooting of thought, which dominates the world, to return to the peace and ease of being at home, the strange flow of gentleness must enter into the geometry of infinite and cold space. Its name is woman.

The return of self, this gathering or appearance of *place* in space, does not result, as in Heidegger, from the gesture of building, from an architecture that shapes a countryside, but from the interiority of 'the House' – the reverse [*l'envers*] of which would be place [*l'endroit*], but for the essential moderation of feminine existence living there, which is habitation itself. She makes the corn into bread and the flax into clothing. The wife, the betrothed, is not the coming together in a human being of all the perfections of tenderness and goodness which subsists in themselves. Everything indicates that the feminine is the original manifestation of these perfections, of gentleness itself, the origin of all gentleness on earth.

The conjugal bond is therefore simultaneously a social bond and a moment of self-consciousness, the way in which a being identifies and rediscovers itself. The oral tradition insists upon this. Did not God give the name 'Adam' to man and woman joined together, as if the two were one, as if the unity of the person were able to triumph over the dangers lying in wait for it only by virtue of a duality inscribed in its very essence? A dramatic duality, for conflict can well up, and catastrophe; the female friend can become the most terrible enemy. It is not without risk that unperturbed spirit, which blows unconditionally where it will, returns to itself and rests in happiness. But 'without woman man knows neither good, nor succour, nor joy, nor blessing, nor pardon'. Nothing of what would be required for a soul! Rabbi Joshua ben Levi added: 'neither peace nor life'. Nothing which transforms his natural life into ethics, nothing which permits living a life, not even the death that one dies for another. Some say, finally, that 'man without woman diminishes the image of God in the world'. And this leads us to another dimension of the feminine – maternity.

II

In one sense, woman in Judaism will have merely the destiny of a human being, in which her femininity will figure only as an attribute. The institutions which define her legal status attest to this condition of moral being. Their revolutionary character in relation to the usages and customs of the period and the oriental civilizations in which the world of the Bible is situated is striking, despite the ritual forms that status takes on. The rites that the Book of Numbers lays down, for example, for the woman suspected of adultery consist, in fact, in respecting the 'human person' in her, in removing her from the arbitrary power of the husband, in 'taking the heat out of' blind jealousy by a long procedure, in leaving arbitration and decision to the priests, the public power, a third party.

These juridical principles express in fact only one of the permanent themes of Jewish thought. The femininity of woman can neither deform nor absorb her human essence. 'Woman is called *islah* in Hebrew, for she comes from man – *ish*', the Bible tells us. The Doctors seize on this etymology to affirm the unique dignity of Hebrew, which expresses the very mystery of creation – namely, that woman is derived quasi-grammatically from man.

This is a very different derivation from biological development. Two distinct acts of creation were necessary for Adam – the one for the man in Adam, the second for the woman – affirms a rabbinic text. Another text takes pleasure in calling attention to the priority Sarah had over Abraham on the level of prophecy. Eve heard the divine word. As an interlocutor of God, woman can no longer lose this dignity, and according to a bold saying of the sages, even on the level of her biological existence she always greets her masculine partner face to face. The relation of person to person precedes all relation.

The total originality of the 'feminine' compared to the 'female' principle is expressed in another parable (to be read chastely, in that context of purity in which the Talmud knows how to speak of the sexual). In this parable, Adam was approached by all living things that had received their names from him, but he remained unsatisfied until the appearance of Eve, who was greeted precisely as an equal being. The legend also insists that Eve can appear only when awaited and called forth by every wish in Adam. She did not offer herself to Adam as ready-made and earmarked for 'biological needs', in the name of an apparent necessity of nature. The calamity of which she was the cause itself indicates a social calamity, for which men carry responsibility and in which one cannot incriminate fate, or nature, or God.

If woman completes man, she does not complete him as a part completes another into a whole but, as it were, as two totalities complete one another – which is, after all, the miracle of social relations. The discussion between the schools of Rav and Shmuel on the creation of Eve can be viewed from this perspective. Did she come from Adam's rib? Was this rib not a *side* of Adam, created as a single being with two faces that God separated while Adam, still androgynous, was sleeping? This theme perhaps evolved from Plato's *Symposium*, but it is one which in the Doctors takes on a new meaning. The two faces of the primitive Adam from the beginning look towards the side to which they will always remain turned. They are faces from the very outset, whereas Plato's god turns them round after separation. Their new existence, separated existence, will not come to punish the daring of too perfect a nature, as in Plato. For the Jews, separated existence will be worth more than the initial union.

'Flesh of my flesh and bone of my bone' therefore means an identity of nature between woman and man, an identity of destiny and dignity, and also a subordination of sexual life to the personal relation which is equality in itself.

These ideas are older than the principles in whose name modern woman struggles for her emancipation, but the *truth* of all these principles lies on a plane that also contains the thesis opposed to the image of initial androgyny and attached to the popular idea of the rib. It upholds a certain priority of the masculine. The latter remains the prototype of the human and determines eschatology, in relation to which maternity itself is described as the salvation of humanity. The justice which will rule the relations between men amounts to the presence of God among them. The differences between masculine and feminine are blurred in this messianic age.

In the rabbinic interpretation of love, maternity is subordinate to a human destiny which exceeds the limits of 'family joys': it is necessary to fulfil Israel, 'to multiply the image of God' inscribed on the face of humanity. Not that conjugal love has no importance in itself, or that it is reduced to the rank of a means of procreation, or that it merely *prefigures* its fulfilments, as in a certain theology. On the contrary, the ultimate end of the family is the actual *meaning* and the joy of this present. It is not only prefigured there, it is already fulfilled there. This participation of the present in this future takes place specifically in the feeling of love, in the grace of the betrothed, and even in the erotic. The real dynamism of love leads it beyond the present instant and even beyond the person loved. This end does not appear to a vision outside the love, which would then integrate it into the place of creation; it lies in the love itself.

The birth of the first children, Cain and Abel, was brought about during the time in Paradise, according to a passage from Tractate Sanhedrin, on the very day of the creation of Adam, which was also the day of the creation of Eve and the day of their first loves, before the original disobedience. They mounted the nuptial couch as two and came down from it as four. 'They came down from it as six', according to another apologue, since 'the wives of the children were born with the children'. The consequence of the Fall was precisely the separation of voluptuousness from procreation, henceforth stretching out successively in time. From now on, the pains of pregnancy and childbirth are subjugated to an end that is distinct from the one which draws the lovers. In the state of perfection the true essence of love was revealed.

From that time on, it is no longer unworthy of God 'to adorn Eve as a betrothed' before bringing her to Adam, nor to spend 'the free time that remains to Him since creation' in matching couples. To give pleasure to newlyweds is one of the most meritorious acts of Jewish piety. A brass basin in the court of the sanctuary, containing water for the ablutions of the priests, is a symbol of purity. According to legend, the metal of the basin was taken from mirrors that Jewish women, coming out of Egypt, had piously offered. Instruments of a chaste coquetry, which reawakened desire in a despairing generation and guaranteed the continuation of Israel. The meaning of love does not, then, stop with the moment of voluptuousness, nor with the person loved. Love does not take on a romantic significance.

This dimension of the romantic, in which love becomes its own end, where it remains without any 'intentionality' that spreads beyond it, a world of voluptuousness or a world of charm and grace, one which can coexist with a religious civilization (and even be spiritualized by it, as in the cult of the Virgin in medieval Christianity), is foreign to Judaism. The forms of the romance that one finds in the Bible are at once interpreted by the *Midrash* in such a way as to bring out the eschatological side of the romance. Classical Judaism will not have art in the sense in which all the people of the earth have had it.

Poetic images of amorous life are discreet in the Bible, outside the Song of Songs, which is soon interpreted in a mystical sense. Pure eroticism is evoked, in a clearly pejorative sense, in the Romance of Amnon and Tamar or, in certain respects, in the loves of Samson. What one calls sentimental love, virtually separated from all eroticism and marked by gripping images – the romances of Isaac and Rebecca, Jacob and Rachel, David and Bathsheba – undergoes a de-poetization in the *Midrash*. This is due not to prudish timidity but to the permanent opening up of the messianic perspective – of the immanence of Israel, of humanity reflecting the image of God that it can carry on its face.

The Eternal Feminine, which an entire amorous experience carries from the Middle Ages through to Dante, up to Goethe, is lacking in Judaism. The feminine will never take on the aspect of the Divine, neither the Virgin Mary nor even Beatrice. The dimension of intimacy, not the dimension of loftiness, is opened up by woman. Doubtless the mysterious interiority of feminine existence will be used to experience, like a betrothed, the Sabbath, the Torah itself; and sometimes the divine Presence in the nearness of men, the *sheckhinah*. The images do not in any way become feminine figures. They are not taken seriously. Amorous relations in Scripture are interpreted symbolically and denote mystical relations.

III

But at the same time as the dignity of this principle restores, we might say, a soul to the spirit, the feminine also reveals itself to be the source of all decline. This appears in an ambivalence in which one of the most profound visions of the ambiguity of love itself is expressed. The delicious weakness which, in the swoon of inner life, saves the human being from rootlessness takes place on the verge of letting go. Woman is complete immodesty, down to the nakedness of her little finger. She is the one who, *par excellence*, displays herself, the essentially turbulent, the essentially impure. Satan, says an extremist text, was created with her. Her contemplative vocation – attested to by the rib from whence she came, a clothed and invisible organ – is allied to all indiscretion.

Rabbinic thought ventures further. Death seizes man before original sin. On the very day of the creation of Eve his destiny was sealed. Until then, like Elijah, the prophet – single, like Elijah, because alone like him – he was able to escape death. True life, joy, pardon and peace no longer belong to woman. Now there rises up, foreign to all compassion for itself, spirit in its essence, virile, superhuman, solitary. It recognizes itself in Elijah, the prophet without pardon, the prophet of anger and punishment, a suckling of crows, inhabiting deserts, without kindness, without happiness, without peace.

Excessive opinion, permanent temptation of the Jewish soul, disdainful of equivocal loves in which the pure and the impure are mixed, scornful of cultures where blood and death are joined to voluptuous pleasures, where the forms of art and enchantment accept supreme cruelties.

But the biblical figure which haunts Israel on the paths of exile, the figure that it invokes at the end of the Sabbath, in the dusk where it will soon remain behind without help, the figure in whom is stored up for the Jews all the tenderness of the earth, the hand which caresses and rocks his children, is no longer feminine. Neither wife nor sister nor mother guides it. It is Elijah, who did not experience death, the most severe of the prophets, precursor of the Messiah.

The Diary of Léon Brunschvicg

I

Passing the point on the avenue Georges-Mandel where the rue Scheffer gently slopes into it, one thinks of Léon Brunschvicg. I recall the soft features in a pink face that retained a kind of childlike candour, an illusion, or intuition, reinforced by big blue eyes that were very pure and a discreet sucking movement, too gracious to be a nervous tic, like that of a schoolboy melting a toffee into his mouth. He was one of the most intelligent men in the university of his day.

The unique impression experienced in this rue Scheffer which leads nowhere, a place that has been somehow diverted from its natural destination, is that of a whole neighbourhood fallen into disuse! I should like to tell those who never knew him of the kind of perfect humanity Léon Brunschvicg represented. I want to show all the young people enamoured, often gloriously, of action, who denounce the Sorbonne and are scornful of knowledge (which sometimes they have not even tasted), how much heart there was in this Reason that was integrally reason, and how much attention it paid to life. And I want to remind Jewish youth who, after their recent experiences, may have had enough of Europe – its 'Western culture', its 'Christian humanism', or whatever – how much civilization was embodied in this European Jew. The youth that aspires to the simple life on a soil that is worked and defended with self-sacrifice and heroism arouses our admiration. But perhaps two thousand years of participation in the European world, culminating not just in Auschwitz but also in a personality like Léon Brunschvicg, should not simply be forgotten. Perhaps the basic toughness and straight-forwardness that helped to conquer Palestine should not remain the final virtues of renewed Judaism. Perhaps we should derive from the Diaspora something more than the qualities of farmers and soldiers.

We should recall that in addition to the heroic surpassing of oneself, there is also the surpassing of grace, the essential non-heaviness, the soaring of the intelligence that thinks totally, careful not to get weighed down – even with a brutal affirmation – lightening the fatal load of affirmation by being ironic, even about irony. With Léon Brunschwicg, in fact, one never knew to what degree the irony was to be taken: 'A fall of snow maintains the warmth of the earth: from irony to surface in order to keep intact the depth of our faith. Anger is merely a wind that makes everything evaporate', notes a still young Brunschvicg on 23 December 1892. And certainly, he in no way ignores the contradiction between thought and action: 'The biggest ideas can be put into practice only by narrowing down and being exclusive.' But this does not entail renouncing action: 'It is therefore important to raise ourselves to the level of an idea so true and pure that it will having nothing to fear from practice.' These problems and solutions are characteristic of happy men and periods of peace. But, after all, does not man's vocation lie in peace?

II

The quotations I have just given come from a curious book published under the title *The Rediscovered Diary, 1892–1942* by Editions de Minuit, and edited by the daughter of Léon Brunschvicg, Adrienne R. Weill-Brunschvicg, and Jean Wahl, a professor at the Sorbonne. Jean Wahl prefaced the slim volume with an introduction and appended an 'ideological classification'. Madame Weill, with a discreet emotion so typical of Brunschvicg himself, recounted the history of the published notebook. It was one of Brunschvicg's old diaries, dating from 1892, when, as a young philosophy graduate, he taught at Lorient grammar school. Every day he recorded a thought for the benefit of his lifelong friend, the future historian Elie Halévy, from whom he was separated on leaving the Ecole Normale Supérieure. Elie Halévy likewise kept a diary for Brunschvicg. The two friends exchanged notebooks.

On the death of Elie Halévy in 1937, Brunschvicg returned his friend's notebook, which he had kept for forty-five years, to his widow. Shortly afterwards, Madame Halévy found Brunschvicg's, and gave it back to him. In the tragic climate of 1942, prevented by Vichy from taking part in any activity, Léon Brunschvicg turned his attention to those youthful reflections, creating a remarkable dialogue between self and self and bridging the gap of over fifty years that separated 'a young man and a man still young', to use Jean

Wahl's felicitous phrase. 'It is extraordinary how I resemble my-self', exclaimed Brunschvicg on rereading his old diary. This remark hides, however, the degree to which Brunschvicg's being, which appeared in personal relationships to be superior to duration, involved a daily conquest over self, and no doubt a series of failures and compromises – in short, life. For the self starts off by being a stranger to itself [*le moi commence par être étranger à soi*]. On 15 January 1892 Brunschvicg notes: 'The self that is unbearable to the self, that is me' [*le moi insupportable au moi, c'est moi*]. In 1942 he recognizes that 'after 50 times 365 days of mutual concessions, they none the less seem to be getting used to one another'.

I do not intend here to summarize the thoughts of this little book, or to measure the degree to which it contains in embryonic form or encapsulates Brunschvicg's whole philosophical work. Jean Wahl has already done this with his usual meticulous, subtle and pro-found approaches in his magnificent introduction and his 'ideo-logical classification'. Instead I want to talk about the man.

But how can we talk about the man when that man is Brunschvicg? By enumerating his virtues? They were many and great, but his value goes beyond virtues. By retracing his bio-graphy? It does not encompass his life, one in which nothing was mean-spirited, even in those external matters 'which do not depend on us'. Each of its conditions acted as a springboard. He led the life of a teacher, but also that of a Master; an academician, but also a scholar; a father, but equally a man of the world, and indeed of high society. A privileged life, as he acknowledges in his diary without either false modesty or ingratitude. A happy life. But there is also a lucidity that is already liberating the man from this happiness. The result is a happiness that can be contemplated without scorn or envy, a human happiness above happiness: 'I passed for a happy man; from the experience and the memory of happiness, I hope I have managed to retain the art of knowing how to do without it' (1942).

Certainly, the particular historical conditions in which Brunschvicg lived made such a human achievement possible. It was an age of material security in which political problems remained, at least in appearance, separate from social ones and in which every revolution was already over; an age of 'European equilibrium' with the 'great powers' stable and evenly balanced, in which Germany was Germany and not a metaphysics, Russia was Russia and not a messianism. But the political and social contingencies which were agreeable to a Brunschvicg do not in the least compromise the impression gained at meeting him of human perfection and civilization.

The abundance in which he lived placed him in an area of nobility that preserved his innate nobility from all change. And rather than use excess, his grandeur expressed itself in equilibrium – grace, finesse and a kind of absence.

In conversation he used short replies, phrases that avoided degenerating into maxims, while his teaching displayed a predilection for expressions that were light but rich in possiblities and already breaking open the verbal envelope. This was the marvellously civilized speech of Brunschvicg. It remained aloof from the writer's simple concerns, and was even less interested in speechifying. But the way in which thought trembled in its verbal form constituted for him the very tremble of thought itself. The mind manifested itself by spilling over the admittedly necessary limits of language. The resistance put up by language excited thought. It is in this that Brunschvicg's speech bore witness to his French training at the Ecole Normale Supérieure and to everything that is most nobly French about the traditions of that school. 'And my most beautiful thought', writes Brunschvicg on 29 May 1892, 'is to say that one cannot express thought.' In 1942, he adds: 'if it is true that the expression, albeit by its own beauty, betrays the thought that it should have served, the effort to subdue the rebellious slave is the very life of thought.'

III

I once saw Brunschvicg unhappy. I remember a Sunday morning on rue Scheffer in autumn 1932. It was raining or clouding over, and in his large first-floor study Brunschvicg was sitting by his vast work table in his slippers, waiting for his students to arrive. It was early, and no one had yet come. 'The men of my generation', said Brunschvicg, 'have known two victories: the Dreyfus Affair and 1918.' Outside it was now really raining, and in Germany there was mounting anger. 'And now', went on Brunschvicg, with that air of having no air that was unique to him, 'those two battles are being fought all over again ... unless this is just an old man's lament', he added after a moment's silence, already distancing himself from what he had just said.

In the Diary, we find an even more dispairing Léon Brunschvicg: 'The war: contagion of sufferings, without explanation or consolation, which multiply a billion times' (9 February 1942). 'In short, in my life, stupefaction dominates ... yesterday in the face of the mediocrity surrounding me, today in the face of the horror of inhumanity' (3 June 1942). 'When one has dreamed a lot, there are very few things that surprise you in reality (7 December 1898) ... In 1892 maybe, but in 1942!' (7 December 1942). 'When we have to bear, as we do today, the weight of the whole world, examining our conscience is something that risks exhausting us without being of much use' (10 August 1942).

Who is this 'us' that supports the weight of the whole world? It is not the Jew, it is the man who had won the Dreyfus Affair and the First World War. A Reason, a Conscience. To speak of the man Brunschvicg is to speak of the whole generation of which he was both a part and which he summed up, those who fought during the Dreyfus Affair. They remembered less the fact that such an injustice had been possible in a civilized age than the triumph recorded by justice. This memory marked them. They were to be found occupying every chair in higher education up to the middle of the so-called interwar years. Their faces seemed to radiate light. They were men who had proved the existence of justice – that was their civil status. In their brains, ideas which had become vulgarized were thought through with acuity. They showed the power of truth spreading through proof and not through propaganda, that terrorism of the mind. Their motives lay in justice and not in the will to power, their criteria originated in moral conscience rather than in the horrible prestige of the Sacred.

To identify with human conscience appears to have been the human life of a Brunschvicg. That is why we do not find, in the Diary's entries for the whole of 1942, the slightest trace of a specifically Jewish reaction. Brunschvicg is wounded only in his human conscience, and certainly there is no dissimilation in this silence. He was a member of the Central Committee of the Israeli Alliance from well before the war and never tried to forget his origins. But it is perhaps through this that he represents, even for those who feel they are men only through their Judaism, a profoundly respectable form of successful assimilation (which is so decried, and justly). Assimilation for Brunschvicg proceeded not from betrayal, but from adherence to a universal ideal to which he could lay claim outside of any particularism.

IV

'Neither sensitive, nor sentimental; my soul exists completely in a subtle sentiment; I should call myself *sentimenteux*, a word that seems beautiful to me; chemically, it indicates its weak intensity; literally, the suffix of disdain indicates its intellectuality; grammatically, the feminine forms a profound pun: *sentimenteuse* [sentimental/false]' (22 February 1892). This mistrust of sentiment is required by mind. 'If we had only sentiment, we should suffer only from what is: but we have an intelligence in order to suffer from what is merely possible and a conscience in order to suffer from what should be' (20 December 1892) ... 'To avoid platitudes, three dimensions seem necessary in grief as in space' (1942). There is nothing fixed in this need for intelligence: 'An *idée fixe*: if one has one, one thinks of nothing, if one does not have one, one believes in nothing ... at least so long as one has not managed to differentiate between the idea that seizes us and the idea that we seize upon.' Beyond static ideas, creative thought manifests itself. But Brunschvicg was accused of intellectualism and being unfit for inner life.

I remember the 1937 Descartes Congress. New philosophical tendencies were already being affirmed: existentialist thought, Catholic thought, Marxist thought. Anguish, death, care, were increasingly popular topics. In the course of one session, Gabriel Marcel launched a fiery attack on those thinkers 'deprived of any gift of inner life', blind to God, blind to death. At which point Brunschvicg, still with that air of having no air, said: 'I think that the death of Léon Brunschvicg preoccupies Léon Brunschvicg less than the death of Gabriel Marcel preoccupies Gabriel Marcel.' Neither the sadness of old age nor the thought of death is absent from Brunschvicg's Diary, but all that sadness is tempered by irony, and he uses a wise man's smirk to defend the gates of philosophy.

The inner life for Brunschvicg is not confused either with mysticism or with religious anxiety. His inner life is composed of reason and enlightenment. He is much more wary of religions and Christianity than of God. He knows another way to reach Him, one based on the coincidence of rational activity and moral consciousness: the God of Descartes, certainly not that of Pascal, nor the God-Object of the eighteenth-century *philosophes*. But although Brunschvicg ignores Judaism, since he does not know it, does he not discover its essential strains by affirming that at the heart of the Infinite, where the intellect dwells, there is an independent man, master of his fate, who communicates with the Eternal, in the clear light of intellectual and moral action? 'One can only work effectively for the future if one wishes to realize it immediately' (24 October 1892) ... 'and totally, which does not lighten the task'

(1942). That is the thought of a Jew, a thought echoed in the famous verse by Bialik: 'And if justice exists, let it appear immediately'. This atheism is much closer to the One God than the mystical experiences and horrors of the Sacred to be found in the supposed religious revival of our contemporaries.

Naturally, our generation could not derive from the experience of Hitler what Brunschvicg's generation derived from the Dreyfus Affair. If the 1945 victory demonstrates that in history, vice is ultimately punished and virtue recognized, we do not wish once more to bear the brunt of this demonstration. But let us hope that today's Jewish youth, when it sets off for new spiritual and sometimes geographical horizons, does not purely and simply shake the dust of the world it is leaving off its feet. There is gold in that dust.

Being a Westerner

For our fathers, the twentieth century signified a success. The elegance of the rounded figure lent a certain triumphal tone to this age of reason. Since then, two wars have given this triumph a lugubrious resonance and the successful outcome of humanity is taking on the appearance of an ending. Henceforth, it is understood that the terms progress and science bear witness only to the primary spirit [*esprit*] and that only a thirst for the irrational takes the place of human dignity. A religion incapable of quenching this thirst is proscribed – unless it invents, from various bits and pieces, the irrational element it lacks.

Perhaps, however, the discredit into which reason has fallen has to do not with the century's moments of anguish and ecstasy but with the isolation into which that reason is obliged to retire by virtue of its very nobility. A Cantor or an Einstein has no doubt fewer contemporaries than a Descartes or a Newton once had, says Léon Brunschvicg in 'On True and False Conversion', a series of articles published before the war in the *Revue de Métaphysique et de Morale* which have just been published in volume form.[1] Perhaps this work from beyond the grave will have the salutary effect of giving a bad intellectual conscience to those who have forgotten, using the pretext of youth, what has after all, for three centuries, now gauged the exact gap between thought and childishness.

But is it urgent to think? Vital questions assail us: our daily bread and that of our fellow man; the destruction threatening the world, our country, our families. Respectable questions, but questions which the instinct for conservation cannot justify. What must be preserved beyond our private existence? What are the lessons for being? The humblest of discourses, the most hesitant stuttering, covers itself with grand words without which the cries of naked existence put man to shame. Defending the West, defending civilization, defending the mind [*esprit*]! That horrible word 'mind' – a refuge, like hell itself, for every good intention and unkind action.

What does it mean to be a Westerner? Is there in this allegiance to the West the expression of belonging to a high form of society, one that is more than a coalition of interests, a professional or confessional grouping, more than adherence to local customs, a philosophical or literary credo, or even a Review, a study circle, an 'original' doctrine all of which, furnished with a social reason, quoted according to the roles of the passionate game of letters in the neighbouring Review or study circle, gave their adherents, collaborators and subscribers the illusion of entering history and renewing civilization? Léon Brunschvicg believes in the existence of an absolute society: Galileo, Descartes, Kepler, Huyghens, Newton, Cantor, Einstein – and a few others. A society made up of minds of the first order. And let all the rest be literature. He also thinks that the intellectual activity of the members of this company coincides exactly with the moral generosity and religious purity that guarantee man's dignity.

The results of physics and mathematics map out a real universe behind the verbal universe of conceptual abstractions. But above all, these conceptual abstractions, which raise themselves up with a disturbing speed to the level of the Divine, in reality remain prisoners of perception, which is egocentric and ultimately egoist like animality. Only mathematical thought manages to free itself from the camouflaged egoism of scholastic knowledge and its mystical and rationalist relics. It is a creative thought. 'We are no longer in fact concerned with stable forms presented once and for all, but with moving forms, subtle relations constructed by the mind in the course of its free workings': this piece of Brunschvicg reationalism was written by Jean Wahl, a man curious to examine every new idea while stubbornly defending every valuable idea. It is a truly inner thought. Within mathematical evidence thought frees itself from its biological condition: simultaneously subservient to and dominating truth, it is pure self-intimacy, 'the transition from the temporal present to the eternal present' (p. 177).

> Born to be a simple animal, man broke the fetters of his biological finality. Knowledge was a means, and he made it into an end, one which, thanks to the establishment of certain forms of behaviour relating to mathematical co-ordination and experimental control, conquered the dignity of an intrinsic value. (p. 177)

That a spiritual life should be one devoid of egoism – *egoism as a striving for salvation* – is in his view the lesson to be learned from the West.

47

The preoccupation with our salvation is a remnant of self-love, a trace of natural egocentrism from which we must be torn by the religious life. As long as you think only salvation, you turn your back on God. God is God, only for the person who overcomes the temptation to degrade Him and use Him for his own ends. (p. 258)

Certain students and those whom Brunschvicg terms 'the twentieth-century Precartesians' are free to hold forth on the crisis of the scientific spirit and turn with enthusiasm to mystery. 'Beneath the envelope of mystery, psychologists, historians or sociologists manage to rediscover the remains of a primitive mentality ... I do not understand why the irrationalists of the present day pride themselves on having killed off the old concepts and then immediately set about adoring their shadow,' exclaims Léon Brunschvicg on p. 259. His books, based on the calm truth of science and of the world which science understands, are like that sudden rush of good sense in certain families when the childish behaviour of adolescents is tolerated until the moment when they are about to do something stupid, at which point one cries: 'That's enough'.

The concern for salvation, even when it raises itself above immediate needs and seeks only to triumph over death, still stems from the biological *self*; the biological self cannot dispense with mythology and war. These are the points on which Brunschvicg's intransigence is infinitely close to us. Judaism also appeals to a humanity devoid of myths – not because the marvellous is repugnant to its narrow soul but because myth, abeit sublime, introduces into the soul that troubled element, that impure element of magic and sorcery and that drunkenness of the Sacred and of war that prolong the animal within the civilized.

'Can the God of the wars of religion be the God of Religion?' asks Brunschvicg.

Just as we cannot look away from sacrifices that are joyfully made and heroically offered, as an exaltation of faith, so we cannot avoid gazing on the suffering violently imposed by everything in the way of bloody fury and so-called charitable crimes that is conversely entailed in that same exaltation. Is it on this that we are going to build a theory of Divine Providence?' (pp. 120–21)

This is a profound text: not because it involves the extrinsic witness of history, but because it denounces the very ambiguity of exaltation – abnegation and cruelty. Because cruel acts find themselves conditioned precisely by the residual elements that are uncontrolled and impure in their supposedly pure and simple love of the transcendent God. The Churches claim in this way to go beyond the austere spirituality of the Law. Is this not the ultimate purpose for 'the blindness of the Synagogue', which refuses the splendour and levitations of salvation by faith? What Christian theologians present as a stubborn attachment to the letter is in reality a refusal of that which is too easily called spirit [*esprit*]. Authentic Judaism thinks of itself in terms of an inner morality, not an outer dogmatism. The supernatural is not an obsession for Judaism. Its relationship with divinity is determined by the exact range of the ethical.

Brunschvicg quotes two verses from the epistles of John: 'No one who denies the Son has the Father. He who confesses the Son has the Father also' (I John 2:23); 'No man has ever seen God; if we love one another, God abides in us and his love is perfected in us' (I John 4:12). He comments that the mythological content of the first verse brings thought back to a point short of the Old Testament, which 'no doubt is written in an anthropomorphic style, in which the unity of God is none the less maintained with a jealous care' – while the second verse, affirming the pure spirituality of God and His interiority, 'places us beyond the New Testament, for the distinction between divine persons ceases to be denied and affirmed all together by the magical virtue of a formulary' (p. 143). How can we fail to admire the astonishing intuition, in a man initiated into Judaism via Christianity, that allows him to devine that the Jewish Bible possesses the style of anthropomorphism? But how can we fail to recognize, in opposition to Brunschvicg, that the inspiration for the second text is no newer – is in fact older – than the New Testament; that it is the very inspiration for the Old Testament.

The piety with which we keep alive the memory of Léon Brunschvicg prevents us from claiming him as our own – he who was so superbly independent when it came to belonging to any confessional mode. We rejoin him only at the point where he discovered the essence of the West by conversing with the greatest spirits.

Means of Identification

The very fact of questioning one's Jewish identity means it is already lost. But by the same token, it is precisely through this kind of cross-examination that one still hangs on to it. Between *already* and *still* Western Judaism walks a tightrope.

What identity does it cling to? One that refers only to itself and ignores all attributes: one is not a Jew by being this or that. Ideas, characters and things can be identified in so far as they differ from other ideas, characters and things. But people do not produce evidence in order to identify themselves. A person is not who he is because he was born here rather than there, and on such and such a day, or because he has blond hair, a sharp tongue or a big heart. Before he starts comparing himself to anyone else, he just is who he is. In the same way, one just is a Jew. It is not even something one adheres to, for that already suggests the possibility of estrangement. It is not something one is possessed by, for adherence to a doctrine soon turns into fatalism. Through the ill that it inflicts on itself, this extreme intimacy linking the Jew to Judaism is like a day-to-day expression of happiness or the sense of having been chosen. 'You are born a Jew; you don't become one.' This half-truth bears out the ultimate feeling of intimacy. It is not a racist remark, thank God. For one can indeed become a Jew, but it is as if there had been no conversion. Can one subscribe to whatever is human? Certain Jews have a way of saying 'Jew' instead of the word 'mankind', as if they took Judaism to be the subject and humanity the predicate.

But this absolute and unshakable sense of identity, which is founded on an adherence that pre-exists any form of allegiance, is not expressed in uncontrollable terms, as being a subject that is stirred by unfathomable feelings. On the contrary, it is alien to any sense of introspection or complacency. Instead of just paying attention to the outside world, it exhibits a perpetual attentiveness that is exclusive and monotheist. It listens and obeys like a guard who never expects to be relieved [*relève*]. This was recognized by Rabbi Hayyim Volozhiner, the favourite disciple of the Gaon of

Vilna, when, in 1824, in the *Nefesh ha'Hayyim* (a work little known
in the West but one in which the living elements of Judaism
converge), he wrote that a Jew is accountable and responsible for
the whole edifice of creation. There is something that binds and
commits [*engage*] man still more than the salvation of his soul. The
act, word and thought of a Jew have the formidable privilege of
being able to destroy and restore whole worlds. Far from being a
serene self-presence, therefore, Jewish identify is rather the
patience, fatigue and numbness of a responsibility – a stiff neck that
supports the universe.

This primordial experience is expressed in a more tolerable way
by Zionism, even if it gets turned into politics and nationalism in the
process. For many Israelis, their identity card is the full extent of
their Jewish identity as it is, perhaps, for all those potential Israelis
who are still in the Diaspora. But here Jewish identify runs the risk
of becoming confused with nationalism, and from that point on, a
loss of Jewish identify is probably the price to be paid in order to
have it renewed.

The Western mentality to which the Jew became assimilated, to
such a degree that henceforth he touched only the surface of
Judaism, is perhaps defined by its refusal to adhere to anything
unless it performs an act of adhesion. In the nationalist movements
which it has promoted, this mentality uncovers something savage.
Any special attachment is marked by the feeling that it is shared by
all. From that point on, one must not simply accept one's own
nature spontaneously; instead, one begins by stepping back, looking at oneself from the outside, pondering about oneself. To
compare oneself to others involves analysing and weighing oneself
up, reducing the personal identity that one *is* to a series of
signs, attributes, contents, qualities and values. The institution that
embodies such a mentality is called the university.

To the extent that the loss of an immediate Jewish identity
proceeds from such a feeling and such demands, it does not
represent a merely regrettable moment in the evolution of Judaism.
A Western Jew must still pretend, as Descartes puts it, that he has
still to be converted to Judaism. He feels duty bound to approach it
as a system of concepts and values that are being presented for his
judgement; even the exceptional fate of being the man who supports
the universe is one he sees petrified in the statue of Atlas. It is his
duty, then, to reformulate everything in the language of the
university. Philosophy and philology are the two daughters of this
universal speech (wherein we must guard against the younger

devouring the elder). It is up to Judaism to support this language, even if it was important one day to turn this language back on the civilization nurturing (and nurtured by) the university.

But this legitimate demand for a system or doctrine – in short, for a conscience – is shown to be completely naive when it proceeds as though it were drawing up an inventory of values in the attempt to discover something original in Judaism. A great civilization does not make an inventory of itself, but opens itself up to study through grammar, the dictionary and scholarship. It does not define itself in a cut-and-dried manner on the basis of a few facile antitheses which are inevitably going to be fallacious. It is universal – that is to say, it is precisely capable of whatever can be found in any other civilization, of whatever is humanly legitimate. It is therefore fundamentally non-original, stripped of all local colour. Only those civilizations labelled exotic (or the exotic and perishable elements of civilizations) can be easily distinguished from one another. To the extent that they lose their 'curiosity' value, they find it increasingly difficult to define themselves, since it is only through them that everything is defined. It is not to originality that civilizations owe their excellence, but to their high degree of universality, to their coherence – that is to say, to the lack of hypocrisy in their generosity. We can tolerate the pluralism of great civilizations and even understand why they cannot merge. The very nature of truth explains how this is impossible: truth manifests itself in a way that appeals to an enormous number of human possibilities and, through them, a whole range of histories, traditions and approaches. But even when this multiplicity is acknowledged, it does not absolve the individual from a rational choice. Such a choice cannot be based on the vagaries of subjective taste or some sudden whim. At such moments the amateur and the brute come together again. The only criteria on which we can base the rational examination that is required are those of the maximum degree of universality and the minimum degree of hyprocrisy.

This examination cannot be reduced to the level of testimony: it is not enough to take stock of what 'the rest of us as Jews' are, and what we feel these days. We should run the risk of taking a compromised, alienated, forgotten, ill-adapted or even dead Judaism to be the essence of Judaism. We cannot be conscious of something in whatever way we wish! The other path is steep but the only one to take: it brings us back to the source, the forgotten, ancient, difficult books, and plunges us into strict and laborious study.

Jewish identity is inscribed in these old documents. It cannot be annulled by simply ignoring these means of identification, just as it cannot be reduced to its simplest form of expression without entering into the discourse of the modern world. One cannot refute the Scriptures without knowing how to read them; or muzzle only philogy without doing the same to philosophy; or put a halt, if necessary, to philosophical discourse, without still philosophizing.

Is this worm-eaten old Judaism to be preferred to the Judaism of the Jews? Well, why not? We don't yet know which of the two is the more lively. Are the true books just books? Or are they not also the embers still glowing beneath the ashes, as Rabbi Eliezer called the words of the Prophets? In this way the flame traverses History without burning in it. But the truth illuminates whoever breathes on the flame and coaxes it back to life. More or less. It's a question of breath. To admit the effect that literature has on men is perhaps the ultimate wisdom of the West in which the people of the Bible may recognize themselves. King Josiah ordered a kingdom to be established around an old lost book which was rediscovered by his clerks (*The Book of the Torah* in 622 BCE). It is the pefect image of a life that delivers itself up to the texts. The myth of our Europe as being born of a similar inspiration was called the Renaissance.

The Ark and the Mummy

Let us add a few words in prose to the lyricism of Judaism, to all that merry sprituality towards which we all find ourselves so borne.

Jews are men who live in Israel, Europe, America and elsewhere. They are Israeli, French, English, American. . . . Their moving fate, which is played out above history, is played out within history. Their participation in the terrestrial world is, believe me, the essential factor in this supernatural history. I believe that their role, in this history, consisted above all in creating a society, a type of man who lives in a demystified, disenchanted world, a type of man to whom, as it is somewhat vulgarly put, *one has nothing more to say*. Mystery is the excuse used for many a crime.

Enthusiasm is, after all, possession by a god. Jews wish not to be possessed, but to be responsible. Their God is the master of justice; He judges in the open light of reason and discourse. This God cannot see to all man's sins; the sin committed against man can be pardoned only by the man who has suffered by it; God cannot pardon it. For His glory as a moral God and for the glory of the man who has come of age, God is powerless.

The people who wish to demystify the world none the less have a life that is subject to those numerous prohibitions which constitute the practices of Jewish ritual. This provokes admiration and indignation in the world at large. One rarely speaks of it. But the learned foundations of these disciplines, whose admirable architecture was recently described by Pierre Maxime Schuhl, was for centuries the guarantee of this independence of spirit.

If the majority of present-day Jews have become detached but contrive to reply: 'I am a Jew', it is because a minority, without worrying about the eschatological perspectives that permit them to write beautiful books, perpetuate this disciplined and highly inconvenient life.

So much freedom allied to so many superannuated usages! So much freedom and so little 'spirituality'! What an atrocious anachronism, what a fossil! Toynbee worked in vain!

But this paradox was one the Wise Men of Israel were aware of, and in fact claimed for themselves.

Across the desert, one *midrash* tells us, the Israelis coming out of Egypt carried the remarks of Joseph in an ark alongside the ark of Him who lives eternally.

Passers-by were astonished. What did these two arks in the desert signify? They were told: 'This one is the coffin of a dead man and that one is the ark of Him who lives eternally.'

Then the passers-by – like people today, like Toynbee – asked: 'What is the coffin of a dead man doing beside the ark of Him who lives eternally?'

The reply was: 'He who lies in the coffin of the dead man has accomplished all that is written on the Tablets lying in the ark of Him who lives eternally.'

Have you understood what this means?

The living God can be found among this free people in the desert only if the memory of him who has rigorously obeyed marches alongside.

II
COMMENTARIES

One biblical verse may convey several teachings
(Tractate Sanhedrin 34a)

Messianic Texts

The commentaries you are about to read refer to four passages from the final chapter of Tractate Sanhedrin. They concern the different aspects of messianism.

Several pages of this chapter in fact put forward a profusion of theses dealing with the notion of messianism. This notion is complex and difficult; only popular opinion regards it as simple. The popular concept of the Messiah – translating entirely into terms of concrete perception, on the same level as our daily relations with things – does not satisfy thought. One has failed to say anything about the Messiah if one represents him as a person who comes to put a miraculous end to the violence in the world, the injustice and contradictions which destroy humanity but have their source in the nature of humanity, and simply in Nature. However, popular opinion retains the emotional power of the messianic ideal, and we daily abuse this term and this emotional power.[1]

The central problem dealt with in each of the passages commented on here is indicated by a subtitle. In reality, the problems treated overlap.

The following pages transcribe papers given at the third and fourth conferences of Jewish intellectuals, organized by the French section of the World Jewish Congress in 1960 and 1961. Their form remains that of the spoken texts. They are presented in the same order as that in which they were spoken without taking account of the order in which the talmudic texts commented on actually figure in the Tractate Sanhedrin. References to the talmudic pagination none the less indicate that order.

The exposition of a talmudic text by someone who has not spent his life studying rabbinic literature in the traditional way is a very daring enterprise, even if the person attempting it has been familiar since childhood with the square letters, and even if he has derived much from these texts for his own intellectual life. The traditional knowledge of talmudic texts, in all their scope, by itself would not satisfy a Western thinker, but this knowledge is none the less the necessary condition of Jewish thought. The following essay is an attempt to broach such knowledge.

The Notion of Messianism (Sanhedrin 99a)

> R. Hiyaa b. Abba said in R. Johanan's name: All the prophets prophesied [all the good things] only in respect of the messianic era; but as for the world to come, '*the eye hath not seen, O Lord, beside thee, what he hath prepared for him that waiteth for him*'.

The final part of this text, 'the eye hath not seen', is a free translation, to put it mildly (as talmudic translations very often are), of a verse from Isaiah (64:4) which the Bible of Zadoc Kahn translates as follows: 'no eye has seen a God besides thee who waits for those who wait for him'.

A free Talmud translation, to put it mildly! This is not the time to justify such freedom. In any case, it takes nothing away from the talmudist's real thoughts, to which it gives expression.

The translations – always unique, sometimes bizarre – of the talmudists try to open up the simple lesson of the text to new perspectives which, in reality, give access to the very dimension in which the deep meaning of the simple reading can alone be constituted.

R. Hiyya b. Abba, in R. Johanan's name, first puts forward a classic Jewish thesis (not always familiar to Jews) that there is a difference between the future world and the messianic era. He then states that the messianic era – a charnel house between two eras rather than an end to History – consists in fulfilling all the prophecies, a promise of a delivered and better humanity. One can, in effect, group the promises of the prophets into two categories: the political and the social. The injustice and alienation introduced by the arbitrary workings of political powers in every human enterprise will disappear; but the social injustice, the power the rich hold over the poor, will disappear at the same time as political violence. The talmudic tradition represented by R. Hiyya b. Abba, speaking in the name of Rabbi Johanan, views the messianic era as the simultaneous achievement of every political and social promise.

As for the future world, it seems to exist on another level. Our text defines it as the privilege of 'him that waiteth for him'. It therefore concerns a personal and intimate order, lying outside the achievements of history that wait for humanity to be united in a collective destiny. The future world cannot be announced by a prophet addressing everyone. Judaism, like an objective institution, like a Synagogue, teaches only the truths that concern the Good of the community and the public order. It teaches and prophesies justice. It is not an insurance company. The personal salvation of men, the descreet and intimate relationship between man and God, escapes the indiscretion of the prophets; no one can fix in advance the itinerary of this adventure.

But this is how the text goes on:

> Now, he disagrees with Samuel, who said: This world differs from [that of] the days of the Messiah only in respect of servitude to [foreign] powers.

This well-known text will be taken up again by Maimonides when he tries to synthesize the opinions of Samuel and Johanan. But this opinion, which is supposedly the opposite of Johanan's, is expressed in such a way that one initially has the impression that it is announcing an era that differs from its predecessor on a point of detail: the messianic era indicates only the end of political violence. And no doubt this concerns the end of the political servitude suffered by an Israel that was dispersed among the nations. But Samuel's thinking must be examined in depth, in order to open up a vaster horizon in which Israel's hope resides and without which these private hopes cannot remain on the level of thoughts.

In other texts, Samuel takes political power just as seriously. The era in which political power is reduced, in which politics no longer presents an obstacle to man's moral enterprise, or reduces it to nothing, or puts up all the arguments against it, marks the high point of history and merits the name 'messianic era'.

Can the end of political violence be separated from the end of social violence? Does Samuel announce a capitalist paradise in which there is no more war, no more military service, no more anti-semitism, in a way that leaves savings untouched and the social problem unsolved? A parallel text – for there are many parallel texts in the Talmud – possibly indicates the reasons put forward by Samuel in support of his thesis:

> There is no difference between this world and the days of the Messiah except [that in the latter there will be no] bondage of foreign Powers, as it says: *For the poor shall never cease out of the land* (Deuteronomy 15:11).

It is evidently impossible to attribute to a Doctor of the Talmud the opinion we have just caricatured, according to which the members of the messianic era can be complacent about social injustice. In the passage from Deuteronomy quoted by Samuel, not far from the verse which states that 'the poor will never move out of the land', there is another verse which advises that 'there will be no poor among you' (Deuteronomy 15:4). Samuel cannot have ignored it; his opinion must therefore mean something completely different. Does the disagreement between Rabbi Johanan and Samuel not concern instead the meaning that is positively taken on by the messianic era? For Rabbi Johanan, the messianic era resolves all political contradictions and puts an end to economic stability as it inaugurates a non-alienable contemplative or active life. Perhaps this life is one of absolute knowledge or artistic action or friendship, but at all events it is a life above the political and the social, which have been rendered inoffensive. In this light, Samuel's position acquires its full force: for him, spiritual life, as such, cannot be separated from economic solidarity with the Other – the *giving* is in some way the original movement of spiritual life, which cannot be suppressed by the messianic outcome. The latter allows one a complete blossoming and the greatest purity and the highest joys, by warding off the political violence that distorts the *giving*. Not that the poor should survive so that the rich have the messianic joy of nourishing them. We must think more radically: the Other is always the poor one, poverty defines the poor person as Other, and the relation with the Other will always be an offering and a gift, not an 'empty-handed' approach. Spiritual life is essentially a moral life and likes to operate in the economic sphere.

Consequently, Samuel also has a very high opinion of the messianic era, but he does not believe that the Other, as a poor man, is merely the accident of a regrettable historical regime. The 'future world' – that is to say, that plan of life to which the *individual* accedes through the possibilities of inner life and which is not announced by any prophet – opens up new perspectives. The messianic era as part of history (where the meaning of our real historical responsibilities is consequently revealed) is as yet unaware of these perspectives.

Contrary to Samuel, who does not therefore separate the messianic era from the difficulties encountered by morality and its attempts to surpass them, Rabbi Johanan envisages a pure and gracious spiritual life that is in some way stripped of the heavy load of things which is made concrete by economics. In his vision one can have direct relationships with the Other, who no longer appears as poor but as a friend; there are no more professions, only arts; and the economic repercussions of actions no longer have any bearing. Rabbi Johanan in some way believes in the ideal of a disincarnated spirit, of total grace and harmony, an ideal exempt from any drama; while Samuel, on the other hand, feels the permanent effort of renewal demanded by this spiritual life.

And in fact, our text goes on to relate two other lessons of Rabbi Johanan transmitted by R. Hiyya b. Abba:

> R. Hiyya b. Abba also said in R. Johanan's name: All the prophets prophesied only for the repentant sinners; but as for the perfectly righteous [who had never sinned at all], *'the eye hath not seen, O God, beside thee, what he hath prepared for him that waiteth for him.'*

There then follows a digression, to which I shall shortly return:

> R. Hiyya b. Abba also said in R. Johanan's name: All the prophets prophesied only in respect of him who marries his daughter to a scholar, or engages in business on behalf of a scholar, or benefits a scholar with his possessions; but as for scholars themselves, – *'the eye hath not seen, O God, beside thee etc.'*

Rabbi Johanan teaches us about one new theory: for whom the prophets prophesied. They prophesied first and foremost for repentant sinners. The future world is reserved for the perfectly righteous who have never sinned at all. The righteous who are repentant inherit the messianic era, a world enjoyed by the perfectly righteous who have never sinned at all. Who are these perfectly righteous who have never sinned? They are people without drama, kept apart from the contradictions of the world. Always the ideal of a disincarnated and gracious spirit imposes itself on Rabbi Johanan.

Let us compare the first text with the second, which I have just quoted. The prophets prophesied for those who continue with their daily economic life but do not abandon themselves to the actual determinism of such a life: for those who found a family, of course, but who already dedicate their family to the disinterested life of the intellect incarnated in the scholar who has direct access to the Revelation and the knowledge of God; for those who engage in business but dedicate this work to the scholar; for those with possessions who benefit a scholar with them. Family, work, law – these institutions from pre-messianic history can be shielded, for Rabbi Johanan, from the necessities of history by individuals who are as yet incapable of direct relations with the disinterested spirit but can participate in it indirectly, using the scholar as intermediary. The messianic era would therefore bring them up a notch, enabling them to enter the life of the disinterested and gracious mind of the scholar, who is called upon to attain the highest rank: that of the future world, about which I shall speak shortly.

Let us note – for it is characteristic of the way in which the Talmud broaches questions – that the opposing positions of Rabbi Johanan and Samuel, like every position taken up by the Doctors, reflects two positions between which thought somehow oscillates eternally. Does the spirit indicate a quasi-divine life that is free of the limitations of the human condition, or does the human condition, with its limits and its drama, express the very life of the spirit? It is important to emphasize that these two conceptions come within the area of Jewish thought, for these two conceptions express man. It is also important to be on one's guard against the simplistic use of antitheses indulged in by thinkers anxious to sum up the apparent options within Jewish thought.

Let us now look at another aspect of the (eternal) discussion between Rabbi Johanan and Samuel. Rabbi Johanan thinks that the advent of the messianic era and the happiness it heralds depend on merit. Is it not Samuel who has asked: 'For whom did the prophets prophesy?' It is as if for him, their promises concerned the whole world. In a second text I wish to comment on, Samuel expressly denies the link between the coming of the Messiah and merit. Samuel conceives of the advent of the messianic era as an event that does not depend simply on the moral perfection of individuals. For Rabbi Johanan, the political problem is resolved at the same time as the social problem, and their joint solution lies in the hands of man, since it depends on one's moral power. There is a natural move from moral activity to messianic era. Nothing can alienate moral activity; the good I wish to do, of which I am conscious, spills over into reality, without getting lost in the conflict. It provokes the desired social transformation, which in turn leads to a political transformation. The moral agent remains the true agent of what he does; his intentions are not inverted through spilling over into historical reality.

For Samuel, on the other hand, something foreign to the moral individual exists, something which must first be suppressed before the messianic era can come. The Messiah is, first and foremost, this break. For the lucid conscience in control of its intentions, the coming of the Messiah carries an irrational element, or at least something which does not depend on man, which comes from outside: the outcome of political contradictions. What is interesting is the very category of an event which has come from *outside*. It matters little whether this outside is the action of God or a political revolution that is distinct from morality: the Talmud is often interested much more in the category than in the event iself about which it speaks. R. Johanan's conception puts everything down to human freedom and moral action. Samuel's conception places between the moral enterprise, between human freedom and the resulting good, an obstacle of a completely new type: political violence which must be surmounted by the messianic coming.

That is the gist of what I have to say about the first text, but it contains a digression that I ignored and a final part that I also want to examine.

When Rabbi Hiyya b. Abba says in Rabbi Johanan's name that the prophets prophesied only for repentant sinners, but that the perfectly righteous who has never sinned at all will have a fate that 'the eye hath not seen, O God, beside thee', etc., someone disagrees. Rabbi Abbahu, speaking in Rav's name (which is not at all certain, since a parallel text in Tractate Berakoth does not mention Rav) says: 'The place occupied by repentant sinners cannot be attained even by the completely righteous.'

This last text is often quoted. The advantage given to repentant sinners over the completely righteous evokes the *'felix culpa'* and flatters our taste for pathos, a sensibility nourished on Christianity and Dostoyevsky. Is not the labourer hired at the eleventh hour the most interesting one? Repentance is worth more than an uninterrupted existence spent in good, or boring, fidelity. The discussion between R. Hiyya b. Abba and R. Abbahu shows that the latter's opinion represents only one option: the essence of moral effort for R. Abbahu lies in returning to Good after experiencing the adventure of evil; the real effort would be revolutionary and dramatic. The other opinion persists. It chooses a blameless purity and a perfection untainted by history, absolutely protected against any error and removed from natural determinism. This option also demands effort and virility. The Talmud is content to emphasize the ambiguity of the problem. The dialogue between R. Hiyya b. Abba and R. Abbahu is an eternal dialogue taking place within human consciousness. Both support their thesis by drawing on the same

verse: 'Peace, peace, to him that is far off, and to him that is near.'
This concern to relate the 'opinions' and 'options' back to the
crossroads of the Problem, where they become dignified into
thoughts, is the true spirit of the Talmud.

I come now to the final part of my text: 'the eye hath not seen ...'.
And yet! One would like the completely righteous to have a glimpse
of this promised thing! What is promised to the wise men, and not
only to those who participate indirectly in wisdom and perfection,
providing for the upkeep of scholars and giving their daughters in
marriage? What is the recompense which, beyond the messianic era,
sets the value of the future world? To what does the phrase 'the eye
hath not seen' refer?

> R. Joshua b. Levi said: To the wine that has been kept
> [maturing] with its grapes since the six days of Creation. A
> famous vintage! An ancient wine that had not been bottled,
> or even harvested. A wine not given the least opportunity to
> become adulterated. Absolutely unaltered, absolutely pure.
> The future world is this wine. Let us admire the beauty of
> the image, but none the less question the meaning it might
> have.

Have you never despaired of understanding an ancient text? Have
you not been scared by the many interpretations lying between the
text and yourself? Have you never been discouraged by the
ambiguity in every word, however straight and precise, as it
immediately fades into adulteration and interpretation? Isn't the
future world the possibility of rediscovering the first meaning,
which would be the ultimate meaning, of every word? The magnificent image of wine remaining unaltered in the grape since the six
days of Creation offers the original meaning of the Scriptures lying
beyond all the commentary and history by which it was subsequently changed. But it also offers the hope of understanding every
human language, announcing a new *Logos*, and with it another
humanity. The image unties the tragic knot of the world's history.
   One curious coincidence is that wine in Hebrew is *yayin* and the
numerical value of its letters adds up to 70, as with the three letters
forming the word *sod*, or mystery. Commentators pick up on this.
But the word *sod*, or mystery, in talmudic symbolism signifies the
ultimate meaning of the Scriptures, the one reached after searching
for the literal meaning, or *pohate*, which then raises us to the

allusive meaning, or *Remèz*, from which we reach the symbolic meaning, or *Drache*. But the true mystery stays within the original simplicity, more simple again than the literal meaning. Only the original meaning, in its unaltered simplicity, will be practised in a future world where history has already been covered. Time and history are therefore required. The first meaning, 'older' than the first, lies in the future. We must pass through interpretation to surpass interpretation.

Calculating numerical values proves nothing, of course. Is it not just a standard clause used in the Talmud to pass the idea of unintelligibility from scholar to scholar, and attack the 'bourgeois' dazed by the strange coincidence of numbers? We must always look for a logical link beneath the numerical one. This is an excellent rule of exegesis when interpreting rabbinic texts. In the case in point, the image of the first wine of Creation, unaltered in the grape, is at least as convincing as the amusing numerical comparison.

But a second opinion exists on the future world's miracles which have been promised, according to some, to the perfectly righteous and, according to others, to repentant sinners. There is always a second opinion in the Talmud; without necessarily opposing the first, it raises another aspect of the idea.

> Resh Lakish said: To Eden, which no eye has ever seen; and should you demur, where then did Adam live? In the garden. And should you object, the garden and Eden are one: therefore Scripture teaches, *And a river issued from Eden to water the garden.*

There is therefore a difference between Eden and the garden in which Adam lived. The argument is specious, but Resh Lakish teaches us that the future world is not simply the equivalence of a return to the lost paradise.

The lost paradise itself was irrigated by that 'which no eye has ever seen', which we shall find near the end. It was not its spring, or source. History is not simply a diminished and corrupted eternity, nor is it the mobile image of immobile enternity; history and evolution have a positive meaning, an unforeseable fecundity; the future moment is absolutely new, but it requires history and time in order to come about. Adam, even in his innocence, has not experienced such a moment. Here, once again, we encounter the idea of the *felix culpa*: being thrown out of paradise and thrown into time are actions that herald a greater perfection than that of the happiness tasted in the garden of paradise. It is this idea of the fecundity of time and the positive value of history that Resh Lakish wishes to add to R. Johanan's opinion.

A few words about the method my commentary has adopted up until now, to which I'm also going to adhere for my following texts. In no way do we wish to exclude from the reading of our texts the religious meaning that guides the reading of the mystic or naive believer, nor the meaning that a theologian would extract. But we none the less begin with the idea that this meaning is not only transposable into a philosophical language, but refers to philosophical problems. The thought of Doctors of the Talmud proceeds from a meditation that is radical enough also to satisfy the demands of philosophy. It is this rational meaning which has been the object of our research. The laconic formulae, images, allusions and virtual 'winks' through which thought finds expression in the Talmud can relase their meaning only if one approaches them from the angle of a concrete problem or social situation, without worrying about the apparent anachronisms committed as a result. These can shock only the fanatics for historical method, who profess that *it is forbidden for inspired thinking to anticipate the meaning of all experience* and that not only do there exist words that, before a certain time, are *unpronounceable*; but that there are also thoughts which, before a certain time, are unthinkable.

We begin with the idea that inspired thinking is a thought in which everything has been thought, even industrial society and modern technocracy. It is by beginning with real facts and problems that these formulae and images (through which these scholars speak to scholars over the heads of the masses), which are shown to be more precise, studied and daring than they at first seemed, reveal at least part of their thought. Without this, Judaism, of which they make up most of the content, would be reduced to folklore or anecdotes from Jewish history and would not justify its own history, nor even be worth continuing. It is not a question of contesting the value of the historical method and the interesting perspectives it opens up; but to remain at the level of this method is to transform into incidents and little local histories the truths that have given life to Judaism. Even if these truths were determined by circumstances, conflicts and polemics long since forgotten and rendered insignificant, the words of the Doctors of Israel fix categories, intellectual structures that are absolute in thought. This confidence placed in the wisdom of the wise men is, if you like, a faith. But this form of faith which we proclaim is the only one that does not have to be kept discreetly to oneself, acting like those shameless professions of faith that echo indiscreetly in every public square.

Is the Coming of the Messianic Era Conditional or Unconditional?

Our second text is on pages 97b and 98a of Tractate Sanhedrin. We witness virtually the same protagonists as before. Samuel is there, but his contradictor is not R. Johanan but Rab, Samuel's usual protagonist in the Talmud.

> Rab said: All the predestined dates [for redemption] have passed, and the matter [now] depends only on repentance and good deeds. But Samuel maintained: It is sufficient for a mourner to keep his [period of] mourning.

We can see that for Rab, the objective conditions for deliverance have come together: history is over. One need not have waited for the *Phenomenology of the Spirit* and the nineteenth century to recognize the end of history. It is not that there is no more future, but the objective conditions required for the appearance of the Messiah have already materialized in the third century of the common era.*Everything depends on repentance and good deeds*: the messianic coming is to found *at the level of the individual effort that can be produced in full self-control*. Everything is already thinkable and thought; humanity is mature; what is missing is good deeds and repentance. Moral action, *the individual's work*, is not alienated by a history that denaturalizes it and, consequently, does not have to attempt to impose itself by taking the detour of politics and having recourse to reasons of State.

To bring a just course to triumph, one is not obliged to become politically allied to assassins, so separating the action from its moral source and its real intention. All the predestined dates have passed: good deeds are efficacious. That is the Messiah.

This stands in contrast to Samuel's thesis. He attached importance to political realities. Only messianism can undo the destructive effects they wreak on a moral life. For him, in a word, *messianic deliverence cannot ensue from individual effort* which it makes possible only in terms of efficacity and harmonious play. What does Samuel say? – 'It is sufficient for a mourner to keep his period of mourning.' To understand this sibylline statement, we must first of all find out who it is who is said to be in mourning. There are three opinions.

The first states that it is God Who is in mourning. This can be said in another language: objective will, which directs history, is in mourning. God is in mourning and He has kept His period of mourning – *The objective order of things cannot remain eternally in check*: it cannot remain eternally in a state of disorder; things will work out, and they will do so objectively. One does not need to wait for the individual effort, which is virtually negligible and gets drowned in the magnificent and reasonable course of historic events. The individual effort depends, on the contrary, on this arrangement. The mourner, who suffers because of this different humanity – in theological language God, at all events the will that guides history, torn assunder by its contradictions – will bring about deliverance and return to order whatever happens. But this appeal to a necessary and objective arrangement of history is not only a rationalist demand; as we shall see, it is an opinion absolutely necessary to religion.

The second conception believes that the mourner is Israel. Israel is in mourning. Israel is suffering. This suffering, in the absence of repentance, is the condition for its salvation. This interpretation brings together Samuel's thesis and Rab's conception. The objectivity of deliverance here postulates, all the same, a moral event at its source. But this event is not repentance, in which the individual, fully conscious of evil, undertakes a fully conscious action in order to rectify the situation. It is suffering which is the condition for deliverance. *While laying hold of the individual, it is received from outside*, and so does not place the individual at the absolute origins of his deliverance, but leaves him only the status of a second cause.

This idea of a suffering distinct from repentance situates the martyrdom suffered by Israel throughout the terrible years, as throughout its whole history, somewhere between life in the strict sense of the term and the dignity of the victim who, without having deserved it, suffers absurdly the repercussions of historical necessities. This creates a dignity that is not merited as such.

The third conception belongs to a seventeenth-century commentator, who figures in the classic editions of the Talmud – namely, Maharsha. His view is that the mourner is indeed Israel, but Israel's suffering does not by itself determine deliverance. The commentator is probably shocked by the idea of a redemption which is obtained by the sole effect of suffering and without any positive virtue being required, something that reeks of Christianity. It is sufficient for a mourner to keep his period of mourning – suffering incites him to repentance. And it is repentance that causes deliverance.

In the economy of being, therefore, suffering has a special place: it is not yet moral initiative, but it is through suffering that *a freedom may be aroused*. Man receives suffering, but in this suffering he emerges as a moral freedom. The idea of outside intervention in salvation becomes reconciled in suffering with the idea that the source of salvation must necessarily lie within man. Man both receives salvation and is its agent. Samuel, sensitive to the political obstacle – that is to say, the outside obstacle encountered by morality – and calling on an outside act to bring deliverance, an act transcending simple morality, concurs with Rab, who believes the time has come, and 'the matter now depends only on good works'.

It is perhaps interesting at this point to relate another passage of the Talmud, a very beautiful one, which certainly illustrates Rab's radical position but can also act as a fourth reply to the question: 'Who is the mourner?' The mourner is the Messiah.

R. Joshua b. Levi had the good fortune one day to meet the prophet Elijah. Such meetings happen in the talmudic apologues. The prophet Elijah, as we know, is the Messiah's precursor. R. Joshua asks him the only interesting question: 'When will the Messiah come?' The prophet Elijah cannot answer; he is just an underling: 'Go and ask him himself.' 'Where is he sitting?' – 'At the entrance. He is sitting among the poor lepers.' R. Joshua goes to him, and finds him in a veritable court of miracles. The bodies of these poor wretches are covered in bandages. They untie them, treat their sores, and rebandage them. He has no trouble in recognizing the Messiah. To treat his sores, he does not untie all the bandages at once, as do the others: at any moment he might be called upon to appear as the Messiah. So instead of untying all the bandages at once, he tends each sore separately, uncovering the next wound only when he has rebandaged the previous one. He must not be delayed by the time it takes to perform one medical act.

R. Joshua recognizes him, rushes up to him and asks: 'When wilt thou come, Master?' 'Today', is the answer. R. Joshua returns to the prophet Elijah, asking: Was this 'today' not false? But Elijah answers: 'This is what he said to thee, *Today, if ye will hear his voice*', a reference to Psalm 95, verse 7. Today, on condition that...

What we have here, therefore, is a Messiah who suffers. But salvation cannot ensue from the pure virtue of suffering. None the less, the whole of history has been crossed, and every time completed. The Messiah is ready to come this very day, but everything depends on man. And the suffering of the Messiah and, consequently, the suffering of humanity which suffers in the Messiah and the suffering of humanity for whom the Messiah suffers, are not enough to save humanity.

The two theses propounded by Rab and Samuel seem clearer: they testify to a basic alternative. Either morality – that is to say, the efforts made by men who are masters of their intentions and acts – will save the world, or else what is needed is an objective event that surpasses morality and the individual's good intentions.

Our text then says, in effect, that the discussion between Rab and Samuel takes up an old debate between Tannaim, which set R. Eliezer against R. Joshua.

> R. Eliezer said: If Israel repent, they will be redeemed; if not, they will not be redeemed.

Here we are given Rab's thesis:

> R. Joshua said to him: If they do not repent, will they not be redeemed! But the Holy One, blessed be He, will set up a king over them, whose decrees shall be as cruel as Haman's whereby Israel shall engage in repentance, and he will thus bring them back to the right path.

Here we can recognize Samuel's thesis in the interpretation given it by Maharsha. R. Joshua repudiates the idea of a free deliverance. The phenomenon of Haman (or Hitler) is placed in the perspective of messianism. Only repentance can cause salvation, but objective events of a political character produce this repentance which is both a manifestation of human freedom and a product of an external cause. Samuel's thesis appears in a form much closer to Rab's position, to judge from the version of it which we have just read in the discussion between the Tannaim. *But this is only one version.* Our text reproduces another, given by the *Baraita* – that is to say, by the collection of teachings of the Tannaim which were excluded from the Mishnah and compiled by R. Hiyya and R. Oshaia at the end of the second century.

We are confronted by a characteristic passage of the Talmud in which we have the impression that we are simply witnessing a combat that trades verses like blows.

R. Eliezer said: If Israel repent, they will be redeemed, as it is written, *Return, ye backsliding children, and I will heal your backslidings* (Jeremiah 3:22).*

This time R. Eliezer supports his opinion with a verse beginning 'Return'. The children of Israel are being invited to return. When this return has occurred, the Messiah will come. Salvation depends on man.

R. Joshua said to him: But is it not written, *ye have sold yourselves for nought; and ye shall be redeemed without money* (Isaiah 53:3). *Ye have sold yourselves for nought*, for idolatry; *and ye shall be redeemed without money* – without repentance and good deeds.

Curiously, the Tanna identifies selling oneself with the vanity of idolatry, and money with repentance and good deeds.

R. Eliezer retorts: But is it not written, *Return unto me, and I will return unto you* (Malachi 3:7).

There is still insistence on the word *return*, the condition for salvation.

R. Joshua rejoined: But is it not written, *that I am master over you: and I will take you out of a city, and two of a family, and I will bring you to Zion* (Jeremiah 3:14).

R. Joshua seems to forget the start of the verse quoted which also begins with the word 'Return', supporting his thesis by pointing to the violence of 'I will take you' and 'I will bring you'. This forgetfulness is already an indication that the argument is less formal than it appears.

R. Eliezer replied: But it is written, *In returning and rest shall ye be saved* (Isaiah 30:15).

Here R. Eliezer is playing, we might say, on words, for he is giving the verse from Isaiah a translation that is not impossible, but

---

* *Translator's note*: In each case I have given the Talmud version, rather than Collins.

doubtful: 'In returning and rest you shall be saved'. As always, he is subordinating deliverance to repentance.

R. Joshua goes on the attack again:

> But is it not written, *Thus saith the Lord, the Redeemer of Israel and his Holy One, to him whom man despiseth, to him whom the nations abhorreth, to a servant of rulers, kings shall see and arise, princes also shall worship?* (Isaiah 49:7).

This is an unconditional promise.

We then get R. Eliezer's fourth retort:

> But is it not written, *If thou wilt return, O Israel, saith the Lord, return unto me?* (Jeremiah 4:1).

R. Eliezer reads this with the sovereignty of someone who has his own idea: *if you return, O Israel, to me you should return.* R. Eliezer once again proves the priority of repentance over free salvation.

But R. Joshua does not have to search hard to find another verse in support of his thesis:

> But it is elsewhere written, *And I heard the man clothed in linen, which was* upon the waters of the river, when he held up his right hand and his left hand unto heaven, and swore by him that liveth for ever that it shall be for a time, times and a half; and when he shall have accomplished to scatter the power of the holy people, all things shall be finished. (Daniel 12:7).

In this verse R. Joshua reads the announcement of unconditional deliverance.

And R. Eliezer? R. Eliezer remains silent. This is at first surprising. Has he run short of verses? The combat between erudite scholars could have continued indefinitely. Could not more verses have been found which begin with 'Return', as well as others announcing: 'I shall none the less save you ...'? But R. Eliezer remains silent.

To interpret the strange text I have just been questioning, we must first neglect the points that initially seem to carry the force of the summarized argument, and we must neglect less the verses themselves to which the interlocutors have recourse.

The first force of the arguments seemed indeed to reside in the fact that R. Eliezer produced verses which place a moral condition on deliverance, whereas R. Joshua located his argument in texts dealing with unconditional deliverance.

Let us take the first argument. R. Eliezer said: 'Return, ye backsliding children, and I will heal your backsliding.' The essential words are 'I will heal'. Man's backslidings involve such a radical corruption that this corruption needs medication, a medication also considered ineffectual without some initial effort on the part of the sick person. For R. Eliezer, if evil corrupts being to the extent that medication is required, the cure cannot be obtained from outside, like grace. The external act no longer has any hold over a corrupted being. Nothing can penetrate a person closed in on himself by evil. He first of all has to get a grip on himself in order to be healed from outside. Precisely, *because evil is not simply a 'backsliding', but a profound illness in being, it is the sick person who is the first and principal worker of his own healing*. This is a unique logic, and the opposite of the logic of grace. I can save you on condition that you return unto me. The sick person must retain sufficient lucidity to return to the doctor; if he cannot his illness is madness – that is to say, the state of one who cannot even spontaneously summon the doctor. This is the eternal requirement of a thought that regards sin as breaking with the eternal order, a free being in selfish isolation.

However, R. Joshua's reply emphasizes a requirement that is no less eternal. The sin that separates and isolates is based in turn on a lapse, and a lapse is open to the outside action of teaching. If for R. Eliezer every backsliding is a sin, for R. Joshua a sin, in turn, is based on a lapse. Moral perversion rests on an indifference of culture. This lapse is idolatry. For R. Joshua's Judaism, it is at the base of all moral depravity, but on its own it is just a lapse. 'Ye have sold yourselves for nought', says Isaiah, and R. Joshua is quick to add: 'for nought, for idolatry'.

An offence committed against man proceeds from a radical evil. It can be effaced only when the offended party offers pardon and demands reparation from the offender. An offence against God is something God takes care of. It is due to lack of education. This is precisely what R. Joshua replies: Is there not something intellectually inadequate at the root of a sin that cannot be redeemed by purely external intervention and requires good deeds and an attempt at regeneration that comes from the individual? Should the fall brought about by a (gratuitously) inconsistent lapse not be redeemed from outside without expecting good deeds (money)? Isn't the human fall primarily intellectual and doctrinal? And doesn't this mean that the Messiah must come through the outside influence of teaching? This is why R. Joshua will always be right (just as R. Eliezer will be). Beyond the corruption of evil, he perceives an intellectual flaw which can and must be redeemed from outside.

Let us come now to the other arguments. *Return unto me, and I will return unto you.* Here R. Eliezer once again affirms the eternal requirement of morality: the total *reciprocity* between free people, the equality found between freedoms. What I am in relation to God, God is in relation to me. It is in the name of such freedom that man's salvation must have its origins in man.

The whole discussion is, as I have already said, curiously opposed to the Christian logic of grace: a lapse needs external aid, for true knowledge cannot be self-learned; but sin can be atoned for only from within.

What is R. Joshua's response? This sovereign freedom being put forward is by no means cut and dried. Doesn't freedom rest on a preliminary commitment to the being with regard to whom one puts oneself forward as free? Are not the two free beings, God and man, like an engaged couple freely deciding to be united, when they could reject such an option? Are they not tied henceforth by a bond similar to marriage? It is precisely this image of conjugal union in which the initiative belongs to one of the spouses that is evoked in the verse quoted by R. Joshua. Is God a partner Whom one accepts or rejects? Has one not accepted Him even when one rejects Him? Does not freedom in general presuppose a commitment that precedes the very rejection of such a commitment? Let us transpose all this on to the political plane, for example. Has the person who rejects the State not been formed for this rejection by the very State he rejects?

If one of our speakers from the previous conference were here, he would certainly have protested against R. Joshua's idea, this contestation of freedom, this 'if you deny me, it is because you support me; if you are looking for me, it is because you have already found me'. His protest would not put him outside of Judaism; he would find himself agreeing with R. Eliezer.

R. Eliezer's third argument is: 'In returning and rest shall ye be saved.' Here he once again involves an eternal condition of messianism or deliverance: the possibility of suspending the hold things have on us, and of distancing ourselves from them. This is the place and leisure of being aware, the freedom of thought. Without it, self-renewal, the returning, is not possible. It is the prerogative of any conscience as conscience, assuring us of this renewal and this mastery over our inner destiny.

R. Joshua's reply is peremptory. What about the servant, the worker, the underdeveloped nations, 'him whom man despiseth'? Have not these people already alienated their self-consciousness, do they have peace and leisure, which are the conditions for becoming aware of oneself again? Isn't external intervention in this case necessary?

If moral action must therefore begin from inside, from the 'interval' of consciousness and meditation, in a concrete situation a preliminary and objective event must fulfil its conditions. There has to be outside intervention, whether in the shape of the Messiah or revolution or political action, if only to allow men to accede to that leisure and self-consciousness.

Finally, there is the fourth argument, which gives the debate a dramatic turn. For the first time, the particle 'if' figures in the quoted text: *Return unto me, and I will return unto you.*

To require absolute morality is to require absolute freedom. This creates the possibility of immorality. What will happen in fact if men do not return to God? The Messiah will never come, the world will be turned over to the wicked and atheist belief that it is governed by chance, and evil will triumph. Morality requires absolute freedom, but within this freedom there already exists the possibility of an immoral world – that is to say, the end of morality. The possibility of an immoral world is therefore included in the conditions for morality. It is for this reason that R. Joshua's final argument consists in brutally affirming the deliverance of the world by a fixed date, whether or not men deserve such deliverance.

And this is why R. Eliezer on this occasion remains silent. He does so because this time the requirements for morality reach a point where, in the name of man's absolute freedom, they deny God – that is to say, the absolute certainty of the defeat of Evil. There is no immorality without God; without God morality is not preserved against immorality. God emerges here in His purest essence, one distant from all imagery of incarnation, through the moral adventure of humanity. God is here the very principle of the triumph of good. If you do not believe this, if you do not believe that in any case the Messiah will come, you do not believe in God. This helps us to a better understanding of the famous paradox that the Messiah will come when the world is wholly guilty. This statement is the extreme consequence of an obvious proposition: even if the world is absolutely plunged in sin, the Messiah will come.

R. Eliezer remains silent, but his argument has not been abandoned. It will be resuscitated in the age of Rab and Samuel. And it is still alive. Judaism adores its God while remaining acutely aware of all of atheism's reasons, or Reason.

The Contradictions of Messianism

The passage concerning the internal contradictions of the messianic coming, which is also taken from Tractate Sanhedrin (88b), will be commented on more loosely.

Here is the start of the text:

> Ulla said: Let him [the Messiah] come, but let me not see him. Rabbah said likewise: Let him come, but let me not see him. R. Joseph said: Let him come, and may I be worthy of sitting in the shadow of his ass's saddle.

Abbaye enquires of Rabbah the reason for such an attitude. The coming of the Messiah is accompanied by catastrophes; is it this that causes you fear? But is it not written that the man of good deeds who studies the Torah will escape the upheavals of the messianic era? Are you not that good deed, are you not the Torah itself?

But Rabbah is unsure of being without sin, and unsure of his future: Jacob had received every promise from God, yet he was greatly afraid and distressed to face Esau. Was he not afraid that sin might somehow cause the nullification of God's promise?

And why did Israel on the flight out of Egypt to the Promised Land benefit from miracles, when no miracle occurred on the return to Babylon? Do we not know that miracles were promised for both circumstances, since in the Song of Moses about the Red Sea, we read: 'till thy people, O Lord, pass by [out of Egypt], till the people pass by whom thou hast purchased [in Babylon]' (Exodus 15:16). But sin caused the promise not to happen.

The subject is therefore never a pure activity, but is always placed in question. The subject is not in possession of himself in a relaxed and unalienable way. He always has more asked of him. The more just he is, the more harshly is he judged. Can one therefore enter the messianic state without fear and trembling? The hour of truth is fearsome. Can man match the clarity he wishes to call up? Through the growing demands which it places on the Self and the scruples by which it lives, does not morality exclude the messianic era in which things are brought to fruition?

This text is Pharisaic, but of a kind unknown to the Gospels. Note the precise nature of Rabbah's reply. He refers to Jacob facing Esau and Israel's returning from Babylon, Jacob and Israel, Mr Israel and All Israel. The nations in revolt are no more sure of their cause than are individuals.

But there is a second reason for evading the messianic era. R. Johanan said likewise: 'Let him come, and let me not see him.' Resh Lakish asks:

> Why so? Shall we say, because it is written, *As if a man did flee from a lion, and a bear met him; or went into the house, and leaned his hand on a wall, and a serpent bit him?* (Amos, 5:19).

But is this situation more horrible than the era in which we already live? Have we something to lose in the horrors of revolution?

That is not, then, what R. Johanan fears. Instead, he anguishes over a verse from Jeremiah:

> Ask ye now, and see whether a man doth travail with child? Wherefore do I see every man with his hands on his loins, as a woman in travail, and all faces are turned into paleness? Alas! that day is so great there is none like it (Jeremiah 50:6–7).

This is the verse that frightens R. Johanan, for he naturally reads it in his own way. 'Every man' [*geber*] is not the totality of man; every man designates Him who is virility itself [*geburah*]. 'Every' is here the abverb 'all'. He who is every man is all man, all humanity, all virility. At the end of time God holds His hands on His loins, as though in labour. Why does He hold His hands on His loins? Because at the messianic moment He must sacrifice the wicked to the good. Because in the just act there is still a violence that causes suffering. Even when the act is reasonable, when the act is just, it entails violence.

But the verse is not finished. R. Johanan discerns two other partners, those whose faces are turned into paleness. He says: 'This refers to God's heavenly family [i.e. the angels] and his earthly family [i.e. Israel]'.

The heavenly family and the earthly family are pale. Why? Because they are afraid in case God changes His mind and removes sanctions. For the family on high, the angels, pure Reason, injustice must be punished and justice rewarded. They apply the reasonable law of Reason strictly and cannot understand hesitation. The family below, the victims of evil, whose flesh feels the formidable price of injustice that has been pardoned, and the danger of the gracious remission of crime: they are perfectly informed. And this time the persecuted and the rigorously reasonable join forces, afraid that God will renounce His just justice.

But the miracle of the text is that in spite of the certainties of the heavenly and earthly families, in spite of their perfectly valid reasons and experience, He who is all virility – not woman, nor gentleness, nor sentimentality, nor Mater Dolorosa, nor tender son of God – hesitates in the face of violence even when it is just.

This is also why the necessary commitment [*engagement*] is so difficult for the Jew; this is why the Jew cannot commit himself [*s'engager*] without also disengaging himself [*se désengager*], even when he commits himself to a just cause; the Jew can never march off to war with banners unfurled, to the triumphal strains of military music and with the Church's blessing.

Beyond Messianism (Sanhedrin 98b–99a)

> R. Giddal said in Rab's name: The Jews are destined to eat [their fill] in the days of the Messiah. R. Joseph demurred: Is this not obvious; who else then should eat – Hilek and Bilek?

All my listeners must have made the same mental objection as Joseph: 'Who then, if not Israel, is promised the messianic era?'

But what do the words 'Hilek' and 'Bilek' mean? The first meaning given by the commentators is that Hilek and Bilek are the first people who might happen to come along – any Tom, Dick or Harry, in other words. R. Joseph is therefore surprised that R. Giddal announces the coming of the Messiah for Israel, for it goes without saying: Israel, and not just any Tom, Dick or Harry, will enjoy the messianic era. The messianic era is not just anyone's to enjoy. One must be worthy of it, and in this messianism differs from the end of History wherein objective events free everyone, everyman who has the grace or good fortune to be present at the final hour of History.

According to another commentator, the names 'Hilek' and 'Bilek' (great thoughts are often linked to small things) designate two judges. But these judges are special – they are the judges of Sodom.

R. Joseph's objection therefore becomes: 'Do you believe the messianic era exists for the judges of Sodom?'

What is new about this objection which excludes the judges of Sodom from messianism? Perhaps Sodom should not be limited to its historical and geographical significance. A little of Sodom is to be found everywhere. So the judges, even if they are judges of Sodom, in their capacity as judges place their action under the sign of universality. The judges of Sodom are people who are still familiar with political life and the State; and according to the theoreticians of the end of History, people who act under the sign of universality act just for their era. All politics, through the universality of its designs, is moral and every universal intention is directed towards the unfolding of history. Our text would therefore teach us that the simple fact of acting under the sign of universality does not justify entry into the messianic era, and that the messianic era does not correspond solely to the universality entailed in a Law or a human Ideal. It also has a content.

Hilek and Bilek, judges of Sodom, are not judged in relation to their historical situation – they are at any moment ready for the absolute judgement. No historical relativism to excuse man! Evil can take on universal forms, and the very meaning of the messianic promise perhaps consists in admitting that by itself evil can assume universal forms and become a *State*, but for a supreme will which prevents it from triumphing.

But if the messianic era incontestably concerns Israel, why bother to say so? Is R. Giddal teaching us something banal? In reality, he speaks in order to repel an adverse thesis that is surprising to everyone, except to those who have heard Vladimir Jankélévitch guess by a sort of pre-established harmony the next part of our text: Israel no longer holds the messianic promise. This is how the text continues:

> This [the fact that it is obvious that the Jews will eat their fill in the days of the Messiah] was said in opposition to R. Hillel, who maintained that there will be no Messiah for Israel, since they have already enjoyed him during the reign of Hezekiah.

First we must point out that this R. Hillel is not the famous Hillel the Elder. But he is a Rabbi – that is to say a Tanna, a Doctor of the era before the end of the second century. In the whole of the

Talmud, we have only this one affirmation from him: 'there will be no Messiah for Israel'. For Israel messianism has been superseded, since it has already been enjoyed during the reign of Hezekiah, several thousand years before R. Hillel. And since then? Is there the promise of something higher?

For R. Hillel, at all events, messianism corresponded to a primitive and very ancient Israel. Perhaps R. Hillel also meant that for the prophets messianism is yet to come, whereas it has already come for Israel. The Messiah of the Jews already come (eight centuries before Christ), the Messiah of the peoples still in the future – we must measure the enormity of this affirmation. It is so enormously audacious that tradition repels the thesis.

First our text, through R. Giddal, who speaks in Rab's name, begins by rejecting it. R. Giddal contests the aberration in the fantastic idea of a messianism that has been superseded. But this thesis is still rejected several lines further on, in the passage following our text:

> R. Hillel said: There shall be no Messiah for Israel, because they have already enjoyed him in the days of Hezekiah. R. Joseph said: May God forgive him [for saying so].

R. Hillel's rejected opinion none the less still figures in some way in the minutes of the discussion. His opinion is not purely and simply passed over in silence. When one knows the structure of talmudic thought wherein a valid thesis is never effaced, but remains as one of the poles of a thought that circulates between it and the opposite pole, one can measure the true value of R. Hillel's affirmation.

But we must finally say how the commentators interpret him. This will allow us to show the positive thought that guides his critique of messianism. With one voice the commentators let R. Hillel know that if for Israel the Messiah has already come, this is because Israel is waiting to be delivered by God Himself. This is the highest aspiration of all! R. Hillel's opinion is suspicious of the messianic idea or redemption through the Messiah: Israel awaits a higher aspiration than that of being saved by a Messiah. This surpassing of the messianic idea can be interpreted in several ways. One could do worse than adopt Jankélévitch's view that if the moral order is incessantly improving, this is because it is always on the move and never provides an outcome. A moral outcome is immoral. The notion of morality having an outcome is as absurd as the immobilization of time which it assumes. Deliverance by God coincides with the sovereignty of a living morality that is open to infinite progress.

In passing I wish to mention here that the manner in which I read the talmudic text (a manner I have not invented, for it was taught to me by a prestigious master) consists in never giving the word 'Israel' only an ethnic sense. When one says that Israel is worthy of a greater excellence than messianism, this does not concern only the historical Israel. It is not by virtue of being Israel that excellence is defined, but by this excellence, the dignity of being delivered by God himself, that Israel is defined. The notion of Israel designates an elite, of course, but an open elite and an elite that is defined by certain proprieties that concretely are attributed to the Jewish people. This enlarges every perspective opening on to the talmudic texts and helps us once and for all to get rid of the strictly nationalist character that one would like to give to the particularism of Israel. This particularism exists, as you will see, but it certainly has no nationalist sense. A certain notion of universality is expressed in the Jewish particularism.

To return to R. Hillel's thesis – we must not, all the same, think that it expresses a pure paradox. In the Talmud, it appears only once. R. Hillel never said anything else; perhaps he said something sufficiently important to spare him the necessity of minor works. But his thesis conforms to an old tradition. I am not saying that this is the only tradition of Judaism. Whether the Messiah is a man or a king, salvation by the Messiah is salvation by procuration. To the extent that the Messiah is a king, salvation by the Messiah is not one in which each person is saved individually, for that supposes that we enter a political game. Salvation by the king, even if he is the Messiah, is not yet the supreme salvation open to the human being. Messianism is political, and its completion belongs to Israel's past – that is the force of R. Hillel's position.

I can show that this position is not exceptional by recalling the Book of Samuel where, for the first time, Israel moves towards a political existence and the tension between the political and the purely religious is affirmed with the utmost rigour. I remind you of the resistance put up against this political aspiration by the prophet Samuel, who eventually, but always reluctantly, gave in to popular demand. Each time he resigns himself to reuniting the people in this way, he himself remains hard and contemptuous. He reproaches the people for entering into a political existence and consequently offending God. What is, in concrete terms, a people that has only God for king, if not an existence in which nothing is done by procuration, but where each person participates entirely in what the people have chosen and is entirely present to that choice? This creates a direct link between man and God devoid of any political mediation. This goes beyond a messianism that remains political and has only a limited duration, in the opinion of Tractate Sanhedrin. Judaism does not therefore carry with it a doctrine of an end to History which dominates individual destiny. Salvation does not stand as an end to History, or act as its conclusion. It remains *at every moment* possible.

You can see, then, that R. Hillel's thesis expresses a fundamental possibility of Judaism. Of course, the Bible attests that God orders Samuel to give way to the people. It is probably not possible to maintain for everyone a form of existence in which God alone is King. But it is this form of existence which appears ideal, worthy of Man, to Samuel, and probably to R. Hillel, who carries on its tradition.

Those who refute R. Hillel certainly also agree on the excellence of Israel's destiny when compared to the destiny of nations that are simply political; but if, in their opinion, Israel has been promised to the messianic era, it is not because Israel is alone in being worthy of it, but because this era is not unworthy of Israel.

The two lines I am going to isolate from what then follows above all confirm the idea that messianism does not exhaust the meaning of human history for all the wise men of Israel. In effect, we are told the following:

> Rab said: The world was created only on David's account. Samuel said: On Moses' account. R. Johanan said: For the sake of the Messiah.

Of the three masters quoted, only R. Johanan sees in the Messiah the meaning of the universe and of creation. Rab and Samuel look elsewhere for such a meaning.

'King David' is distinguished here from the Messiah. He is the author of the Psalms, where poetry merges with prayer and prayer spills over into poetry. The word has meaning from the moment adoration is produced in this world, where a finite being stands before something which goes beyond him, but where this presence before the Most High becomes the psalm's exaltation. For Samuel, the world has been created on Moses' account: the creature is justified from the moment the Torah enters the world. The possibility of a moral life fulfils the creature.

R. Johanan estimates that the Messiah is still necessary to the world where there is already prayer and Torah, and his opinion is no doubt plausible. It is not the opinion of everyone.

Who is the Messiah?

I come now to a paragraph which poses a problem that seems futile. Perhaps it bears a hint of anti-Christian sentiment. It consists of questions about the name of the Messiah, and his name in no way resembles that of the founder of Christianity. But the text's real meaning does not show up at first glance.

> What is his [the Messiah's] name? – The School of R. Shila said: His name is Shiloh, for it is written, *until Shiloh come* [Genesis 49:10]. The School of R. Yannai said: His name is Yinnon, for it is written, *His name shall endure for ever: e'er the sun was, his name is Yinnon* [Psalms 72:17]. The School of R. Haninah maintained; His name is Haninah, as it is written, *Where I will not give you Haninah.**

What is being discussed here? They wish to identify the name of the Messiah. There are three possibilities: Shiloh, Yinnon and Haninah. The three names resemble the names of the teachers of the respective schools. The experience in which the messianic personality is revealed therefore comes back to the relationship between pupil and teacher. The pupil-teacher relationship, which seemingly remains rigorously intellectual, contains all the riches of a meeting with the Messiah. This is the truly remarkable thing: the fact that the relationship between pupil and teacher can confirm the promises made by the prophetic texts in all their grandeur and tenderness is perhaps the most surprising novelty in this passage. It is not the resemblance between the name of the teacher R. Shila and the

---

* *Translator's note*: I have followed normal practice in giving the Soncino Press translation, but both here and later, this translation fails to bring out the play on words to which Levinas is pointing. The Collins edition of the Bible gives Psalms 72:17 as: 'May his name endure for ever, his fame continue as long as the sun!' The difference lies in the play on the Hebrew 'Yinnon', meaning 'shall be continued'. Similarly, 'I will not give you Haninah' is an alternative to the Collins 'I will show you no favour' (Jeremiah 16:13), for the Hebrew 'haninah' means favour or 'pity'. In the extract each school is displaying its admiration of its teacher by using the play on words to name the Messiah after the teacher.

mysterious name to be found in Genesis 49 that our text relates, but the presence in the teaching of the coming of the Pacific (Shiloh is translated as 'pacific', linking it with 'Chalvah', meaning 'peace') which the peoples will obey, the presence in the teacher's lessons of peace and abundance whose image follows this coming in the text ('his eyes shall be red with wine, and his teeth white with milk' [Genesis 49:12]).

Similarly, it is not the resemblance of the name Yannai to the word 'yinnon', which strictly speaking (but only strictly speaking) can be read in the Psalms as a proper noun, that is important, but the way the teaching successfully carries out the promise of the messianic Psalm 72. This psalm initially speaks not of peace but of justice and aid to those who can find neither. It deals with a King who gives justice to the poor and crushes the oppressor, a King whose dominion stretches from sea to sea and from the River to the ends of the earth: 'Liphné chemech Yinon chmo'. The Talmud translates this freely as 'e'er the sun was, his name is Yinnon'. E'er the sun was – before Nature, before Creation. Justice precedes and conditions visible splendours. The psalm in fact subordinates abundance itself to social justice. The prestige enjoyed by the Messiah over the other peoples depends on whether he is disposed to give justice and defend the people. A content is therefore loaned to messianism, but this content gleams forth in the face of the teacher. The teacher-pupil relationship does not consist in communicating ideas to one another. It is the first radiant sign of messianism itself.

The third name reveals a new aspect of messianism: favour, or love. Up to now we have been concerned with peace and justice, and the way in which they can be universally extended, and the rational law sustaining them can no doubt be discerned in the teacher's face. But now even the messianic plentitude of pity and love is anticipated by teaching. The passage from Jeremiah (16:13) to which our text refers is the very one that announces exile. The teacher's presence is like the deliverance, the return from exile, the finding of favour.

And that brings us to the next section which I should like you to read with me:

> Others say: His name is Menahem the son of Hezekiah, for
> it is written, *Because Menahem* ['the comforter'], *that*
> *would relieve my soul, is far* (Lamentations 1:16).

The comforter does not appear in the teacher's face, he is announced outside the teaching. The comforter goes further than the man of peace, justice and favour. Peace, justice, favour concern a collectivity, but the comforter has an individual relationship with the person he consoles. One can favour a species, but one consoles only one person.

Consequently, Menahem, the fourth presumed name of the Messiah, where these names define messianism, characterizes the messianic era as an age in which the individual accedes to a personal recognition beyond the recognition he receives from belonging to humanity and the State. It is not within his rights that he is recognized but within his person, his strict individuality. Persons do not disappear within the general nature of an entity. We find ourselves back with R. Hillel's theme: we are saved by God Himself, not be procuration.

Here I am closely akin to the famous talmudic apophthegm which announces in the same spirit: 'the day when the truth can be repeated without concealing the name of the person who first stated it, is the day when the Messiah will come'. The day when truth, in spite of its impersonal form, will retain the mark of the person who expressed himself in it, when its universality will preserve him from anonymity, is the day when the Messiah will come. For that situation is messianism itself.

Let us finally note the general attitude of the text: while preserving the exceptional significance of the messianic coming, the text locates this significance at the heart of the heritage that already belongs to Judaism; the foretaste and more besides of this exceptional experience are already known:

> The Rabbis said: His name is 'the leper scholar'.

The use of the plural form, 'the Rabbis', introduces an opinion of great weight.

> The Rabbis said: His name is 'the leper scholar', as it is written, *Surely he hath borne our griefs, and carried our sorrows: yet we did esteem him a leper, smitten of God, and afflicted* (Isaiah 53:4).

This concerns the famous chapter in Isaiah 53, whose prophecy seems so precise to the Christians. It heralds precisely the leper scholar. It heralds, beyond the individual Messiah, a form of existence whose individuation is not located in a single being.

Once again we find what I said earlier about the familiar character of the messianic experience in Judaism. We are told in the next lines that 'if he is of the living, it might be Rabbi himself, or Me,* if of the dead, Daniel'. Judaism, reaching out for the coming of the Messiah, has already gone beyond the notion of a mythical Messiah appearing at the end of History, and conceives of messianism as a personal vocation among men.

> R. Nahman said: If he [the Messiah] is of those living [today], it might be one like himself, as it is written, *And their nobles shall be of themselves, and their governors shall proceed from the midst of them* (Jeremiah 30:21). Rab said: If he is of the living, it would be our holy Master; if of the dead, it would have been Daniel the most desirable man.

The Messiah is no longer regarded in terms of his relationship with us, but in terms of his own essence. The Messiah is the suffering man. He is already the leper we encountered in the school of R. Judah the Nasi, a simple individual – unless the Messiah is a man invested with a certain authority. Rabbi's leper scholar, even if he is just, is therefore not the first to come. The first to come is Rabbi himself, who has assumed the suffering. Or else it is Daniel, 'the most desirable man', who remains just, despite the tests inflicted on him by Nebuchadnezzar. He too was invested with certain powers by the political authorities. The age does not alter the matter. Each age has its own Messiah.[2]

Between these two eventualities (the Messiah is the leper scholar of the Rabbi school and the Messiah is Rabbi himself or Daniel the most desired man), there is the remarkable text which we have not yet commented on:

> R. Nahman said: If he [the Messiah] is of those living [today], it might be one like myself, as it is written, *And their nobles shall be of themselves, and their governors shall proceed from the midst of them* (Jeremiah 30:21).

---

* *Translator's note*: Levinas uses the word 'Me' both here and in the following quotation from Tractate Sanhedrin: 'S'il est d'entre les vivants, c'est alors Moi'. The word is not reproduced in the Soncino edition; instead R. Nahman says: 'it might be one like myself'. Both refer to the fact that the description from Jeremiah fits R. Nahman, who, as the son-in-law of Resh Galutha, enjoyed great power and prestige. But Levinas goes on to comment specifically on the word 'Moi'.

The text from Jeremiah to which R. Nahman refers announces the age of deliverance in which Israel will be governed not by a strange king, but by a king who will be one of themselves. This is what the verse appears to mean at first glance. How can such a verse support R. Nahman's opinion that 'it might be me' [*Moi*]? What do the commentators have to say?

Rachi is silent. The man who normally explains every detail (there is no better teacher for the Talmud than Rachi) says nothing.

Maharsha claims that R. Nahman is descended from King David. He therefore offers the following reasoning: if Jeremiah announces to Israel the return of political power to a sovereign who is one of their own, nothing precludes R. Nahman from aspiring to a messianic destiny. Maharsha is obviously preoccupied with a theological problem: does R. Nahman's claim not signify a Messiah who is not descended from David?

I venture to propose an interpretation of this text that is less special. If we must be extremely timid when interpreting biblical texts because the Talmud has already said something about them, audacity is allowed with the talmudic texts, which immediately address themselves to our intelligence, soliciting interpretation and always saying *Darchenov*. Jeremiah's text concerns an age in which sovereignty will return to Israel. The Messiah is the Prince who governs in a way that no longer alienates the sovereignty of Israel. He is the absolute interiority of government. Is there a more radical interiority than the one in which the Self [*Moi*] commends itself? Non-strangeness *par excellence* is ipseity. The Messiah is the King who no longer commands from outside – this idea of Jeremiah's is brought by R. Nahman to its logical conclusion. The Messiah is Myself [*Moir*]; to be Myself is to be the Messiah.

We have just seen that the Messiah is the just man who suffers, who has taken on the suffering of others. Who finally takes on the suffering of others, if not the being who says 'Me' [*Moi*]?

The fact of not evading the burden imposed by the suffering of others defines ipseity itself. All persons are the Messiah.

The Self [*Moi*] as Self, taking upon itself the whole suffering of the world, is designated solely by this role. To be thus designated, not to evade to the point of responding before the call resounds – this is precisely what it means to be Me [*Moi*]. The Self [*Moi*] is one who has promised itself that it will carry the whole responsibility of the world, the *Samo-Zwanetz* denounced by Jankélévitch, who is the *Samo-Zwanetz par excellence*, one who invests himself with responsibility. And this is why he can take upon himself the whole suffering of everyone: he can say 'Me' [*Moi*] only to the extent that he has already taken on this suffering. Messianism is no more than this apogee in being, a centralizing, concentration or twisting back on itself of the Self [*Moi*]. And in concrete terms this means that each person acts as though he were the Messiah.

Messianism is therefore not the certainty of the coming of a man who stops History. It is my power to bear the suffering of all. It is the moment when I recognize this power and my universal responsibility.

> Rab Judah said in Rab's name: The Holy One, blessed be He, will raise up another David for us, as it is written, *But they shall serve the Lord their God, and David their king, whom I will* raise up unto them. (Jeremiah 30:9).

The verse quoted does not say 'whom I raise up' but 'whom I will raise up'. The use of the future points, therefore, to the coming in the future of a new king who will be called David.

> R. Papa said to Abbaye: But it is written, *And my servant David shall be their prince [nasi] for ever*? [Ezekiel 37:25]*

From this text R. Papa extracts the idea that the David of the future is not a new David, but the old David.

The conclusion (worthy of the promise!) is:

an emperor and a viceroy.

The new David shall be the king, and the former David shall be his viceroy. Where does the Talmud get its imagination from? A Messiah and a Vice-Messiah!

This strange text defies historians because it affirms the existence of two Davids and, perhaps even more profoundly, it affirms that every historical character possesses a double. For a long time Israelis, and even notably Ben-Gurion, have expressed indignation at the freedom taken by the Talmud with the biblical characters, transforming the historical David, a fiery, bloodthirsty warrior, into a sugary-sweet rabbi, limiting his interests to questions of purity and impurity (in a domain I dare not make public) by making him

---

* *Translator's note*: The French version given by Levinas quotes more of the verse which, in the Collins edition, is: 'they and their children and their children's children shall dwell there for ever; and David my servant shall be their prince for ever'.

get up early and go to bed very late, contrary to the custom of every king in the world.

Is it not enough to read the Book of Samuel to know that the historical David is fiery, bloodthirsty, merry and amorous – in short, possessing every quality of the kings on earth?

Have the Doctors of the Talmud foreseen Ben-Gurion's indignation in the text concerning us? At all events, they think that the David of History is merely the second of the two, his own understudy, and that the significance taken on by David, beyond his time, commands the real David. The ancient David is merely the viceroy of this other David, 'whom I shall establish for them' and who is the real David, the new non-historical David. There is no historical character who is not doubled by this supernatural phenomenon. Each historical event transcends itself, taking on a metaphorical meaning that guides its literal significance. The metaphorical meaning commands the literal and local meaning of events and ideas. In this sense, human history is a spiritual work. The historical character is transcended by the suprahistorical character who is his Master. The historical character who founds the State has meaning only when he obeys the as yet unreal character who is yet more real and effective than the real king.

Rab therefore studied the relationship between the Messiah and history – or between messianism and the concrete ages of historians.

Messianism and Universality

> R. Simlai expounded: What is meant by, *Woe unto you, that desire the day of the Lord! to what end is it for you? the day of the Lord is darkness, and not light?* (Amos 5:18).

What does this text mean at first glance? It probably concerns those who keep coming out with 'Ah! if justice were finally to be had, if only there were some justice on this earth!' As though they were innocent! Would they not be the first people to be annoyed by the establishment of justice on earth?

The identification of 'the day of the Lord' with darkness no doubt carries this first meaning. Nothing apocalyptic in this prophecy. The messianic dream, and even the simple dream of justice that so delights human foolishness, promise a painful awakening. Men are not only the victims of injustice; they are also the perpetrators. The biblical text rebels against the idyllic messianism of universal pardon and reminds us of the stark severity entailed in justice and judgement.

But the Talmud gives this vision of the prophet a deeper significance. The day of darkness does not merely signify the severity of judgement: it emphasizes the existence of souls incapable of receiving the light and ill-suited to salvation. This is how the text goes on:

> This may be compared to a cock and a bat who were hopefully waiting for the light [i.e. dawn]. The cock said to the bat, 'I look forward to the light, because I have sight; but of what use is the light to thee?'

The Messiah comes only to him who waits. There is no objective deliverance. No messianism for the bat! The cock and the bat: the cock is the 'specialist' of the light, it is its element. It not only has eyes to receive it, it also has, if I can put it this way, a 'nose' for light. The lark may greet the sun, but anyone can do as much. Everyone is capable of greeting the dawn. But to glimpse the dawn, the proximity of light, in the midst of night, before it shines forth, is perhaps the mark of intelligence. I was always puzzled by the daily blessing: 'Blessed be the Lord who gave intelligence to the cock that it may discern the night from day.' Or, if you like, I was always puzzled that in this blessing, 'Sekhvi' – to be blessed with intelligence – was always translated by the word 'cock'. I also thought that no great subtlety was needed to discern night from day. Our wise men judged differently. The cock that perceives the dawn, that senses in the night, a few moments in advance, the approach of light: what an admirable symbol of intelligence! An intelligence that knows the meaning of History before the event, and does not simply divine it after it has happened.

The bat represents one who does not see the light. The commentators say that the bat has no light, it lives in darkness. Darkness weighs on it, unhappy it lies in darkness. But the light, alas, says nothing to it. This is the very image of damnation, provided that damnation is not added to evil as an external sanction, imposed by violence; provided that damnation is more deeply tragic than violence. The bat suffers from darkness, but the light will give it nothing.

A cruel messianism. The Messiah is refused to those who are no longer capable of enlightenment, even if darkness weighs on them.

But the text now takes up what has just been said and transforms it once again. It passes from the idea that the truth is given only to the person who is ready inside to the idea that the truth is not universal in the logical sense of the term.

> And thus a *Min* said to R. Abbahu: 'When will the Messiah come?' He replied, 'When darkness covers those people who are with you.'

What is a Min? A member of the early heretic sect of early Jews. It is possible that he is a Christian. The question could, in fact, come from a Christian. I can feel its irony: do you know when the Messiah will come? Are you sure the Messiah has not already come?

R. Abbahu's reply is in fact merciless: 'When darkness covers those people who are with you'. 'You have condemned me!' exclaims the Min. Or, put in today's terms, your messianism is not universalist. You are a man of closed morality, Bergson was right to denounce you. To say that salvation will come when darkness covers the Min is to claim exclusivity in the matter of salvation.

What will R. Abbahu's reply be? Discussion with those who know the Book is not difficult. They are obliged to recognize the authority of the verses admired by all. Dialogue is possible.

> He [R. Abbahu] retorted: 'It is but a verse: *For, behold, the darkness shall cover the earth, and gross darkness the people: but the Lord shall shine upon thee, and his glory shall be seen upon thee.*' (Isaiah 60:2).

This verse is no more universalist than the thesis it props up, but this is so only if we ignore the verse that follows: 'And nations shall come to your light, and kings to the brightness of your rising.'

The Messiah will arrive when darkness has completely covered those people. The conjunction 'and' of the biblical text is transformed into 'when' and designates not a simple simultaneity of two events – darkness weighing on some and light bathing others – but the conditioning of the one by the other. The darkness is needed to create this light! Does that not tell us about the quality of this light? We could of course see all this as no more than the wickedness of Jews cruelly savouring their privileged triumph in the midst of universal desolation. But the quotation from Isaiah can leave us with this impression only if we separate it from the following verse, which announces the light to nations and kings – that is to say, to the whole of humanity involved in political evolution. I suspect, as a result, that R. Abbahu wishes precisely to describe the universality of the messianic coming, which is not to be confused with the universality that might be called catholic, which is sought by political life and formulated by Aristotle.

What is in fact the march towards universality of a political order? It consists in confronting multiple beliefs – a multiplicity of coherent discourses – and finding one coherent discourse that embraces them all, which is precisely the universal order. A coherent discourse is already open to the universal when the person holding it, who up until now has remained enclosed within his individual circumstances – though his discourse may have been coherent – concerns himself with the inner coherence of discourses other than his own, and so surpasses his own individual state.

This situation can also be described as the beginning of philosophy. But it is precisely the destiny of Western philosophy and its logic to recognize that it is a political condition, to the point where the free expression of truth and the constitution of the universal State (through wars and revolutions) coincide. The conflicts between men, the opposition of some to others, the opposition of each one to himself, create the sparks of an enlightenment or a reason that dominates and penetrates antagonists. The ultimate truth is set ablaze [*s'embrase*] by all these sparks as the end of History embraces [*embrasse*] all histories. The two events become one. The truth of each one attains its true state within universal truth rather than pale before the latter's splendour.

Suppose for a moment that political life appears not as a dialectical adjustment which men make towards another, but as an infernal cycle of violence and derision; suppose for a moment that the moral ends which politics prides itself on achieving, but amends and limits by virtue of achieving them – that these ends appear steeped in the immorality that claims to sustain them; suppose, in other words, that you have lost the meaning of the political and the consciousness of its grandeur, that the non-sense or non-value of world politics is your first certainty, that you are a people outside peoples (and that is what, in good prose, is meant by 'a people living apart – or a people not counted among the peoples'); suppose that you are a people capable of diaspora, capable of remaining outside, alone and abandoned: then you have a totally different vision of universality, one no longer subordinated to confrontation.

The light will be produced when the darkness covers 'all your people'; when silence falls on all those teachings that call you to fallacious confrontations, when all the prestige of exteriority fades and is as though it never existed. At the moment when the political temptations of the light 'of others' is overcome, my responsibility is the more irreplaceable. The real light can shine. At this point the real universality, which is non-catholic, can affirm itself. It consists in serving the universe. It is called messianism.

Is this a dangerous conception (each person risks promoting his own truth and affirming it without compromise) or is it a conception which, beyond such a primitive subjectivism, glimpses the dangers of the politicization of truth and morality? According to the *Midrash*, the first man was as big as the universe: 'from the Earth to the Heavens' for some, and 'from East to West' for others. Big as the distance separating East from West. This is the man who concerns himself with the discourses which he hears about him, and universalizes his truths according to a political rhythm. Jewish universalism is that represented by the man who stands as tall as the gap between the heavens and the earth. It signifies above all that Israel does not measure its morality by politics, that its universality is messianism itself.

To conclude: I sincerely wonder if, since the Emancipation, we are still capable of messianism. Can we still believe that History has no meaning, that no reason makes itself manifest therin?

Judaism thought that for a long time. It thought it in the Middle Ages. It felt it lived in an arbitrary world, in which no reason commanded political evolution. Certain texts of the medieval 'decisionaries' cannot explain themselves in any other way. Even in the Talmud the historical confusions and anachronisms committed by the Rabbis are not the result of ignorance but attest to a refusal to take events seriously, or to credit them with a valid significance. Instead, events unfolded in an informal cycle of violence and crime.

But since the Emancipation, we can no longer separate reason and history so radically – perhaps because since the eighteenth century, reason has penetrated History. Be that as it may, to deny the universality of confrontation by refusing to grant political life a significance and a source of truth would be a strange attitude for a modern Jew to adopt. He would sooner deny messianism if he knew it to hold such peculiar presuppositions, and would embrace the accusation made by the enemies of Judaism against the apparent egoism or utopianism of Israel's messianic thought. Emancipation has been something other than a practical and juridical reform of Judaism and the welcome it received from the nations. Emancipation has been for Judaism itself an opening – not on to humanity, for which it always felt responsible, but on to the political forms of that humanity. It enabled it to take history seriously. Thus messianism in the strong sense of the term has been compromised in the Jewish consciousness since Emancipation, ever since Jews participated in world history. If we cannot feel the absurd element in history, a part of our messianic sensibility is lost. One cannot lay claim to the prophetic vision of truth, and go on to participate in the values of the world which has surrounded us since the Emancipation. There is nothing more hypocritical than the messianic prophetism of the comfortable bourgeois.

The messianic sensibility inseparable from the knowledge of being chosen (which is perhaps, ultimately, the very subjectivity of the subject) would be irremediably lost – and this will be my final remark – if the solution of the State of Israel did not represent an attempt to reunite the irreversible acceptance of universal history with the necessarily particularist messianism. This universalist particularism (which is not Hegel's concrete universal) can be found in the aspirations of Zionism, and associated with a recognition of History and a collaboration with it. This collaboration begins with a withdrawal, a movement out of History in which we have located ourselves as assimilated Jews ever since the Emancipation. It is in the preservation of this universalist particularism, at the heart of History in which it is henceforth to be found, that I see the importance of the Israeli solution for the History of Israel. The hypocrisy of those who consider themselves to be outside History while benefiting from it is annulled by the dangers and risks that the Israeli solution entails. To judge the outside world, deny reason to a reality that pleads only its reality, and then lay claim oneself to the glorious title of 'reasonable man' is permissible only if one confronts the dangers of History. For centuries this was represented by the danger of persecution.

Israeli Judaism has accepted this danger in its life in the form of the State of Israel and what the State of Israel is to its whole Judaic contents, its vanguard groupings are to the State itself. The unique fate of being a Jew presents itself to different degrees, with a growing number of exponents. Within the State, all its small grains scattered in the desert, all the remote frontier kibbutzim, men established themselves. These men are indifferent to the seething world whose human values they none the less serve. They display their indifference in their daily lives, lives composed of work and risks.

III
POLEMICS

'The Lord of hosts.' The history of the Hebrews shows that this has to do not only with stars, but also with the warriors of Israel. ... This blasphemy was unknown to all the other (peoples).

(Simone Weil, *Letter to a monk*)

Not by might, nor by power, but by my Spirit, says the Lord of hosts.

(Zachariah 4:6)

Place and Utopia

It is perhaps not urgent to renew the disputes between Christianity and Judaism. The misunderstanding has lasted twenty centuries. Now we can wait. Who could dispel it in any case? No simple, or even complex, formula could imprison the vast movements of ideas, feelings and wishes. In the first place, the facts themselves prove nothing. If Christianity strikes the imagination by the way it has conquered the Western world, Judaism astounds us by its refusal to recognize that conquest. The stiff neck of this people is truly the supernatural part of its anatomy. Whatever anyone says, this stubbornness, which is stronger than persecution or temptation, is not pride, but freedom.

So why do I come back to it? We are not living at a time in world history when Christianity is threatening our inner lives in any particularly disquieting way. In the midst of so many other horrors, the extermination of six million defenceless beings, in a world that in two thousand years Christianity has not been able to make better, in our eyes robs its conquest of Europe of much of its prestige. Of course, we must never forget the purity of individual acts by Christians, and there were an impressive number of them who were faithful to the spirit of France in saving the lives of us, the survivors, during those terrible years. We cannot forget the courage of the Church hierarchy in France. But Christianity's failure on the political and social level cannot be denied. It is particularly notice-able today, when the importance of earthly things appears not only to base souls. This is the moment at which to reflect on what seems to us to be a utopia.

The belief that the things of this world are important has never been denied by Christianity, but it simultaneously overestimates and underestimates the weight of the reality which it wants to improve. It overestimates it because it sees in it a total resistance to human action. The relationships that man entertains with himself and his neighbours seem to him fixed, unalterable, eternal. He underestimates it, for he hopes that a miraculous intervention on the part of Divinity will transfigure this brutal weight. This double attitude shows why revolutionary Christianity, which uprooted the individual from the strongest links binding him to his condition, was horribly conservative: bowing before the established order, afraid of scandal, paradoxically associating its horror of a nature of grace with the poetry of naivety, fields of wheat, the virtues of being warrior-like and putting down roots, of being a man-plant, a humanity-forest whose gnarled joints of root and trunk are magnified by the rugged life of a countryman.

If Judaism is attached to the here below, it is not because it does not have the imagination to conceive of a supernatural order, or because matter represents some sort of absolute for it; but because the first light of conscience is lit for it on the path that leads from man to his neighbour. What is an individual, a solitary individual, if not a tree that grows without regard for everything it suppresses and breaks, grabbing all the nourishment, air and sun, a being that is fully justified in its nature and its being? What is an individual, if not a usurper? What is signified by the advent of conscience, and even the first spark of spirit, if not the discovery of corpses beside me and my horror of exiting by assassination? Attention to others and, consequently, the possibility of counting myself among them, of judging myself – conscience is justice.

To be without being a murderer. One can uproot oneself from this responsibility, deny the place where it is incumbent on me to do something, to look for an anchorite's salvation. One can choose utopia. On the other hand, in the name of spirit, one can choose not to flee the conditions from which one's work draws its meaning, and remain here below. And that means choosing ethical action.

I do not know if Judaism has expressed its metaphysics of the spirit in the terms I have just outlined, but I do know that it has chosen action, and that the divine word moves it only as Law. This action does not tackle the Whole in a global and magical way, but grapples with the particular. All the same, it cannot efface the given facts of a problem rather than resolving it. It is historical, it exists in time. History is not a perpetual test whose goal is the diploma of eternal life, but the very element in which the life of the spirit moves.

The incomprehension that greets the ethical essence of the spirit – due in large part to forgetting Hebrew, reading a Bible frozen in translation, being unable to go back to the Talmud, which boldly unfolds the Bible in a way that reveals the whole spectrum of the human drama it assumes – today propels a whole young generation who wish to be faithful to notions that are totally foreign to Judaism. The Sacred – together with the fear and trembling, as well as the ecstasy, aroused by its luminous presence – becomes the key word, if not the grand concept, of a whole religious revival. What contemporary sociology discovered in the prelogical mentality of Australia and Africa assumes the status of a privileged religious experience. It is triumphantly set against the dry and mind-deadening moralism of the nineteenth century, that abomination of abominations. Do these young men suspect the merciless war declared by the Bible and the Talmud on the Sacred and sacraments?

When monotheist teaching is passed down to men by word and by scripture, it captures humanity in its savagely real state. What it seems to reflect of a bygone age is what precisely constitutes its force and testifies to the way it adjusts to the human condition: a world in which there are wars and slaves, sacrifices and priests, material interests and crime – jealousies, hatreds and murders which fraternity itself cannot resolve. The Bible does not begin the building of an ideal city in a void. It places itself inside these situations which it must assume, in order to overcome them. It seems to transform them by pursuing them right into their dialectical return, which is the enslavement of man by man after the suppression of slavery, the survival of mythologies after the crumbling of idols. To recognize the necessity of a law is to recognize that humanity cannot be served by at once magically denying its condition. The faith that moves mountains and conceives of a world without slaves immediately transports itself to utopia, separating the reign of God from the reign of Caesar. This reassures Caesar.

Utopia seems not just vain in itself, it is also dangerous in its consequences. The man of utopia wishes unjustly. Instead of the difficult task of living an equitable life, he prefers the joy of solitary salvation. He therefore refuses the very conditions in which his bad conscience had set him up as a person. He is nothing but Desire: disturbed by the dazzling day of his human conscience, he pursues a dream as though he were still sleeping, as though another day should dawn within his day, and with it another waking that would rid him of his suffocating nightmares.

To speak of law is not to remain at the stage surpassed by the Redemption. To speak of Redemption in a world that remains without justice is to forget that the soul is not the demand for immortality but the impossibility of assassinating, and that consequently the spirit is the proper concern of a just society. It involves making Israel. To move towards justice while denying, with a global act, the very conditions within which the ethical drama is played out is to embrace nothingness and, under pretext of saving everything, to save nothing. The God of monotheists Whose Revelation coincides with the very awakening of conscience, of the accounts kept against nature — an action that henceforth doubles our energy expenditure – does not give Himself over to human fantasies. A heavy suspicion weighs over the feeling of divine presence and mystical ecstasy and every aspect of things sacred: are they not a seething, subjective mass of forces, passions and imaginations? Moral action must not be confused with the tedium of sermons. It involves the reasoning and the humour of the talmudists, the overwhelming certainties of the prophets, and the virile confidence of the psalms. It even involves the possibility of those feelings that have lost their innocence. These days even Jews scarcely appreciate the scope, the difficult but real complexity of relationships, and the dramatic turns and implications of the ethical order. But it is on the basis of this ethical order that these metaphysical abstractions, the toys of our oratory, take on significance and effectiveness. It is on this basis that we can once more find a meaning to the love of God, His presence and His consolations.

The ethical order does not prepare us for the Divinity; it is the very accession to the Divinity.

All the rest is a dream.

A New Version of *Jesus Narrated by the Wandering Jew* by Edmond Fleg

The new edition of *Jesus Narrated by the Wandering Jew* is read with a new emotion. Perhaps because it simply furnishes the occasion to reread the book, to reread Fleg, to let oneself be once more assailed by the torrent of images, simultaneously noble and grotesque, by all the mischievousness of the *Midrash* which, as a master of anachronism (that is to say, of eternity), confuses times and places and is wary of abstractions that are always prematurely rigid and clear.

But the emotion has perhaps another cause: the revisions made to this definitive edition touch us very directly, for they refer to certain events which took place between 1933 and 1945 in Christian Europe, and certain others which have happened since, in a corner of Asia, where, for the first time, Jews can live without obsessive fear of Christianity. If the suffering of the just atones for evil, one may wonder, after these new chapters of a bimillennial history, who endured the Passion, who fulfilled the prophecies about universal expiation, who was resurrected two days after his death. With the small shopkeepers and craftsmen who lived by their wits, with those small vergers and rabbis in little towns throughout Eastern Europe, the purity went out of this world. Certainly, they had no divine substance to dispose of in order to play out a metaphysical drama with confidence; but behind the exotic dress, the picturesque gesticulations and the irregularities which an inhuman world was eager to denounce, there was a humanity that was both perfectly lucid and perfectly pure — that is to say, which was not intimate with true Evil. Fleg thinks that the resurrection of this world in the country of Israel is the true guarantee of the coming messianic era.

His wandering Jew bears the mark of this world which had disappeared and is being reborn. But as he is free of all the conventional characteristics of allegory, he is marvellously alive. His irony, which is that of a man who has returned from everything, for he has walked a great deal, expresses an experience that is outside Evil – profound, maybe, but outside. He speaks like a character out of Shalom Aleichem. This narrator constitutes the work's great success. The book is important because it speaks of the wandering Jew and his great adventure, his refusal to accept Christianity. But it is important above all because this refusal begins at a very early moment.

The Western Jew, who is so legitimately proud of his integration into the great modern nations, does not fulfil the final part of his assimilation. He often cites the differences separating Jews from his Church. It is a convenient cliché: the teacher of the Gospels is attractive; medieval history is repulsive. Enormous efforts are then made to seek out in the Palestinian landscape the trace of the steps, the salt of the tears, the echo of the prayers belonging to the man they call 'the last prophet of Israel'. Poets try to get emotional by pondering on the fact that he was a Jew and the son of Jews, as though local colour were needed in order to feel sympathy for suffering or recognize a just man. Or else, scrutinizing the figures in the Gospels in an effort to come up with myths that excite the brain, intellectuals create a metaphysics out of them and basically strive to resolve problems whose given facts they do not in reality accept.

Fleg's remarkable originality consists in surprising the first hesitations of the wandering Jew, when faced with Jesus himself. The wandering Jew has confidence in the ideal image of Jesus. The man who paints that image sincerely wants to understand and love it. But it is on contact with this Jesus, whose charm is felt by Fleg, that his initially imperceptible reservations appear. The gap begins to widen and climaxes at the very moment of crucifixion, when his pity for the two thieves on the cross, who are going to their deaths without glory or any certainty of resurrection, outweighs the pity he feels for the crucified Christ.

What certainly rings out from the scene is one of the characteristic tones of the Jewish 'No'. The misery that calls out for our pity, our justice, our freedom and our work, is replaced by an ambiguous passion in which grief is transformed into ritual and sacrament, and unfolds like a scenario. It is as if its human meaning were not sufficiently full, as if another mysterious night enveloped the night of human suffering, as if some celestial salvation could triumph without ridding it of visible misery. The efficacity of the work is replaced by the magic of faith; the austere God appealing to a humanity capable of Good is overlaid with an infinitely indulgent divinity that consequently locks man within his wickedness and lets loose this wicked yet saved man on a disarmed humanity.

All that, with the delicate touches of accomplished art, is suggested from the opening pages, for all that is deeply felt – more deeply felt, no doubt, than the attraction of Christ's personality. So Fleg's march towards Judaism, from his childhood when he first encountered Jesus, culminates, despite his lingering at certain crossroads, with his complete return.

But is it really the Church that prevents us from rejoining Christ? The Church is, after all, what we understand best. The old neighbour! There is a level other than that of dogma and mystery on which we encounter it. It has absorbed many elements from rationalist humanism since it absorbed Aristotle. The Greek wisdom which the talmudists admired, the ideas of the revolution which it has admitted since Leo XIII and the Rallying, have created a common language for us. Here is a great modern institution which directs the lives of millions of our citizens. The evil it has inflicted on us in the past cannot make us deaf and blind. How can we deny the possibilities for good and the spirit of sacrifice of so many of its men in whose debt, moreover, we lay though the recent terrible years, and to whom many of us owe our lives? But this friendship which comes from being neighbours must have nothing in common with an intimacy going back to origins. Fleg is right when he perceives a strange message in the gentleness of the man whose marvellous charm he wants us to feel, but no Jewish writer speaking of Jews has been able to communicate his enchantment. Dear and venerated Edmond Fleg, you are no more! The most bizarre of all Greek myths speaks to our intelligence. The figures of the Gospels leave us cold and stupid; we feel we are lying to ourselves when we take them up again. Explain that by uneffaceable memories, invoke psychoanalysis, speak of stubbornness. Two thousand years of Jewish history is worth the triumph of Christianity, in order that our refusal should not be suspected of utopia. It is not enough to call Jesus Yechou and Rabbi to bring him closer to us. For us, we who are without hatred, there is no friendship. It remains far off. And on his lips, we no longer recognize our own verses.

The Spinoza Case

The anathema pronounced against Spinoza by the religious authorities of his day, and the project proposed by Ben-Gurion to lift this condemnation, certainly have no significance for the glory and influence of Spinoza in the world. A case of posthumous justice: Spinozas do not lie. 'One does not judge conquerors', said Catherine the Great, sacrificing justice to success. Neither does one fly to the assistance of victory.

Does it therefore involve saving the honour of the Jewish people? But the Jewish people is a large enough entity to permit itself a conflict, even with Spinoza. One must not remain locked within the timid attitude of the nineteenth-century Jewish Haskalah, which joined to an admirable confidence in the future of Judaism a strange suspicion of any of its values that remained unvulgarized or unaccepted by the Gentiles. This was the chink in the armour of admirable men who, fifty years on, created the State of Israel! Free from any national 'inferiority complex', they hide the fact within a spiritual order in which concupiscence for the modern man is the only thing without censure. At a dinner given in Paris for a high-up Israeli political figure, the host asked his guest of honour to admire a Yiddish translation of a Talmud tractate. He was informed that Israel needed neither the translation nor the original. A treatise on bee-keeping would have been more successful, as no doubt would have been the *Tractatus Theologico-Politicus*!

The condemnation or rehabilitation of Spinoza none the less concerns the Jewish people. At stake is an essential question that has arisen since the Emancipation of the Jews throughout the world on the one hand, and the creation of the State of Israel on the other. Israelites and Israelis see themselves as Westerners. What do they think they retain from the West?

'West' signifies freedom of spirit [*esprit*]. All its virtues and some of its vices follow from this. Freedom of spirit, in a very precise manner, announces the wish to maintain an inner link with truth: to be self-effacing before the truth, but to feel the master in this effacement, like the mathematician who bows before the evidence, conscious of a supreme freedom. This marvellous coincidence of obedience and commandment, subjection and sovereignty, bears a well-worn but handsome name: reason. It is to reason that Spinoza's work offers supreme and certainly approving homage. It is ultimately the interiority of rational relations, and the equivalence to the highest forms of life, that are illuminated by the *Ethics*. Judaism cannot separate itself off from this, just as it cannot turn its back on mathematics; it cannot remain disinterested in democracy and social problems, any more than it can choose to ignore the injuries man and things inflict on man in favour of the intelligible relations such as dialogue, gentleness and peace. Beyond its credo and its ritualism, Judaism in its entirety, by means of its faith and its practices, has perhaps sought only to bring an end to mythologies and the violence they exert on reason and perpetuate in customs.

Rationalism does not menace the Jewish faith. What do theological subtleties matter if myths are finished! There is a beautiful talmudic text which isolates two moments in religious infidelity: the abandonment of truth and the adherence to myth. These two faults perhaps follow on from one another, but they are not to be confused. Though they may scandalize pious souls, those Jews who do not practise their faith and believe themselves to be atheists remain Jews all the same. But for how much longer? The question does arise, and it is a serious one. The moral reservations which have accumulated over centuries of self-mastery, suffering and study still show up as an instinct for what is just and unjust. This has created a certain hierarchy of values which seems natural to some and a certain vision of history which moves others. In our day, the history of ideas is the godless theology that stirs the soul of unbelievers. It is the secret garden in which their own basic values bloom forth. Spinoza exerted an influence on this history of ideas that was decisive and anti-Jewish.

It does not have to do with biblical criticism, which he inaugurated. Biblical criticism can ruin only a faith that has already been weakened. Does not the truth of eternal texts shine forth all the more when they are denied the external support of a dramatic and theatrical revelation? When they are studied for themselves, do they not bear witness to the divine value of their inspiration and the purely spiritual miracle of their union? This miracle is all the more miraculous the more it consists of numerous and disparate fragments, and all the more marvellous for the way in which rabbinism develops a form of teaching that tallies with it. The reading of the texts can nurture a fidelity to Judaism: the conviction that the Old Testament contains the definitive terms of civilization, that the forms can evolve without our having to renew the way in which we think them through, that every category has already been given, that the Old Testament completes history and is consequently modern, that its truths no longer call up new revelations. In this sense, Hermann Cohen, when asked by a Christian if he did not long for Jesus, quoted the Psalm: 'The Lord is my shepherd, I shall not want'.

We entirely agree with the opinion of our late lamented and admirable friend Jacob Gordin: Spinoza was guilty of betrayal. Within the history of ideas, he subordinated the truth of Judaism to the revelation of the New Testament. The latter is of course surpassed by the intellectual love of God, but Western being involves this Christian experience, even if it is only a stage.

Henceforth we cannot ignore the harmful role Spinoza played in the decomposition of the Jewish intelligentsia, even if for its representatives, as for Spinoza himself, Christianity is only a penultimate truth, and the adoration of God in spirit and in truth must still surmount Christianity. Acknowledging that the Gospels are an inevitable stage on the road to truth is more important today than actually professing one's faith. It was by prefiguring Jesus with Judaism that Spinozism managed to introduce a movement into irreligious Judaism which, when it was religious, it opposed for seventeen centuries. How many Jewish intellectuals detached from all religious belief do not regard the figure of Jesus as fulfilling the teaching of the prophets, even if this figure or these teachings are succeeded in their minds by the French Revolution or Marxism? For a Léon Brunschvicg, whose memory we venerate, or a Jankélévitch, whom we admire, a quotation from the New Testament is much more familiar than one from the Old Testament, and it is often the former that illuminates the latter.

There is perhaps no danger of proselytism in a society in which the religions have lost their influences and form part of a private order, like aesthetic preferences and culinary tastes. This despite the fact that Christianity is in Europe the religion of the strong, the humility of good form, and we have reverted to a time when, in Reinach's words, conversion conferred only the advantage of being ill-received in a salon. Thanks to the rationalism patronized by Spinoza, Christianity is surreptitiously triumphing, bringing conversion without the scandal of apostasy. People who are often remarkable and well loved, like those warriors not wanted for battle by Gideon, hold to certainties which they belie by their reflexes. The thinkers who, in the aftermath of the Emancipation, conceived of a West without Christianity, such as Salvador in France, remained without disciples. The recent work of Franz Rosenzweig, whose homage to Christianity consists in showing it a different destiny to the one Judaism accomplishes, remains unknown. The intimate thought of Western Jewish intellectuals is bathed in a Christian atmosphere. Will it have taken the loss of religious feeling in the world, then, to make Jews aware of the triumph of the Galilean? Do they still know that our great books, which are increasingly ignored, reveal a Synagogue that in no way tries to act as a blindfold? That Spinoza, in his Jewish Studies, perhaps only had teachers of little calibre? Alas! Hebraism, in our day, is such a rare science that it can no longer imagine itself to be nondescript or mediocre.

Israel is not defined by opposition to Christianity, any more than it is defined as anti-Buddhism, anti-Islam or anti-Brahminism. Instead, it consists in promoting understanding between all men who are tied to morality. It seeks their understanding, in the first instance, with Christians and Muslims, who are its neighbours or companions in civilization. But the base of this civilization is the Reason that the Greek philosophers revealed to the world. We are completely convinced that, in an autonomous and even more glorious way, the Mosaism prolonged and interpreted by rabbinism led Israel there; we are completely convinced that Christianity has a different inspiration; we are therefore competely convinced that we still have more chance of finding an unsullied rationalism in Plato and in Aristotle than in Spinoza. All these deep convictions could be kept by us if, for two thousand years, Christian theologians had not presented themselves as the men who perfected, carried out and rounded off Judaism, like those Kantians who, in their studies, perfect Kant and those Platonists who improve Plato. Ah! the workers of the eleventh hour!

Our feeling for Christianity is wholehearted, but it remains one of friendship and fraternity. It cannot become paternal. We cannot recognize a child that is not ours. We protest against its claim on the inheritance and its impatience to take over, since we are still alive and kicking.

The difficult trial has lasted for two thousand years. In proposing that Spinoza's trial be reopened, perhaps Ben-Gurion is seeking to question – more effectively than the missionaries installed in Israel – the great certainty of our history; which ultimately, for Ben-Gurion himself, preserved a nation to love and the opportunity to build a State.

Have You Reread Baruch?

Does Spinoza, in his *Tractatus Theologico-Politicus*, hide his real thought and the mortal blows, visible to anyone who can read, dealt to the authority of the Scriptures and the religions they found? The American philosopher Leo Strauss has in fact invited us to see a cryptogram in the whole of philosophy, even in the work of Maimonides, in which Reason secretly fights against religion. Sylvain Zac, who does not allow himself to be guided by any concern for apologetics and in no way wishes to put himself forward as a defender of the Revelation, none the less breaks with this mixing of philosophical history with detective fiction.[1] In a work whose richness of information, respect for the text, contempt for eloquence and false symmetry, and modesty vie with its own penetration, finesse and philosophical tact, Zac isolates the coherence of the thought overtly expressed by Spinoza, without prematurely drowning it in the possibilities raised by afterthought. He fixes the exact meaning of the text before inducing a hidden meaning.

The esoteric doctrine of the *Tractatus Theologico-Politicus* already appears sufficiently nuanced and, on several points, unexpected. Was it able to play a positive role in the formation of the modern religious consciousness? A special analysis is needed to answer this question. We shall conclude by showing how it remains in any case relevant to a man of today who wishes to be a Jew. What has unquestionably been retained of that doctrine is the way it invited historical criticism of the Scriptures. But Sylvain Zac shows us precisely that this criticism was not Spinoza's basic project.

In possession of a philosophy that represented for him – and for every reasonable being, in his view – wisdom and salvation, Spinoza wishes to guarantee the independence of this high path leading to the intellectual love of God, the true religion that imposes itself without violence, despite the violence with which it can be opposed by Church and State in the name of the ill-read Scriptures. European philosophy, in Spinoza's age, has not yet been reduced to regarding political life as a moment in its own unfolding process, but Reason for Spinoza does enter certain political conditions (p. 232).[2] So it must be demonstrated that there can be no conflict between the Scriptures and philosophy, and that the intention of the Scriptures is not philosophical. Spinoza denounces as 'arbitrary', useless, harmful and absurd' the act of interpreting the Scriptures from philosophy, which has been wrongly pursued by both rabbis and Christian theologians; the Scriptures have only the object of teaching, without proving anything and for the benefit of those who cannot accede to philosophical wisdom, a doctrine of salvation, the Word of God, composed of faith and charity. The idea of applying a historical method to the Bible is therefore born from a concern to protect true philosophy in the City, just as America was discovered by navigators who were expecting to reach the East Indies.

The neutrality of the Scriptures with regard to philosophy presupposes the possibility of interpreting *the Scriptures through the Scriptures*. To prove the truth of a text, it must agree with reality; to understand its significance, it need only be made to agree with itself. By right, of course, every human is explained by Nature – that is, by cause. But before explaining ideas, we understand them in terms of what they signify:

> Spinoza's great discovery consists in showing that, in order to understand the exact meaning of the ideas contained in the sacred texts, we can use a method that is as rigorous as the method of the wise men, without our seeking to explain things in terms of cause. (p. 00)

The artificial coherence of the philosophers is replaced by the history of the editing of the texts. In the expression of the Word of God which tradition took to be as eternal as the Word itself, we must henceforth separate the grain from the chaff. Socrates deplored the fact that in the *Phaedra* the truth of a statement is not questioned before asking 'Who said it' and 'From which country is he?' Spinoza thinks that enquiring about the author of a biblical text and the circumstances surrounding its production allow one to isolate the meaning of the *statement* and separate out the temporal from the permanent.

An enquiry that assumes a vast historical culture confronts texts first in order to bring out their authenticity and provenance, after which the true thought of the authors and the validity of their testimony can be ascertained.

This method has become familiar to us all, even if not all of us share Spinoza's optimism over the results to be obtained or the infallibility of this colligation of literary facts, imposed, according to Zac, by the colligation which Bacon recommends for the intellection of natural facts.

The method of procedure taught by Spinoza lacks any appeal to an anticipatory vision of the whole, which spills out over the positivist colligation of texts and is perhaps rooted in an inevitable commitment to a project. Spinoza thinks that a discourse can be understood without the vision of the truths enlightening it. But isolating the fundamental meanings of an experience while practising an 'epoche' in relation to its truth involved indicating one of the paths along which philosophy may travel, even after the end of speculative dogmatisms.

Text and Content

The fact that Spinoza should have been able to put aside a rational method designed to isolate the meaning of the Scriptures and find a place in the life of the Spirit for the 'prophetic' light beside the natural light, and for a Book containing what, without a trace of irony, he calls the Word of God, together with the fact that this good hermeneutic judgement and this faith should not square with any of the there genres of knowledge, is of the highest importance for the meaning subsequently taken on not only by religious philosophy but by all philosophy. Of course, Spinoza does believe that the Word of God ultimately comes from the nature of God and that if one understood this nature, wisdom and future would derive from it in a rigorously determinist way. But in the complexity of things, this future cannot be known philosophically and it is the prophet who perceives this future, as God's decisions and decrees (p. 95). Since impenetrable complexity of things is not contingent, the Word is not dedicated to the silence of the day in which 'everything will be clear'. This must be underlined, as must the *sui generis* certainly conferred on faith in Spinoza's examination of the Word of God.

It is in vain that he prefers the holiness of teachings to the intangibility of the biblical text which is their vehicle, for he recognizes the appropriateness of this text to the content. We must insist on the role – in which the Jews will recognize themselves – of obedience and hope in the perception of this Word and finally, despite the resentment that Spinoza could have retained for the

Jewish community which had treated him harshly, we must insist on the freedom with which he recognizes an equal value, each according to its perspective, in the two Testaments, and sometimes the superiority of the Old over the New.[3]

Obedience but not Servitude

What does the Word of God say? Addressed to all 'without distinction of age, sex, race or culture, the Word of God must be a principle of love and union for all men' (p. 92). The Bible is not aimed at the true knowledge of God but only at the teaching of a practical rule of living, inspired by the disinterested love of God (p. 85). To know God, as Jeremiah says, is to practise justice and charity (p. 98). Neither sacred things nor sacred words exist in themselves. 'What is sacred is the conduct of men when it is inspired by justice and love.' As for words, if 'they are used to formulate a discourse liable to excite true piety in the hearts of people, we can say that they are truly sacred' (p. 93).

The eternal truths of faith are perceived as commandments from God and constitute 'for the believer the path to Salvation' (p. 95): to love God and one's neighbour. But in this matter the truths which are, of course, not transmitted *more geometrico* – and of which Zac will tell us (p. 76) that it is obvious once and for all that they do not bear in themselves the sign of their certainty – involve a universality. They express an evidence that can be perceived by any sound spirit. Without approaching Spinozism (p. 97),[4] without being 'of the order of reason in the philosophical sense of the word' (p. 99), these truths involve an interiority all their own: the word of the prophet finds an echo in the hearts of men. Scripture teaches the true religion. We must exclude from it the historical side of things (even if it is useful for simple souls) as well as the ceremonial and speculative elements (p. 99). This gives rise to a tolerance towards rites that are not truths but belong to the realm of social custom (pp. 102–3). This is an interiorization of the Bible, a religious liberalism but one devoid of philosophy.

Obedience, not knowledge, is the attitude called for by the Word of God, which cannot separate men as theories do. The Word of God is ethical. It is openly so. As objects of faith, precepts are commanded and must be obeyed, but the motives for obedience are not of *a rational order*. They are motives of an affective order, such as fear, hope, fidelity, respect, veneration and love (p. 107). Obedience and heteronomy, but not servitude, for the believer does not serve the interests of the master, but has a hope for him. 'It is hope', writes Zac, 'that ultimately constitutes the most powerful motive for obedience' (p. 108). On the other hand, obedience comes not from constraint but from an internal and disinterested fervour. Commandments and love do not contradict one another, contrary to Kant; the desire to be conserved, without being torn inside, adheres to the Commandment which generates integrity.

But religious fervour is manifested in acts, never only in words. 'A faith without works is dead' (p. 110). 'Obedience, sincerity, fervour, love and joy – all these notions are indissolubly linked to that of faith.' And Zac does not hesitate to recognize a Jewish style in this, the *simhah shel mitsvah*, the joy of fulfilling the commandment. Of course, such a faith cannot be judged for truth but for fervour, and is accompanied only by 'moral certainty', which is not transmissible *more geometrico*. It is a subjective certainty, a risk, but 'the customs of life and society oblige us to give our consent to a large number of things that we cannot demonstrate'. The moral word has thus a special rank, placed beside speculation and above the realm of the imagination.

Moral faith and certainty. Only the presuppositions of justice and love constitute the simple dogmatic faith of believers. It involves the existence of a God Who is good, omnipotent, powerful, and gifted with providence, requiring only a spiritual, pardoning and merciful worship. This is a religion of moral certainty that is universal, not to be confused with any script-based religion yet irreducible to a religion of reason. Each person is free to resolve the philosophical problems as he understands them. As in Kant, this God of faith reflects the demands of practical reason, but in Spinoza He does not occupy the place left empty by the dismissed impossible metaphysics. We are at a point prior to the Kantian critique: the God of philosophy is for Spinoza both the theoretical and the practical God of reason. Faith is the support of the Scriptures to which the historical religions lay claim. The only conceivable faith is historical faith. It is independent of all philosophy (p. 110) while agreeing with the practical consequences of philosophical reason. This faith therefore possesses a curious autonomy within a rationalist and dogmatic philosophy. Philosophers have no need of it, since instead of believing they know.

Modern man no longer belongs, via his religious life, to an order in which propositions on the existence of God, on the soul, on miracles or a future revealed by the prophets remain, in spite of the abstract nature of the pronouncement, on the level of perceived truth. At least, present-day Western Judaism does not receive them in such a spirit. For a modern religious conscience, the idea that the Scriptures contain the Word of God, but are not that actual Word, frustrates only an infantile representation of the Revelation without discrediting a text to which a Jew nowadays can bring many more resources, when researching into this word, than Spinoza could have imagined. The theoretical formulations of his tradition wash away the accumulated riches of a long inner experience.

The Talmud and rabbinic literature are neither folklore nor a 'purely human invention' (p. 39), as Spinoza still thinks; not a process by which to enclose the Bible within some philosophical system of the day, or to confer a logical order on the alluvial deposits of Jewish history. They sum up the efforts made over thousands of years to go beyond the letter of the text and even its apparent dogmatism, and to restore a wholly spiritual truth even to those passages in the Scriptures called historical or ritual or cere-monial or thaumaturgical. In its scope and lucidity this undertaking has no precedent, but it is guided by the letter of the text, an extraordinary letter since it nurtures and demands this effort. This accounts for the prestige once more enjoyed by the Talmud in the eyes of some contemporary groups of Western Jews. And it is on this issue that they part company with Spinoza.

When one tackles the Bible with such an understanding of the Talmud, the multiplicity of presumed authors of the Scriptures, which biblical criticism since Spinoza likes to multiply still further, no longer questions the religious value of the text. This number can no longer compromise the internal coherence of the religious experience attested to by the Bible and controlled and confirmed by talmudic pluralism. It is perhaps the Talmud which best institutes the idea of a single Spirit at work among those partaking in dialogue and the idea that opposing theses express the Word of a Living God. Once again it is Spinoza who has taught us that we have the right to stick above all to the instrinsic value of a text to the very extent, perhaps, that it attacks the value that the Scriptures would in some way extract from its ink. It would none the less be excessive to demand from philosophy that wishes to think *sub specie aeterni* that it allow lived experience to be one of the conditions for a just appreciation of a text, or allow the historical relativism of ideas to be one of the causes of their fecundity; it would be too much to hope for from such a philosophy to propose that it view the Talmud and rabbinic literature as the very work produced by this historical maturing of intuitions.[5]

As a man of his time, Spinoza must have ignored the true meaning of the Talmud. Between the interiority of the Divine inscribed in the hearts of men and the interiority of fitting thought, on the one hand, and the exteriority of opinion, on the other, Spinoza would not have recognized, in history, a work of interiorization that reveals the inner meaning of something that had previously passed for opinion, But to his credit, Spinoza did reserve for the Word of God a *proper status* outside opinion and 'fitting' ideas.

Zac's book calls our attention to this side of Spinoza which is perhaps the least Spinozist. The fact that non-Spinozism can make an appearance in Spinoza remains itself indicative. We are far from so-called Spinozists to whom the believer-non-believer alternative is as simple as pharmacist-non-pharmacist. What counts is the difference between those who regard the Scriptures, even if they are judged to be inspired or naive, as a test like any other, and those who regard them, in spite of the traces they retain of their evolution, as an essential form of the spirit, irreducible to perception, philosophy, literature, art, science or history, yet compatible with political and scientific freedom. Although incapable of being transmitted *more geometrico*, the Word of God, a religion and not merely wisdom, can be presented as agreeing with philosophy (pp. 118–21). In that lies not its inconsistency but its originality and its universality, its independence in the face of the order that philosophy declared to be final and where it claims to reign without division. This gives it its power to survive at the end of philosophy.[6] Moreover, Spinoza – while substituting, in the *Ethics*, a philosophy for the religion of the Bible – was careful to retain in this philosophy the unimpeachable plenitude of the Scriptures. Spinozism was one of the first philosophers in which absolute thought also tried to be an absolute religion.

Contrary to his contemporaries, Spinoza therefore 'sincerely made concessions to the theologians by recognizing the divinity of the Scriptures' (p. 231). There is a way of reading the Bible that goes back to listening to the Word of God. This approach remains irreplaceable in spite of the privileges to be gained by philosophy (that is to say, Spinozism). Through the multiple authors whom the historical method discovers in sacred texts, the Word of God invites men to obey the teachings of justice and charity. Through historical criticism of the Bible, Spinoza teaches us its ethical interiorization. 'Judaism is a revealed Law and not a theology': this opinion from Mendelssohn came, then, from Spinoza. Can the present-day Jewish religious consciousness deny this teaching of interiorization, when it is capable of giving such teaching a new meaning and new perspectives? Does it want to side with a Kierkegaard in regarding the ethical stage of existence as surpassable?

Is dogmatism, albeit Spinozist, still the prototype of philosophy? We distrust it as much as ideologies! Philosophy does not engender itself. To philosophize is to move towards the point where one sees the light as it illuminates the first meanings, which none the less already have a past. What Spinoza called the Word of God projects this light and carries language itself. The biblical commandments relating to justice are no longer a sublime stammering to which a wisdom transmitted *more geometrico* would restore absolute expression and context. They lend an original meaning to Being. Since Kant, we philosophers know that they open up a Nature to us. They allow us to conceive of a world that the rigorous sciences merely weigh.[7] The ethical significance of the Scriptures, whose irreducibility was perceived by Spinoza's genius and which he highlighted in an age in which axioms, still superb, had nothing to fear from axiomatics, has survived the dogmatism of fitting ideas. Is philosophy not on the point of rising up from such dogmatism, as if from a solitary rock?

Persons or Figures
(On *Emmaüs*,[1] by Paul Claudel)

Could we gain access to the mystery of religions wihout philology?
Vocabulary, conjunctions, syntax only encumber the tortuous paths
of profane civilizations. A whole youth must be spent in explaining
three lines of the *Odyssey*. Religious verses are more rewarding. In
Emmaüs, Claudel offers a personal exegesis of the Old Testament.
Relying principally on the Vulgate, he allows himself to be guided
by Raban Maur of Mayence, a ninth-century scholar of the Holy
Scriptures, the Fathers of the Church and Greek. He knew no
Hebrew.

The history of human beliefs inflames men of every belief. The
literary works which illustrate them and comment on them nurture
our intelligence, charm our sensibilities, and provoke recognition
and admiration for the talent and knowledge of their authors. The
rest of us Jews of the twentieth century lack neither scientific nor
literary tastes. But the Old Testament is familiar to us: for more
than two thousand years we have been reading the original. Our
first commentators brought its disparate elements together and, if I
may venture to say so, became its editors. It is by their work and
knowledge that Christians themselves have inherited the Bible. The
situations are familiar to us, and better than anyone we know their
difficulties, obscurities, contradictions and allusions. So we cannot
avoid the fact that claiming to free the profound meaning of a text
while remaining ignorant of its exact meaning seems to us extreme
poetic licence – even if genius should be excused grammar.

We shall not have the bad taste to mock the inspired nature of St
Jerome's translations. But do the Christian theologians themselves
see such work as being anything other than the Vulgate conforming
to the general spirit of the dogma? Do we have the right, for all that,
to interpret its propositions, exploiting etymologies, verbal simi-
larities and mystical calculations? The representatives of the Church
have not always neglected the tradition of Jewish exegesis or the
return to the original text. It suffices to recall the work of the
Franciscan Nicholas of Lyra who, in the thirteenth century, attributed

the highest value to them to the point of assiduously returning to Rachi's commentary. He demanded for the allegorical interpretation of the Fathers a point of departure in the literal sense.

I know that if these lines come one day under the gaze of Claudel, he will merely shrug his shoulders. He will see them as just one more of the countless attempts to contest the prefiguring of Jesus by the Old Testament. I certainly do not have the unworthy and anachronistic ambition to denigrate the dogma. But, faced with the forms that exegesis takes in *Emmaüs*, one cannot fail to think of the old scholastic principle: in proving too much, one proves nothing. The strange accent that Paul Claudel makes our Scriptures adopt compromises the serious purpose of his undertaking more than the criticisms one could have made. Plutarch, no doubt wishing to embrace the barbaric world with Greek reason, at some point draws a comparison between worship at the Temple of Jerusalem and the cult of Dionysus. On closing *Emmaüs* one understands that there are methods for reaching such conclusions.

With all the respect due to Christian thought, we believe that we have grasped the deep principle guiding this exegesis: *The Passion* contains the ultimate meaning of humanity, and all intelligibility emanates from the events constituting this drama. But must this dignity attach itself to every accessory of the action?

When it is claimed that Noah's Ark is significant only in that its wood prefigures the future Cross, or that the wells sunk by Isaac prepare us for the meeting between the Samaritan woman and Jesus, or that Miriam's leprosy symbolizes Mary's whiteness, or the burning bush prefigures the crown of thorns, all this brings us to a stage of logic that surpasses logic or precedes it. Either that, or the process appears as an immense psychoanalysis practised by the repressed Author of the Bible.

The incoherence or gaps in a text that is refractory to the preconceived idea are redressed or covered with the help of mystical links, symbols and allegories which, at the opportune moment, embrace psychology or history. Take, for example, Bathsheba: 'The name Bathsheba', indicates a naive note, 'appears to mean either the *house of satiety* or the *house of the sabbath*.' David prefigures the Saviour under the yoke of the First Alliance. Uriah has 'the ill fortune, despite being the most honest man in the world, to lend himself to being the figure of the Jewish People'. This does not prevent such an allegory of the Redemption from remaining scabrous. But the divine economy, does sin itself not serve some use? Through sin, David is opened to the joys of repentance and the idea of Salvation enters the world. And the details of the text? 'Raban Maur sees in the whole narrative a series of mysteries.' The way is open to poetry, and the resources of talent will mingle with those of mystery.

It is impossible to summarize *Emmaüs*. All question of exegesis apart, it is a book of profound piety in which Christian sensibility is given free rein. It is also a work in which Claudel's poetic imagination remains fascinating. Ah! that dull thud as Noah's Ark, after long weeks of navigation, hits land, at the top of Mount Ararat! We are not going to deal Claudel the insult of considering him a great poet. But this spirit whom we have admired since our youth cannot just be reproached for being pedantic, not knowing Hebrew, managing to shock us as Jews, and driving us away from the old Testament.

We wonder, in fact, if the idea of prefiguration, legitimate to the extent that it coincides with that of prophecy, does not alter, when it is raised into a system, the very essence of the spirit which Judaism installed. If every pure character in the Old Testament announces the Messiah, if every unworthy person is his torturer and every woman his Mother, does not the Book of Books lose all life with this obsessive theme and endless repetition of the same stereotyped gestures? Does the spiritual dignity of these men and women come to them through reference to a drama operating on a miraculous level, in some mythological and sacred realm, rather than from the meaning that this life, which is conscience, gives itself? Does the monotheist God haunt the roads of the unconscious? When Abraham receives the three visitors, does he receive the Lord because of the trinity which the visitors prefigure or because of his hospitality?

Sacred History is not the interpretation of a *pièce à thèse*, albeit transcendent, but the articulation through human freedom of a real life. Are we on the stage, or are we in the world? Does obeying God involve receiving a role from Him or receiving an order? We distrust theatre, the petrification of our faces, the figure that our person weds. We distrust poetry, which scan and bewitches our gestures; we distrust everything which, in spite of us, throws up a depective illusion in our lucid lives. It is for this reason that the Claudelian exegesis ultimately disconcerts us. Man as a person, as an agent of history, seems less real to him than man as a figure or statue. The freedom of conscious man is enveloped by a kind of sublime and sacramental *fatum* in which, instead of *being*, man *figures*. God the Director effaces God the Creator. He commands actors rather than freedoms. Is the image that, in its marvellous precociousness, Judaism conceived in the midst of peoples who were extremely happy in their pagan enthusiasm, not alienated when the shadow of a destiny falls on our intentions?

I wonder if our Christian friends can understand that Claudel's book leaves us feeling frightened and disorientated: as if our grandparents, parents, sisters and brothers were rigged out in exotic gear, and spoke a strange language. Unknown and hostile. Ethnically and racially transfigured, at each step they deny us. In *Emmaüs* we are more than ever before a people guilty of deicide. Poor Jules Isaac! He worked so hard to consult the Graeco-Roman documents and read the Gospels. These historians will never be able to locate the source. Does not Cain prefigure the Jewish people and Abel the Sacrificed Lamb? This is a courtly explanation of all our woes subsequent to exile, Auschwitz included. Eliphaz of Theman had already offered Job such an explanation, with all his contrition and tact. This is a prefiguration which we accept.

A Voice on Israel

A new book by Paul Claudel, *A Voice on Israel*,[1] abounds with Latin quotations from the Old Testament. Since we are well aware of the pitfalls scattered throughout the Bible, we shall not allow ourselves to discuss this exegesis. In this field, we fear combat less than ridicule.

The interpretation of these phrases or snatches of phrases encounters the same problem as the interpretation of the original ideas: the difficulty, to use the admirable formula of one modern philosopher, lies not in their possibility, but in their compossibility. There is nothing more ridiculous than a verbal battle that trades misunderstood verses! We do not want to take part in this farce, or to force a great poet to take part in it. If exegesis can sometimes become a game, there is no reason why it should be viewed as the only game without rules.

The biblical text does not contain its meaning like a symbol or an allegory, but as an expression contains its thought. This absolute thought given rigorous expression requires rigorous study. The belief that the Word of God can be heard only in study; that it cannot be distributed like bread but requires teachers; that study is not limited to mastering an alphabet, a vocabulary and a grammar reserved for scholars, but also represents the watershed of religious life, is a view that might seem that of a Pharisee. Why not? The word which remains and is not made flesh is not 'the letter which kills by drying up our need for the thing signified: the letter which has become an ideal' (p. 34). The word in its dignity can precisely put up with a stone or a parchment. Only in this way can it arouse a spiritual relationship in an intelligence. In this way it frees moral action and refines the fervour of love. Freedom engraved on a stone! It is for the heart to beat. As for the idol, rest assured – when it comes to unearthing idolatry, we Jews have been specialists for a long time.

Finally, the uncertainties of erudition often lead astray the greatest spirits. When, in an article in *Le Figaro littéraire*, Paul

Claudel, with all the self-confidence gained from cross-reference to the classics, writes to a Jewish correspondent, 'You must recognize, however, that there is a difference between the atmosphere of the Old Testament and that of the Talmud', we tell ourselves that Claudel has not even read a Latin translation of the Talmud, and that sixty years of assiduous reading of the Old Testament have none the less prevented him from seeing that the text – which is no doubt secondary – of the Ten Commandments does not begin *Ten times* with the word *No* (p. 68). We do not wish to reproach these readings for a vulgar lack of attention. We simply believe that it is the atmosphere of the Talmud which, precisely, communicates to the reading of the Bible this exact contact which prohibits impressionistic approximations, just as knowledge of a language makes us immediately aware of any mistake in gender or verb ending made by a speaker.

We prefer to transfer the debate on to a plane that is better adapted to the state of our respective knowledge.

What does *Une voix sur Israël* invite us to do?

Paul Claudel is sincerely overwhelmed by the massacre of the European Jews. In order to speak of it, he adopts a tone that does not deceive us and recalls what we have heard from him in other circumstances. Auschwitz, the State of Israel and the bringing together of the dispersed peoples are to be viewed for him in a religious perspective. Israel visibly returns to the Sacred History which it never left. Once again, a role awaits it in Christian drama. Jews gave the world Jesus. They were to allow him to atone for the whole world on the Cross. A new act now awaits them. It does not just involve a pure and simple conversion that would be the equivalent of a new dispersion through being dissolved into Christianity. 'God did not spend all that time getting used to your interesting physiognomy in order to deprive himself suddenly of the benefits of your curious vocation and personality. It is not every day that one finds a people like Israel to get things going' (p. 49) – Claudel assures us in one of these magnificent movements to which his dramatic work has accustomed us. Israel will do better. Operating from near the church of the Saint Sépulcre, it will declare itself the heir and steward of Christianity and will profitably exploit, with a perfect sense of commerce, this heritage and bind Christianity itself by creating this circulation of values which had once established the reputation of Israel in the stock exchange.

In pages which we regard as remarkable – and in which we find certain ideas belonging to Léon Bloy – Claudel for a moment then raises money and commerce to the level of ontological categories. The very solidarity of Creation, even the link between man and God, are expressed in terms of buying and selling. Commerce presupposes the interdependence of beings. The profit attached to it marks the law of interest which is inherent in love itself and which, at the heart of its generosity, anticipates its reward. 'A disinterested love? I should like to know what that is. There is no love that is not passionately interested' (p. 51). Finally, all money designates the universal amplitude of a solidarity which, instead of being one particular thing, can be attached to everything. In the article already quoted from *Le Figaro littéraire*, with increasing intellectual daring, Claudel explains his thoughts in detail. Love acts at the heart of the most brutal manifestations of reality: in war, humans are searching for one another, while in bestiality animals who half-devour one another are already achieving a communion. These are nevertheless elementary forms of religious life, which bear the mark of the Creator. Everything is indispensable to everything.

All the same, the juxtaposition of beings that half-devour one another and men who give themselves up to commerce seems to diminish the rigour of the analysis which we have just admired. For Claudel it is by no means a question of perceiving, in the commercial relations themselves, the potentiality of a spiritual existence, but only its prefiguration. The real society set up by the exchange of material goods – a society in which a person cannot touch another outside of an economic link and in which, for that precise reason, the coming of Law is announced – remains for Claudel a society of figures and parables. The spirit will descend miraculously on this world in which these figures and parables move like shadows. The brutal fervour of animals eating one another resembles just as much, if not more, the gratuitous nature of relations in a redeemed Creation in which law has been abolished.

But beware! The argument can be turned round. If there is love at the heart of war and bestiality, then is there not a trace of wretchedness within the fervour of feelings? Léon Brunschvicg at least taught us so. In *On True and False Conversion*, he wrote:

> Just as we must recognize those sacrifices that are happily made, and heroically offered up in the exaltation of faith, so we must not turn our eyes away from the suffering violently imposed by everything which that same exaltation entails in the way of bloody fury and so-called charitable crime. (p. 120)

Love is always interested, Claudel himself proclaims. But from that point on, should we not look elsewhere for human dignity? The inevitable appearance, within commercial relations, of Law is surely something that raised an interested act to the order of justice. Here, something new is produced in the midst of universal war. Between justice and charity, there is no relation of *less* to *more*; within the general economy of being, justice and charity designate two diverging tendencies.

It is not that Jews feel they are better merchants than anyone else. But since the Old Testament and the Talmud which carries its atmosphere, since the time they were only an agricultural people, the Jews have thought a great deal about material relations and their equity. These relations are peaceful ones: they are established between persons who confront one another and see a human face, and rather than give in to an ambiguous fervour, they recognize a law. These relations are between people who are solitary but free, and they inaugurate a humanity. They are not simply the tribute paid to our material nature; on the contrary, our material nature is the very fulfilment of solidarity within being. It prefigures nothing. Economic life is the ontological space wherein creature is transformed into spirit – or, if we may use a terminology that has become suggestive, it is the space wherein flesh is opened up to the Word. The idea that every relation is a transaction, that the relation with the Other can be brought about only to the extent that it engages us materially in some way or other, and that consequently everything must be done with justice, is one that leads to true responsibilities. And that makes us unavailable as stewards of the grace which Paul Claudel invites us to accept. We are occupied elsewhere.

Poetry and the Impossible

I

Volume 7 of *Les Cahiers de Paul Claudel* clarifies the poet's position with regard to Judaism and Jews. A succession of studies which vary greatly in theme but are all written with a degree of passion – many of them by Jews and some even by Israelis, all of whom admire his work – trace a remarkable evolution.[1] Claudel ultimately recognizes Judaism, but starts off with a very crude anti-Semitism that is attributed to the age in which he grew up, his family and social background, the violent and integrist directors of conscience with whom he had dealings after his conversion, and a certain intolerance, no doubt, that was part of his character or temperament.

Claudel's discovery of Judaism begins with the Old Testament, to which the commentaries he wrote during the last years of his life will act as counterpoint. A Jewish reader will certainly reject the Christian tones of his interpretation, which are not unexpected in Claudel's case. He will be no less struck by the force of this high word and by the sense of the biblical poetry to which this force attests. One has only to read the extraordinary pages entitled 'The Patriarchs' that come almost at the beginning of this issue of the *Cahiers* in order to measure the effect of certain comparisons when the parallel is drawn from within the Old Testament. It is a personal exegesis that disdains the impoverishment of meaning through which historical criticism re-establishes the coherence of the Scriptures, one that turns out to be above all the coherence of the world in the eyes of critical historians. For Claudel, however, this exegesis is not exhausted by compiling the prefigurations which the Christian faith claims to have fulfilled. This is another aspect of the poet's greatness. The supposedly veiled truth remains extremely attractive to him; it too is irreplaceable and has its own spiritual value. Resounding homage is paid to Jewish writing; Judaism survives the advent of Christianity. One is forced to recognize a sense of continuity running from the biblical Israel to the Israelites, and even Israelis, of our day.

Slowly, Claudel goes this far. He grants modern Jews – and even their aspirations, even Zionism, even the State of Israel – the privilege of continuing Sacred History. On this final stage of Claudel's itinerary there are essential texts in the solid pages of a study by Madame Denise Gamzan ('Claudel encounters Israel') and another, bristling with tense emotion, by Charles Galpérine ('The Exegete and the Witness') who, in addition, assumed the remarkable responsibility of editing the collection. Even so, however, all these texts offer somewhat staggering reading.

It is incredible that Jules Renard, nearly thirteen years after the poet's conversion and after his regular readings of both Testaments, could write in his journal on 3 February 1900: 'He comes back to his horror of Jews, which he can neither see nor feel.' It is incredible that after so many years of relations with Jews, after his friendship with Suarès – ashamed to be a Jew, certainly – but also with Darius Milhaud, who was proud to be one, and after rubbing shoulders with the Jewish elite who fêted him at Frankfurt, and a brilliant diplomatic career among the men of the Third Republic, Claudel could put his name to a document denouncing German anti-Semitism produced in 1936 by the World Jewish Congress but refuse to allow publication of his signature on the pretext that 'everywhere one sees Jews at the head of parties of social or religious subversion'. It is incredible that Claudel could write on 1 August 1939: 'All the sacred writers call Israel a witness, but the Greek word "witness" means "martyr"'; and yet on 6 July 1940, take stock of France after its defeat with these unequivocal words: 'After sixty years, France has been freed from the yoke of the radical and anti-Catholic party (teachers, lawyers, Jews, free-masons).' It is incredible that this evolution therefore took so long, and was so painful and uncertain in spite of his early understanding of the 'mystery of Israel'; that these uncertainties lasted until the eve of Auschwitz, and that it took no less than *that* for him to arrive at a definite reassessment. It seems almost unreal. Evil is infinitely profound, its texture is thick and inextricable. Its impregnable fortresses survive at the heart of a refined civilization and deep in the souls conquered by grace.

The fact that a man of Claudel's stature should find it so difficult to uproot himself is enough to make the survivors of Auschwitz tremble. Hitler has paled the memory of the Jewish blood spilled before 1933–45. People have ended up believing that anti-Semitism was born with National Socialism and that the fall of the Third Reich essentially rid humanity of it, leaving it to lead an anachronistic existence among certain underdeveloped peoples and a few sick spirits who have no grasp of the way things really work. The history of Claudel's 'drying-out', even more than the reawakening of anti-Semitism in such and such a part of the world today, reveals the 'un-condition' of Western Jewish society. It seems assimilated to the ideas, customs, mental balance, social severity, values and revenues of the West, while its writers also can be declamatory, like to move through pathos, and generally revel in the 'paradox of Israel', though evolving within well-established realities. It is for these reasons that we call such a society bourgeois, when in fact it is sitting on a powder keg.

II

It would perhaps have been better for Jews reflecting on their destiny, and their Christian friends trying to understand, to embrace more closely the daily reality of Jewish life. One has to be great like Claudel to use poetry as a means of attaining knowledge.

For contemporary Jewish history unfolds in a series of narratives whose literal meaning goes further than any metaphor. The life and death of Jews under the Nazi occupation, the life and death of Jews who built the State of Israel! To glimpse the profound link that ties one life to the other and one death to the other, to relate the despair of the camps to the new beginning in Israel, is no doubt to speak Sacred History, without rhetoric or theology.

Claudel knew that, under Hitler, the Jews endured an ordeal that is without name, and cannot be placed within any sociological category. It is a lie to locate it within the series of natural causes and effects or to defer to 'human sciences' and seek to explain it by examining the thoughts and 'readings' of an Eichmann, the 'inner crises' of a Goebbels or the 'structures' of European society between the wars. The Jewish people lay at the very bottom of the abyss into which humanity was thrown between 1939 and 1945. In a non-confessional, non-ecclesiastical sense, the Jewish people lived out a religious drama. 'This action is nothing like the extermination of the Mongols', wrote Claudel courageously. 'The difference is between the actions of a ferret in a henhouse, and a religious immolation.' Claudel has the supreme daring to do what no one, in this present period of complete confusion, would attempt: he places the martyrdom of Auschwitz out on its own. To differentiate between different forms of human suffering is certainly not allowed. But Claudel cannot look away from a suffering that is experienced as the abandonment of everything and everyone, a suffering at the limit of all suffering, a suffering that suffers all sufferings. That is no doubt what he is referring to when, without being flippant or guilty of trotting out a tired cliché, he uses the term 'holocaust'.

From that point on, Claudel makes possible an attitude that is adopted by a Christian for the first time: he sees that the Jew as Jew is fully his contemporary.

The Christian is perhaps no longer obliged in this day and age to see the Jew as reproved, as evidence of his own damnation and less related to 'our father Abraham' than anyone baptized. The Pauline text on divine choice without repentance and the conversion of Israel at the end of time has recently been recalled and serves to remind Christians that the 'alienation' of the 'chosen people' is provisional. But to the Jews, this text teaches only one thing: that until the end of time they will not be *out of phase* with Christian society and will make up the ground ineluctably lost only at the expense of an ultimate infidelity. As a 'miraculous and privileged survivor', the Old Testament acts as 'keeper of the key to the New Testament', acceding in the abstract to divine love. But for the Church and churches Judaism, for all that, still remains a stammered version of the Christian truth,[2] and consequently lags behind an era, a stage, a thought, a clarity. The beautiful text, for example, which Stanislas Fumer devoted to the book *When Israel Loves God*, by Father Menasce, which is reproduced by the *Cahiers Paul Claudel*, is astonishingly natural and casual in the way it bestows on the liveliest manifestation of modern Jewish spirituality the merit of being approximations of Catholic manifestations made 'in spirit and in truth'.

Certainly we cannot ask a Catholic to 'put away his Catholicism', but we should despair of humanity if its highest life forms could not assure men of a true contemporaneity. The possibility of a fraternal existence – that is to say, one that is precisely synchronic, without any 'underdeveloped' or 'primitive' peoples – is perhaps the decisive test of the spirituality of the spiritual. Surely equality between men rests on the abstract and geneal idea of Man, or on the way he belongs to the biological species of reasoning animal? As if fraternity, unknown to the individuals constituting the extension of a logical genre, did not before all else define the human genre.

But here Claudel reverses the meaning of the famous Pauline text, in a passage cited by Jacques Madaule and Galpérine. The prediction about 'the mass conversion of Jews at the eleventh hour' is not some quiet liturgical gesture, but the holocaust of millions of victims under Hitler. The mystical participation in the sacrifice of innocence is, when it involves Jews, a real sacrifice of innocent people. The limits of preservation reached in the death camps, without anyone having to mouth a credo, is no longer felt by a Christian as a prefiguration of something, but as a fulfilment. Theology becomes communication. At the level of moral and purely human conscience, a rent is therefore produced that overwhelms and unites consciences. The Jewish people return, for Christian thought, to the heart of the Divine Comedy. For the first time, this incorrigible latecomer to Sacred History is on time.

But what, then, is an event in Sacred History which does not touch the living flesh of humanity, beyond all national differences? And what is the suppression of these differences if not an indivisible humanity – that is to say, one that is entirely responsible for the crimes and griefs of a few? The Arab peoples would not have to answer for German atrocities, or cede their lands to the victims of Hitlerism! What deafness to the call of consciousness! Can every human relationship be reduced to assessing damage and interest and every problem to balancing the accounts? The right to a 'birthplace' invoked by Arab refugees can certainly not be treated unjustly, and Paul Claudel is not one to speak lightly of an attachment to one's native sort and the nostalgic value of the church tower (or minaret). But can the call of the land silence the cries of Auschwitz which will echo until the end of time? Can any human wash his hands of all that flesh turned to smoke? Once again it is the Old Testament that provides Claudel, in the admirable exegesis of the *Patriarchs*, with the image of people who squabble over their inheritance and remain blind to the grand design.

This gives rise to a frightening apostrophe, when Claudel employs an excessive phrase: 'What does all this Bedouin caper matter to us?' A gesture of recognition offered to Israel by the Arab peoples would no doubt be answered by a surge of fraternity that would allow the problem of refugees to lose its unknown quantity. Why remain a prisoner of outmoded sociological categories? The universe will be astounded by the new possibilities that will arise, if, on both of Israel's frontiers, the swords are turned into ploughshares and the tanks become tractors.

Will the vast spaces inhabited by the Arabs not lose some of their majestic dimensions and the Arab Fatherland lose its heart through the amputation of a tract of land whose immensity is measured only in centuries of Sacred History, a history never interrupted by the soul of Israel?

Is it for a Jew to say? But *every survivor of the Hitlerian massacres – whether or not a Jew – is Other in relation to martyrs.* He is consequently responsible and unable to remain silent. He is obligated to Israel for the reasons that oblige every man. These reasons are therefore common to Jew and Arab and ought to help them to talk to each other. So much the worse if one suspects the Jew who evokes these reasons of 'preaching for his saint' (which would not, moreover, conform to his religion). It is impossible to remain silent. There is an obligation to speak. And if politics, arising everywhere, falsifies the original intentions of the discourse, there is an obligation to cry out in protest.

But does politics constitute the ultimate framework of Being and the sole guide to action? Is the poetic vision which transends it for ever doomed to remain *'belles-lettres'* and perpetuate phantasms? Is it not, on the contrary – and this is probably the very definition of poetry – the thing that makes language possible?

Simone Weil against the Bible

I

Simone Weil's intelligence, borne out by her writings, all of them posthumous, was equalled by her greatness of soul. She lived like a saint and bore the suffering of the world. She is dead. Faced with the three abysses that separate us from her, only one of which can be crossed, how can we speak of her and, and above all, how can we speak against her?

'Men ... can think themselves atheists and state that they are so even though supernatural love lives in their souls. They are certainly saved.' This affirmation is our own. It is certainly in the Bible. But Simone Weil hates the Bible. We call the Bible what the Christians designate as the Old Testament. Simone Weil's anti-biblical passion could wound and trouble Jews. To them we must speak.

It is certainly infinitely more ridiculous to come to the aid of the Bible than it is to discuss matters with a dead woman, even if she is a saint and a genius. But Western Judaism's contact with the Scriptures has become so tenuous in the past hundred years – I mean so strange to the talmudic spirit – that it is broken without any resistance beneath the blows of an argument which on top of everything else, has been cultivated in sources outside the 'religious instruction' class.

Simone Weil has been accused of ignoring Judaism – and, my word, she has ignored it in a right royal way. But we are greatly mistaken if we think that present-day culture could have taught her something in this regard. She had the rigour of a system of thought, and we should have offered her those private and intimate meditations that we are uncomprehendingly prepared to accept as our religious life when, for our intellectual life, we need a Kant or a Newton. To meet a real teacher of Judaism has become a matter of luck. This luck depends greatly on the person looking. It is created out of discernment. Most of the time, we let it pass by. It is a difference of intellectual potential between Simone Weil and a science of Judaism that has become 'a forgetting of science', completely transformed into homiletics or philology. This constitutes the tragedy of those troubled by Simone Weil.

If we want to open a debate without presumption, we must therefore refuse to engage in a contest of theologies and texts. We must place ourselves on the level of the theology we share with our non-Jewish contemporaries, and begin from the studies we have both made.

II

There are two troubling theses in Simone Weil's doctrine. She imposes a reading of the Bible such that the origins of Good are always foreign to Judaism, while Evil is specifically Judaic. And she turns Good into an absolutely pure idea, excluding all contamination or violence. Because the second thesis seems evident to the intuition, if not the thinking, of today's European, the first thesis can be a crippling one. Its anti-Judaism is of the gnostic type, concerning more the Hebrews than post-exile Judaism, which happily has experienced the beneficial influence of the Chaldeans, the Egyptians and maybe even the druids, as well as all those authentically monotheist pagans. Nothing in common with Hitler. How comforting!

The idea that biblical Judaism's fundamental blindness towards the Revelation reveals a supernatural privilege and a backward-looking sense of being chosen, which is aggravated by a calling as plagiarist and forger, would all the same prove highly compromising for the position of divine Good conceived as a simple idea. So Simone Weil explains that the Passion took place in Palestine, since it was there that it was most needed. We know the rest.

In reality the process by which Simone Weil establishes this perfidy of the Jews is at the very least original.

It consists first of all in crediting every nation on earth, with the exception of Israel, with a prefiguration of the Passion. This is a thesis that Jews, resistant to Christianity, could accept. It is not up to them to refute it. But it reveals an astonishing bias. The methods of comparative literature are today so familiar to everyone, and world literature is so vast, that one can always come across gestures and symbols and snatches of phrases that resemble in some way particular details from the Gospels. Any figure can be found in the sea of folklore. Simone Weil turns round the argument put forward by criticism: the latter recomposed the Passion with the help of all the mythologies in order to view it as no more than an amalgam of composite beliefs. Simone Weil, however, sees them as prefigurations and the proof of the eternal universality of Christianity. The argument, in both its new and ancient forms, does not touch us greatly. It proves too much.

With regard to the Scriptures themselves (which Simone Weil, of course, knows only in translation) her attitude is ambiguous: she treats them as historical books whenever they support her thesis, and false whenever they disturb it. The existence of a Melchizedek is known to her only through Genesis, but she affirms that he was 'infinitely superior to anything ever possessed by Israel'. Why take genealogies seriously and then immediately add that the Jews falsified them? It is not Israel's past that forms the Bible teaching, but the judgement brought to bear on this history. True or false? This depends not on profane documents that confirm or invalidate the materiality of the facts related, but on the human truth of this teaching.

The biblical teaching does not consist of praise for a model people. It consists of invectives. Israel's sole worth lies perhaps, in having chosen this book of anger and accusation for its message, having made this book its own. Israel is not a model people, but a free people. It is of course, like any people, filled with lust and tempted by carnal delights. The Bible tells us of this lust in order to denounce it, but also knows that it is not enough to deny. It seeks to elevate matters by introducing the notion of justice. It is in economic justice that man glimpses the face of man. Has Christianity itself found a horizon for its generosity other than in famine and drought?

Only Greek, Chaldean, Egyptian and Hindu writings contain an unsullied generosity. Jews possess only a God for armies – how horrible! But what an opportunity it provides to learn, through Simone Weil, the exact translation of *Adonai Zebaoth*!

The Church itself, sometimes militant, is content in its liturgy to transcribe these Hebraic words, no doubt because of modesty. In the *Cahiers* we find the translation of the opening verses of Exodus 6, where the question of names for God is again raised. Why look for definitions when one has only to consult the *Larousse*? the good people ask. The Jewish tradition is more mistrustful. Carrying on an uninterrupted tradition, having brought the Scriptures into the world with its own hands, it feels that the intellection of terms does not lie at the level of the dictionary, but presupposes a science. The passages which Simone Weil finds indigestible should be clarified by the digestible passages, not the other way round. The inner necessity of both must be shown.

Whatever the origins of the different elements of the canon, they have not been welcomed by collectors of folklore. This weakens the philosophical scope of philology if we also admit, for want of the mosaic nature of the Pentateuch, for example, its talmudic authenticity. It is here that we find the full conscience from which the Jewish scriptures flow; a thought is built with so-called alluvial deposits. To be a Jew is to believe in the intelligence of the Pharisees and their masters. It is through the Talmud's intelligence that we accede to the Bible's faith.

What confidence can we henceforth have in Simone Weil's use of world literature? How can we excuse her for referring to worlds which themselves in turn demand a life in order to be penetrated? She contrasts the Bible, which she knows poorly, with 'chosen bits' of civilizations foreign to Europe. Although 'digestible' texts fill the Old Testament, she treats them as exceptions and attributes them to strangers, but with a disconcerting generosity goes into ecstasies over the slightest trace of the Divine, which crosses distant worlds like the Moon. Does she simply wish to know into which barbarous night these fulgurations are absorbed?

III

This arbitrary method can be guided only by an intuition about the essence of spiritual life; the Divine is absolutely universal, and this is why it can be served in purity only through the particularity of each people, a particularity named enrootedness.

The fact that God was known to all the peoples of the earth and, in a certain sense, better served by them than by the Jews, is proclaimed not by Simone Weil but by the prophet Malachi, the most 'nationalist' of the prophets – in a certain sense. For God is both universal and yet not universal. His universality is not accomplished so long as it is recognized only by thought and is not fulfilled by the acts of men. It remains abstract, then. The universality of a mathematical truth is satisfied within the thought of a single man, and the ignorance shown of it by the Other cannot contradict it. The inner recognition of the universality of God is contradicted by the evil present in outer reality. Here interiority does not amount to universality, nor does it equal it in worth. Universality here should become visible from the outside. God must be one and His name must be one. When it is finished inwardly, nothing has yet been finished. When Simone Weil writes: 'the proof that the content of Christianity pre-existed Christ is that there have been no great changes since in the behaviour of men', we believe that the argument can be turned round.

The unity of the name is the unity of language and the Scriptures and institutions. It is the end of naivety and putting down roots. The Church remains faithful to a deep Jewish tendency when it seeks to bring about the religious emancipation of man by 'everywhere imposing Jewish Scriptures, as Simone Weil complains'. Every word is an uprooting. Every institution amenable to reason is an uprooting. The constitution of a real society is an uprooting – the term of an existence in which the 'being-at-home' ['*chez soi*'] is absolute, and everything comes from within. Paganism is putting down roots, almost in the etymological sense of the term. The advent of the Scriptures is not the subordination of the spirit to a letter, but the substitution of the letter to the soil. The spirit is free within the letter, and it is enslaved within the root. It is on the arid soil of the desert, where nothing is fixed, that the true spirit descended into a text in order to be universally fulfilled.

Paganism is the local spirit: nationalism in terms of its cruelty and pitilessness – that is to say, in its immediate, naive and unconscious sense. The tree grows and retains all the earth's sap. A humanity with roots that possesses God inwardly, with the sap rising from the earth, is a forest or prehuman humanity. One must not be fooled by the peace of the woods. If Europe had been spiritually uprooted by Christianity, as Simone Weil complains, the evil would not be great. And it is not always the idylls that have been destroyed by Europe's penetration of the world. Evil perhaps lies in the extreme violence of this proselytism, but is Europe's unhappiness not due to the fact that Christianity did not sufficiently uproot it?

A history in which the idea of a universal God must only be fulfilled requires a beginning. It requires an elite. It is not through pride that Israel feels it has been chosen. It has not obtained this through grace. Each time the peoples are judged, Israel is judged. This is the strict justice that, according to a fundamental *midrash*, separates the Israelites from the Egyptians at the moment when the Red Sea was crossed. It is because the universality of the Divine exists only in the form in which it is fulfilled in the relations between men, and because it must be fulfilment and expansion, that the category of a privileged civilization exists in the economy of Creation. This civilization is defined in terms not of prerogatives, but of responsibilities. Every person, as a person – that is to say, one conscious of his freedom – is chosen. If being chosen takes on a national appearance, it is because only in this form can a civilization be constituted, be maintained, be transmitted, and endure. Abraham was not the first to recognize God, but he was the first to found a monotheist family. 'The feelings of so-called pagans towards their statues', says Simone Weil, 'were probably the same as those inspired today by the crucifixes and statues of the Virgin and the Saints with the same deviations in spiritually and intellectually mediocre people.' We dare not turn round the argument once again. But it exists, and so the phenomenon of spiritually mediocre people, of pagans, also exists.

IV

'To say that God can order men to commit acts of injustice and cruelty is the greatest error that can be committed in his regard.' From this point on, evil itself can inspire only love. The extermination of the Canaanite peoples during the conquest of the Promised Land is the most indigestible passage of all the indigestible passages in the Bible. The texts vainly insist on the evil committed by the Canaanites; it is vain to extrapolate the very idea of perverted and irreparable civilizations, contaminating those who pardon them, which have to disappear for a new humanity to begin – Simone Weil is revolted by such cruelty. The extraordinary thing is that we are with her on this. The extraordinary thing is that the Jewish consciousness, formed precisely through contact with this harsh morality, with its obligations and sanctions, has learned to have an absolute horror of blood, while the doctrine of non-violence has not stemmed the natural course towards violence displayed by a whole world over the last two thousand years. The harsh law of the Old Testament is perhaps not a doctrine based on kindness, but what does this matter, if it is a school of kindness? It is not a question of justifying it by its success. But it is probably in the nature of spirit that an austere God and a free man prepare a human order which is better than an Infinite Goodness for a bad man. Only a God Who maintains the principle of Law can *in practice* tone down its severity and use oral law to go beyond the inescapable harshness of Scripture.

The notion of oral teaching is not the vagueness of a tradition that is added to written teaching or is anterior to it or simply abolishes it. Oral law is eternally contemporary with the written. There exists between them an original relation whose intellection assembles the very atmosphere of Judaism. The one neither maintains nor destroys the other, but makes it practicable and readable. To penetrate daily into this dimension and maintain itself within it is the famous study of the Torah, the famous 'Lernen' which occupies a central place in Jewish religious life. Or, if you like, it is the Phariseeism of which the Gospels have given us such an odious image. The major misunderstanding between Simone Weil and the Bible consists not in having ignored the texts of the Talmud, but in not having suspected their dimensions.

From this point on, the extermination of evil by violence means that evil is taken seriously and that the possibility of infinite pardon tempts us to infinite evil. God's goodness dialectically brings forth something like God's wickedness. This is no more difficult to admit than many Christian mysteries. The idea that divine patience might have come to an end, and that there are sins committed, is the condition for the respect given by God to the fully responsible man. Without this finitude to divine patience, man's freedom would be only provisional and derisory, and history just a game. We must recognize man's coming of age. To acknowledge punishment is to acknowledge respect even for the guilty party's person.

Does divine goodness consist in treating man with an infinite pity that lies within this supernatural *compassion* that moves Simone Weil, or in admitting him into His Society, and treating him with respect? To love one's neighbour can mean already to glimpse his misery and rottenness, but it can also mean to see his *face*, his mastery over us, and the dignity he has as someone who is associated with God and has rights over us. God's supernatural love, in Simone Weil's Christianity, if it goes beyond a compassion for creature's misery, can signify only love of evil itself. God loved evil; this is perhaps – we say it with infinite respect – the most fearful vision of this Christianity and the whole metaphysics of Passion. But our respect is mingled with a strong sense of dread. Our path lies elsewhere.

V

An inspired text, according to Simone Weil, admits the possibility of the misfortune of the innocent. For a Simone Weil, this resignation cannot signify quietude. But it is precisely this inanity of charity – this resignation at the base of the most active charity, to the misfortune of the innocent – which is a contradiction. Love cannot overcome it, since it feeds off it. To overcome it we must act

– and here is the place of action and its irreducibility in the economy of being. Iner man would have been enough, if the innocent had not suffered. The most active charity despairs of its action and has hopes only for itself – it is interiority. The relation with a contradiction like the suffering of the innocents is not overcome in the interiority of love. Here again interiority is not the equal of universality. Here the continuation of evil in the world is a flagrant denial of the perfection of love. Here nothing is finished as long as the external order has not been affected. To give the Other his due, to love him within the framework of justice, is the essence of a true action. The Other is my master and in acting I establish an order that, in itself, is already possible.

To love a creature because it is only a creature or to love man because, in the creature, he transcends the creature, is the alternative of charity and justice.

We cannot reproach Simone Weil's culture for being ignorant of the fact that notions like goodness are not simple, and that they can call up and encapsulate notions which seem opposed to them. And while the dialectic of Christian experience excites her, she is content to remain on the level of immediate notions whenever it involves referring to the Old Testament. Here she casually repeats Voltaire's argument that 'Abraham began by prostituting his wife'.

VI

It is Platonic clarity which haunts Simone Weil. She has glimpsed in the Gospels the same interiorization of religious truth which the Greeks achieved with geometry in the realm of theoretical knowledge. And certainly, there is only Greek geometry and logic. But the universality of a social order does not result from a logical operation. The Old Testament appeared to her as that might of myths, tales, apologues and opinions, pursued by the Word, which in the end speaks without innuendo or approximation. This failure to understand the Old Testament goes back a long way. The Church which sees in it a series of prefigurations is pushed towards this vision not only by apologies but also by the sense that the Book has an absolutely enigmatic character. For us, the world of the Bible is a world not of figures, but of faces. They are entirely here and related to us. The face of man is the medium through which the invisible in him becomes visible and enters into commerce with us.

We do not conceive of relations, we are in relation. It is not a question of inner meditation, but of action. It is in the impunity of the world, which the Old Testament takes on together with all its facts, that purity is made. But it is *made*, it is an act. There is no redemption of the world, only a transormation of the world. Self-redemption is already an action; purely inner repentance is a contradiction in terms. Suffering has no magical effect. The just man who suffers is worthy not because of his suffering but because of his justice, which defies suffering. Suffering and death are the terms of human passion, but life is not passion. It is an act. It is in history.

This history flows not from sin, but from man's creation. The true paradox of the perfect being has consisted in wanting to create equals outside himself, a multiplicity of beings, and consequently action, beyond interiority. It is here that God has transcended creation itself. It is here that God 'has emptied Himself'. He has created someone to talk to.

Loving the Torah more than God

Many of the recent publications devoted to Western Judaism are beautiful texts. There is no shortage of talent in Europe. But true texts are rare. For a hundred years now, Hebraic studies have dried up and we have lost sight of our origins. The knowledge that is still produced is not based on an intellectual tradition. It remains self-taught, even when it is not improvised. And to be read only by those less wise than oneself – what a corruption that is for a writer! Deprived of criticism or sanctions, authors mistake this lack of resistance for freedom and in turn take this freedom to be a mark of genius. Need we be surprised, then, if readers no longer believe this and instead see Judaism, which is still adhered to by several million sinners, as just a mass of petty, boring quibbles that have nothing to do with spiritual matters?

I have just read a text that is both beautiful and true, true as only fiction can be. It was published anonymously in an Israeli journal and translated by Arnold Mandel for *La terre retrouvée*, a Parisian Zionist periodical, under the title *Yossel, son of Yossel Rakover from Tarnopol, speaks to God*. It seems to have been read somewhat emotively, and it deserves a better fate. Its intellectual nature offers a clearer reflection than certain readings by intellectuals – such as the concepts borrowed from Simone Weil, for example, who is, as everyone in Paris knows, all the rage at the moment when it comes to religious terminology. This text, on the other hand, offers a Jewish science in a modest but self-assured manner, and conveys a deep and genuine experience of spiritual life.

The text presents itself as a document written during the final hours of the Warsaw Ghetto resistance. Thus the narrator witnessed all the horrors and under atrocious circumstances lost his young children. He is the last survivor of his family and in his remaining few hours he offers us his final thoughts. It is, of course, a literary fiction; but a fiction in which every one of us who survived recognizes his own life in astonishment.

I shall not recount the whole story, even though the world has ignored and forgotten it. I shall refrain from turning the Passion of Passions into a spectacle, or these inhuman cries into the vanity of an author or director. They continue to resound and reverberate down the centuries. Let us simply listen to the thought which they express.

What can this suffering of the innocents mean? Is it not proof of a world without God, where only man measures Good and Evil? The simplest and most common answer would be atheism. This is also the sanest reaction for all those for whom previously a fairly primary sort of God had dished out prizes, inflicted punishment or pardoned sins – a God who, in His goodness, treated men like children. But with what lesser demon or strange magician have you therefore filled your heaven, you who claim that it is empty? And why, under an empty sky, do you continue to hope for a good and sensible world?

The certainty of God is something Yossel, son of Yossel experiences with a new force, beneath an empty sky. For if he is so alone, it is in order to take upon his shoulders the whole of God's responsibilities. The path that leads to the one God must be walked in part without God. True monotheism is duty bound to answer the legitimate demands of atheism. The adult's God is revealed precisely through the void of the child's heaven. This is the moment when God retires from the world and hides His face. In the words of Yossel ben Yossel: 'He has handed men over to their savage instincts.... And since these instincts rule the world, it is natural that those who preserve a sense of divinity and purity should be the first victims of this rule.'

The God who hides His face is not, I believe, a theological abstraction or a poetic image. It is the moment in which the just individual can find no help. No institution will protect him. The consolation of divine presence to be found in infantile religious feeling is equally denied him, and the individual can prevail only through his conscience, which necessarily involves suffering. This is the specifically Jewish sense of suffering that at no stage assumes the value of a mystical atonement for the sins of the world. The condition of the victims in a disordered world – that is to say, in a world where good does not triumph – is that of suffering. This condition reveals a God Who renounces all aids to manifestation, and appeals instead to the full maturity of the responsible man.

But this God Who hides His face and abandons the just man to a justice that has no sense of triumph, this distant God, comes from within. This intimacy coincides in one's conscience with the pride of being a Jew, and of belonging clearly, simply and historically to the Jewish people: 'To be a Jew means ... to swim eternally against the filthy, criminal tide of man.... I am happy to belong to the most unhappy people on earth, for whom the Torah represents all that is most lofty and beautiful in law and morality.' The intimacy of the strong God is won through a terrible ordeal. By belonging to the suffering Jewish people, the distant God becomes *my God*: 'Now I know that you are really my God, for you could not be the God of those whose actions represent the most horrible expression of a militant absence of God.' The suffering of the just man for a justice that has no triumph is physically lived out as Judaism. The historical and physical Israel becomes once again a religious category.

The God Who hides His face and is recognized as being present and intimate ... is this really possible? Does it involve a metaphysical construction, a paradoxical *salto mortale* in the manner of Kierkegaard? Here I believe we see the specific face of Judaism: the link between God and man is not an emotional communion that takes place within the love of a God incarnate, but a spiritual or intellectual [*esprits*] relationship which takes place through an education in the Torah. It is precisely a word, not incarnate, from God that ensures a living God among us. Confidence in a God Who is not made manifest through any worldly authority can rely only on internal evidence and the values of an education. To the credit of Judaism, there is nothing blind about this. This accounts for the monologue's closing remark, in which Yossel ben Yossel echoes the whole of the Torah: 'I love him, but I love even more his Torah.... And even if I were deceived by him and became disillusioned, I should nevertheless observe the precepts of the Torah.' Is this blasphemy? At the very least, it is a protection against the madness of a direct contact with the Sacred that is unmediated by reason. But above all it is a confidence that does not rely on the triumph of any institution, it is the internal evidence of morality supplied by the Torah. This is a difficult path, both in spirit and in truth, and it cannot be prefigured. Simone Weil, you have never understood the Torah! 'Our God is the God of vengeance,' says Yossel ben Yossel,

> and our Torah is full of venial sins that are punished by death. And yet when the Sanhedrin, the Supreme Court of our people, passed the death sentence for the first time in seventy years, the judges were looked upon as murderers. Yet the God of all peoples commands us to love each creature in his likeness and it is in his name that our blood has been spilled for well nigh two thousand years.

Man's real humanity and gentle nature enter into the world with the harsh words of an exacting God. Spirituality is offered up not through a tangible substance, but through absence. God is real and concrete not through incarnation but through Law, and His greatness is not inspired by His sacred mystery. His greatness does not provoke fear and trembling, but fills us with high thoughts. To hide one's face so as to demand the superhuman of man, to create a man who can approach God and speak to Him without always being in His debt – that is a truly divine mark of greatness! After all, someone in credit is, *par excellence*, a person who possesses faith, but is equally someone who is not resigned to the debtor's refusal. Our monologue begins and ends with this refusal of resignation. Man can have confidence in an absent God and also be an adult who can judge his own sense of weakness. The heroic situation in which he places himself gives the world value and equally puts it in danger. Nurtured by a faith that is produced by the Torah, he reproaches God for His inordinate Greatness and excessive demands. He will love Him in spite of all God's attempts to discourage such love. But 'do not bend the bow too far', cries Yossel ben Yossel. The religious life can end only in this heroic situation. God must show His face, justice and power must join, just institutions must reign on earth. But only the man who has recognized the hidden God can demand that He show Himself. This vigorous dialectic establishes an equality between God and man at the very heart of their disproportion.

This is a long way from a warm and almost tangible communion with the Divine and from the desperate pride of the atheist. It is a complete and austere humanism, linked to a difficult adoration! And conversely, it is an adoration that coincides with the exaltation of man! A personal and unique God is not something revealed like an image in a dark room! The text I have just commented upon shows how ethics and principles install a personal relationship worthy of the name. Loving the Torah even more than God means precisely having access to a personal God against Whom one may rebel – that is to say, for Whom one may die.

An Eye for an Eye

The weekly section of Leviticus, which comprises chapters 21, 22, 23 and 24, closes with the famous passage which, to many modern people seems antiquated. Delicate palates require fresher food. For their refinement, our text emphasizes the very antiquity of the Old Testament. Ah! the *lex talionis*, an eye for an eye. How much pious anger you generate in a world ruled only by kindness and love!

> He who kills a man shall be put to death. He who kills a beast shall make it good, life for a life. When a man causes a disfigurement in his neighbour, as he has done it shall be done to him, fracture for fracture, eye for eye, tooth for tooth; as he has disfigured a man, he shall be disfigured. He who kills a beast shall make it good; and he who kills a man shall be put to death. You shall have one law for the sojourner and for the native; for I am the Lord your God. (Leviticus 24:17–22)

Harsh words, far removed from those which magnify non-resistance to evil. You have no doubt thought of that other page in the Scriptures which tells the just man: 'Let him give his cheek to the smiter, and be filled with insults'. You recognize this passage and recall the reference. It is, of course, Lamentations 3:30 – another fragment of this same Old Testament!

Fracture for fracture! Harsh words, but noble in their strictness. In their rigour, they command from on high. Let us at least admire the concluding part, which states the unity of humankind. This message of universalism has not delayed in issuing us with the resounding message that world-scale industry reveals or imposes human solidarity. One law for all is the principle that the Old Testament, in mocking repetition, repeats almost fifty times on the first Scroll, in lines that are none the less concise and considered. How can we assume from this point on that a thinking which rose to become a vision of humanity, in an age of tribes and clans, has remained at the level of the law of the undergrowth? I should like to show you the wisdom contained in these mysterious words and the drama to which such wisdom responds.

For there is a drama which involves the humanizing of justice.

Eye for eye, tooth for tooth, is not the principle of a method of terror; it is not a cold realism which thinks of effective action, scorns sentimental effusions and reserves morality for the youth club; it is not the exaltation of a superhuman and heroic life from which heart and pity must be banished; it is not a way of revelling in the vengeance and cruelty in which a virile existence is steeped. Such inspirations were foreign to the Jewish Bible. They come from the pagans, or Machiavelli, or Nietzsche.

Rest assured. The principle stated by the Bible here, which appears to be so cruel, seeks only justice. It inserts itself into a social order in which no sanction, however slight, can be inflicted outside a juridical sentence. They have interpreted it in the light of the spirit that pervades the whole of the Bible. We call this method of understanding: Talmud. The Doctors of the Talmud anticipated modern scruples: eye for eye means a fine. Not for nothing is the passage relating to the material damages which the Bible demands for the loss of a beast given alongside the precepts of eye for eye. The passage invites us to reread the verses relating to disfigurement, as if the question of damages should hold sway with the judge over the noble anger provoked by the wrongdoing. Violence calls up violence, but we must put a stop to this chain reaction. That is the nature of justice. Such is at least its mission once the evil has been committed. Humanity is born in man to the extent that he manages to reduce a mortal offence to the level of a civil lawsuit, to the extent that punishing becomes a question of putting right what can be put right and re-educating the wicked. Justice without passion is not the only thing man must possess. He must also have justice without killing.

But here the drama hots up. This horror of blood, this justice based on peace and kindness, is necessary and henceforth is the only possible form of justice, but does it preserve the man it wishes to save? For it leaves the way open for the rich! They can easily pay for the broken teeth, the gouged-out eyes and the fractured limbs left around them. Outrage and fracture take on a market value and are given a price, and this contradiction does not stem only from the law that substitutes a fine for suffering. For everything we pay with a light heart and a healthy body comes down to a fine, and a financial fracture is not a mortal one. The world remains a comfortable place for the strong, provided that they keep their nerve. The evolution of justice cannot move towards this rebuttal of all justice, this contempt for the man that justice wishes to have respected. We must save the spirit of our codes by modifying their letter. The Bible reminds us of the spirit of kindness.

The Bible speeds up the movement that brings us a world without violence, but if money or excuses could repair everything and leave us with a free conscience, the movement would be given a misinterpretation. Yes, eye for eye. Neither all eternity, nor all the money in the world, can heal the outrage done to man. It is a disfigurement or wound that bleeds for all time, as though it required a parallel suffering to staunch this eternal haemorrhage.

The Struthof Case

The recent trial of Struthof is eight years late. It is just, though, that, mingled with the happy or industrious clamour of the street, amid the murmur of midnight breezes or amorous exchanges, the men of 1954 should once again have heard the indiscreet cries of tortured men. A young Pole cries: 'Mummy!' Forgetfulness is the law, happiness and condition of life. But here life is wrong.

The fact that all that could have happened cannot be explained simply by man's bestiality. Bestiality is unwittingly limited by the moderating influence of instinct. Nature, witout knowing it, is law. The horror that once more gripped us on reading the accounts of Metz was engendered in our intellectual paradoxes, our prewar *ennui*, our pusillanimous deception in the face of the monotony of a world devoid of violence, our Nietzschean curiosity, our blasé indifference to the 'abstractions' of Montesquieu, Voltaire and Diderot. The exaltation of sacrifice for the sake of sacrifice, faith for the sake of faith, energy for the sake of energy, fidelity for the sake of fidelity, fervour for the heat it procures, the call to a gratuitous – that is to say, heroic – act: this is the permanent origin of Hitlerism.

The romanticism of fidelity for its own sake, abnegation for its own sake, bound anyone, for any task, to these men who truly did not know what they were doing. Reason precisely involves knowing what one is doing, and thinking of a content. The principle of military society in which discipline takes the place of thought, where our conscience lies outside us but which, in a normal order, is subordinated to a political thinking – that is to say, a universal thinking, from which it derives its *raison d'être* and its nobility – found itself – in the general mistrust of reasonable thought, claimed to be ineffectual and impotent – governing the world alone.

From this point on it could do anything with man. Struthof's trial reminds us, in the face of overproud metaphysical systems, that man's freedom succumbs to physical suffering and mysticism. Provided that he accepted his death, every man in the past could call himself free. But now physical torture, cold and hunger or discipline, things stronger than death, can break this freedom. Even in its final hiding-place, where freedom consoles itself for its powerlessness to act, and remains a free thought, the strange will penetrates and enslaves it. Human freedom is thus reduced to the possibility of foreseeing the danger of its own decay and to protecting itself against such a decline. To make laws and create institutions based on reason which will steer clear of the ordeal of abdication is man's unique opportunity. The romanticism of the heroic stance, and the self-sufficient purity of feeling, must once more be substituted. This substitute must be given its proper place and be put first. It is the contemplation of ideas, something which makes republics possible. These republics crumble when one no longer fights for something but for someone.

The Name of a Dog,[1] or Natural Rights

> You shall be men consecrated to me; therefore you shall not
> eat any flesh that is torn by beasts in the field; you shall cast
> it to the dogs. (Exodus 22:31)

Is the biblical verse guilty, as one will later accuse it, of attaching too
much importance to what 'goes into man's mouth' and not enough
to what comes out? Unless the sight of flesh torn by beasts in the
field seems meat too strong for the digestion of the honest man
who, even if he is carnivore, still feels he is watched over by God.
This flesh torn by beasts in the field, and the remains of bloody
struggles between wild animals that half-devour one another, from
the strong species to the weak, will be sublimated by intelligence
into hunting games. This spectacle suggesting the horrors of war,
this devouring within species, will provide men with the artistic
emotions of the *Kriegspiel*. Such ideas make one lose one's appetite!
In fact, they can also come to you at the family table, as you plunge
your fork into your roast. There is enough, there, to make you a
vegetarian again. If we are to believe Genesis, Adam, the father of us
all, was one! There is, at least, enough there to make us want to
limit, through various interdictions, the butchery that every day
claims our 'consecrated' mouths! But enough of this theology! It is
the dog mentioned at the end of the verse that I am especially
interested in. I am thinking of Bobby.

So who is this dog at the end of the verse? Someone who disrupts
society's games (or Society itself) and is consequently given a cold
reception [*que l'on reçoit comme un chien dans un jeu de quilles*]?
Someone whom we accuse of being rabid when we are trying to
drown him? Someone who is given the dirtiest work – a dog's life –
and whom we leave outside in all weathers, when it is raining cats
and dogs, even during those awful periods when you would not put
a dog out in it? But all these, in spite of their misery, reject the
affront of a repulsive prey.

So does it concern the beast that has lost the last noble vestiges of its wild nature, the crouching, servile, contemptible dog? Or, in the twilight [*entre chien et loup*] (and what light in the world is not already this dusk?), does it concern the one who is a wolf [*loup*] under his dogged faithfulness, and thirsts after blood, be it coagulated or fresh?

But enough of allegories! We have read too many fables and we are still taking the name of a dog in the figurative sense. So, in the terms of a venerable hermeneutics, more ancient than La Fontaine, orally transmitted from early antiquity – the hermeneutics of the talmudic Doctors – this biblical text, troubled by parables, here challenges the metaphor: in Exodus 22:31, the dog is a dog. Literally a dog! Beyond all scruples, by virtue of its happy nature and direct thoughts, the dog transforms all this flesh cast to it in the field into good flesh. This feast is its right.

High hermeneutics, however, which is so caught up here in a word-for-word approach, allows itself to explain the paradox of a pure nature leading to rights.

It therefore unearths some forgotten dogs lying in a subordinate proposition in another verse from Exodus. In Chapter 11, verse 7, strange dogs are struck by a light in the middle of the night. They will not growl! But around them a world is emerging. For this is the fatal night of the 'death of the first-born' of Egypt. Israel is about to be released from the house of bondage. Slaves who served the slaves of the State will henceforth follow the most high Voice, the most free path. It is a figure of humanity! Man's freedom is that of an emancipated man remembering his servitude and feeling solidarity for all enslaved people. A rabble of slaves will celebrate this high mystery of man, and 'not a dog shall growl'. At the supreme hour of his institution, with neither ethics nor *logos*, the dog will attest to the dignity of its person. This is what the friend of man means. There is a transcendence in the animal! And the clear verse with which we began is given a new meaning. It reminds us of the debt that is always open.

But perhaps the subtle exegesis we are quoting gets lost in rhetoric? Indeed?

There were seventy of us in a forestry commando unit for Jewish prisoners of war in Nazi Germany. An extraordinary coincidence was the fact that the camp bore the number 1492, the year of the expulsion of the Jews from Spain under the Catholic Ferdinand V. The French uniform still protected us from Hitlerian violence. But the other men, called free, who had dealings with us or gave us work or orders or even a smile – and the children and women who passed by and sometimes raised their eyes – stripped us of our human skin. We were subhuman, a gang of apes. A small inner murmur, the strength and wretchedness of persecuted people, reminded us of our essence as thinking creatures, but we were no longer part of the world. Our comings and goings, our sorrow and laughter, illnesses and distractions, the work of our hands and the anguish of our eyes, the letters we received from France and those accepted for our families – all that passed in parenthesis. We were beings entrapped in their species; despite all their vocabulary, beings without language. Racism is not a biological concept; anti-Semitism is the archetype of all internment. Social aggression, itself, merely imitates this model. It shuts people away in a class, deprives them of expression and condemns them to being 'signifiers without a signified' and from there to violence and fighting. How can we deliver a message about our humanity which, from behind the bars of quotation marks, will come across as anything other than monkey talk?

And then, about halfway through our long captivity, for a few short weeks, before the sentinels chased him away, a wandering dog entered our lives. One day he came to meet this rabble as we returned under guard from work. He survived in some wild patch in the region of the camp. But we called him Bobby, an exotic name, as one does with a cherished dog. He would appear at morning assembly and was waiting for us as we returned, jumping up and down and barking in delight. For him, there was no doubt that we were men.

Perhaps the dog that recognized Ulysses beneath his disguise on his return from the Odyssey was a forebear of our own. But no, no! There, they were in Ithaca and the Fatherland. Here, we were nowhere. This dog was the last Kantian in Nazi Germany, without the brain needed to universalize maxims and drives. He was a descendant of the dogs of Egypt. And his friendly growling, his animal faith, was born from the silence of his forefathers on the banks of the Nile.

The Virtues of Patience

Having recourse to the judgement of history does not preclude a crime from acquiring a virtuous reputation, nor an acknowledged virtue from being put to shame. But the verdict of the court in which magistrates pass honest judgement on their contemporaries reveals a further ambiguity at the heart of human acts. The most detestable misdeeds are not always perpetrated in the crime: this is an old truth for anyone who bothers to examine the intention. But the intention no longer has the innocent look of a pious thought that flits past as it justifies the unjustifiable. Henceforth, a good intention is an act. For the author of a political crime, whether right-wing or left-wing, involving betrayal or murder, good intentions signify asceticism and renunciation, abnegation and sacrifice, austere obedience and fidelity and, in any case, a violent rejection of a secure and innocuous existence. Obviously, too many virtues are required in order to commit a crime. This creates a sense of confusion in the judgement brought to bear on our neighbour, a refusal to condemn and a refusal to acquit. This sometimes encourages a deliberate blindness which conveniently avoids suspending judgement in a world that demands lively reflexes and immediate outrage. And here, too, we find ourselves having recourse to the judgement of history which, miraculously, we know in advance.

But perhaps these contradictions in morality are produced only by the same impetuosity that incites us to action and the blessing that thinkers give to such impetuosity. Perhaps morality is thus already banished from the domain of behaviour when we ask it just to guide and control such behaviour. The only morality is therefore one of kindness.

But no doubts are possible concerning contemporary violence. It is not just barbarism. It is not just egoism. It claims to unravel the studied web of spiritual crisis. It presents itself as the root of inner equations. It puts itself forward as the path to grace and the soul's cure. Intellectuals are ashamed of their own condition, feeling powerless and decrepit. For almost fifty years now, they have been ashamed of contemplation. The eternal essenses exclude *ennui*. They wish to cut the knot of a problem through action. A violent break with the course of things – whatever that entails in order to keep something that is disappearing or hurry along something that is disappearing too slowly – will bring back their spirit. The slow maturation of things is intolerable. The last life is the most lively and least reflexive one, a life of youthful insolence, as though such youths had already resolved all the questions accumulated by successive civilizations by simple virtue of their wildness. The exception is worth more than the rule; conflict is greater than work. They glorify whatever is harsh and pitiless, adventurous and heroic, dangerous and intense. They flatter adolescents. The renunciation of adventure is denounced as a fear of living, and there is no greater cowardice than this fear.

But from this point on, violence, even when it is inevitable and just, dearly and nobly paid for by the danger or death involved, can cost nothing by itself. The ordeal that should have come from its immorality is dulled by the heroism in which it shows up and in which souls seek and find their salvation. The modern world has forgotten the virtues of patience. The rapid and effective action to which everyone is committed for a single moment has furnished the dark gleam produced by the ability to wait and suffer. But the glorious deployment of energy is murderous. We must recall these virtues of patience not so as to preach a sense of resignation in the face of revolutionary spirit, but so that we can feel the essential link which connects the spirit of patience to true revolution. This revolution comes from great pity. The hand that grasps the weapon must suffer in the very violence of that gesture. To anaesthetize this pain brings the revolutionary to the frontiers of fascism.

IV
OPENINGS

Between times messianic thought filled the world (Franz Rosenzweig, *Stern der Erlösung*, Vol. II, p. 97)

Jewish Thought Today

What does Jewish thinking concern itself with? A whole host of things, no doubt, which we are not going to list. But its basic message consists in bringing the meaning of each and every experience back to the ethical relation between men, in appealing to man's personal responsibility – in which he feels chosen and irreplaceable – in order to bring about a human society in which men are treated as men. The realization of this just society *ipso facto* involves raising man up into the same society as God. This society is human beatitude itself and the meaning of life. This is so much so that saying that the meaning [*sens*] of reality is understood in terms of ethics is tantamount to saying that the universe is sacred. But it is in an ethical sense [*sens*] that it is sacred. Ethics is an optics of the Divine. Henceforth, no relation with God is direct or immediate. The Divine can be manifested only through my neighbour. For a Jew, Incarnation is neither possible nor necessary. After all, the fomula for this comes from Jeremiah: 'He judged the course of the poor and needy; then it was well. Is not this to know me? says the Lord' (Jeremiah 22:16).

Christianity, which evolved from Judaism, seems to the Jews to move away from these propositions in a direction in which the power of these propositions certainly seemed to intensify, but in which Judaism could discern that they changed. This has given rise to a painful history of injustice and misunderstanding, violence and rancour. We are not here going to open a debate on the substance of this history, which is something that centuries of questioning have not managed to resolve. But by listing some of the positions taken up by modern Judaism, we shall have occasion to note its present attitudes towards Christianity.

Three great events, whose shadow was already being cast over Europe long before they were handed down to us, constitute for Jewish thought today the facts of the new situation:

1. The unique experience of the revival of anti-Semitism, which

culminated in the scientific extermination of a third of all Jews by National Socialism.

2. The Zionist aspirations which culminated in the creation of the State of Israel.

3. The arrival on the historical scene of those underdeveloped Afro-Asiatic masses who are strangers to the Sacred History that forms the heart of the Judaic-Christian world.

These three events have given Jewish thought a new and determined physiognomy for those tendencies I shall try to list objectively. As regards the position of Judaism in relation to Christianity, each event has produced contradictory movements in which kings come closer together and then move apart.

I

But let us note above all the position of the Jewish thought born from the Emancipation that occurred in the eighteenth century. This thought preceded these great events and is far from being surpassed today. In this position, which is still that of many Western Jews, Judaism is a religion alongside Christianity, a form of worship in which the supernatural fate of the human soul is decided. Understanding with other men is achieved on the level of the State and the nation, as a fraternity between citizens. Its relations with the other forms of worship are characterized by respect and tolerance, but display none of the drama of a soul in torment as living out its truth, when faced with the fact that there are other truths lived out in the world. Religion is something private, like family memories. Such a vision is possible in a harmonious world, but is not entirely lost in the new situation! This interhuman fraternity outside religion, this respect shown to the other form of worship because it belongs to our fellow citizens, will remain the basis of all future relations with Christianity, which will be marked by an absence of contempt, indifference and even vindictiveness. Many Jews continue to think that the rational aesthetic and political values of Graeco-Roman humanism are the true foundation for the understanding between Jews and Christians, just as they form the basis for understanding among all the religions.

II

The extermination of six million European Jews, which marked the culmination of this century's anti-Semitism, for the Jews signified a crisis for the world that Christianity had modelled for twenty centuries. In this sense, the thought of Jules Isaac goes a very long way. But the fact that the monstrosity of Hitlerism could be produced in an evangelized Europe shook within the Jewish mind the plausibility which Christian metaphysics could have for a Jew used to a long acquaintance with Christianity. This plausibility involved *the primacy of supernatural salvation with regard to justice on earth*. Has not this primacy made at least possible a great deal of confusion on earth, and this extreme limit of human dereliction? The famous incomprehension towards supernatural salvation shown by supposedly worldly Jews – something even assimilated Jews occasionally accused themselves of – and Bergson's thought and Simone Weil's violent passion stem from this self-accusation – this famous incomprehension appeared abruptly not as an example of pigheadedness but as a moment of supreme lucidity, and the Jews began to believe that their stiff necks were the most metaphysical part of their anatomy.

From before the two wars this century, but above all in the aftermath of the Liberation, this created a nostalgia in Western Judaism for its own sources, a return to rabbinic literature as the authentic access to the Bible. In France, the poetry of an Edmond Fleg, inspired by its sources, nourished an entire generation that had lost all access to Hebrew and Aramaic. But the revival of Jewish studies themselves, which is not only due to the sense of prestige conferred on the State of Israel by the Jewish intelligentsia, is the remarkable fact of Jewish life.

These studies aim to return to the rabbinic texts, which offer a true illumination of the Bible, the Law and the prophets. The Old Testament does not prefigure the New: it receives its interpretation from the Talmud. Judaism has always thought this. What is new is this appearance in Western Europe of talmudic houses of study of the type that was traditional in Eastern Europe. They are made up of students who are products of Western Judaism, the type that seemed well and truly assimilated, irreligious or attracted to conversion. What is new is the creation of houses of study and a series of movements, among both the young and adults, which scour the traditional texts of rabbinic literature for a reply to questions that occur to a modern Westerner. The novelty of Jewish thought lies in this Western revalorization of the Talmud, which is no longer treated archaeologically or historically but as a form of teaching.

The possibility that texts developing the law of strict justice – that boring ethics so decried by artists and mystics; the possibility that such texts will lead us to the secret contradictions and the most intimate breathing of the human soul; the possibility that the deployment of this ethics will enable us to hear the footsteps and the voice of the Lord and His ultimate proximity, paternal and smiling without being effusive, in the subtle drunkenness of common lucidity; the possibility that the most concrete, modern, audacious or banal concerns of social and economic justice will pierce you like the very word of that familiar, friendly, irksome and exacting God – these are what create the incredible adventure and the unique, scarcely communicable emotion experienced by the student of the Talmud and rediscovered by the Western Jew. He feels as a result that many essays on the Jew and his God are ridiculous.

Some do not go that far, but the memory of the Passion lived out by Judaism between 1940 and 1945 made some men conscious once more of their exceptional destiny. Thirty years ago, they seemed to slot the whole of their existence into the clearly defined Western categories of nation, State, art, social class and profession (ultimately religion as well, but only very rarely). This happened, moreover, without the structure of their thought in any way changing, or their attachment to the West weakening, or their knowledge of the Jewish sources growing, or their membership of the synagogue taking place. This new experience was no doubt destined to be translated into thoughts and works and to mark the future fate of Jewish thought, but while expressing itself as a negative waiting, it none the less was metaphysical and incontestable and direct.

As Jankélévitch said recently:

> All we have in common is being here, all of us, the survivors. Everything that is most common and essential to us, you will admit, is summed up in our being alive; by accident, we are here ... each one of us, individually, is here ... we don't know how! ... through an oversight on the part of the Gestapo ... we don't know what happened, but we came back ... we have emerged. ... We were forgotten. We passed by or arrived on the scene after the final round-up had taken place. There has been in our lives a series of horrible tragedies which have for ever marked us and set us apart from others ...

But this Passion lived out by Judaism in Christian Europe just as unquestionably represents a reconciliation with Christians. In the collapse of this Europe, Jews entered into a relation with Christian individuals and Christian groups who spoke to them as brothers. Behind Christian dogma and the Christian vision of history, Jews discovered the courage and the charity of real people. Throughout the entire Nazi domination, in a world of brown shirts, the black cassock signified refuge and human warmth. The magnificent clergy of the secular country in which we live won an undying right to our gratitude. This experience was so strong that it has in turn left its mark on the Jewish consciousness. This has created a reconciliation with Christians and Christian groups, despite the crisis in a civilization that has not managed to inject some humanity into the visible world of institutions.

Traditional Jewish thought, moreover, provides the framework in which to think of a universal human society that incorporates the just people of every nation and every belief, with whom it is possible to achieve the final intimacy, the one formulated by the Talmud in reserving participation in the future world for all the just people. And Maimonides' theses on the missionary role of Christianity in the service of monotheism have assumed, in the course of these terrible years, a meaning that is perhaps less optimistic but more direct. Yet even before National Socialism, in the mounting peril of the interwar years, the philosopher Franz Rosenzweig, who died in 1929 but exerts a growing influence on contemporary Jewish thought, plans Judaism and Christianity within the common programme of a religious truth that is certainly not pluralist but dualist. Truth, in itself, would entail a double manifestation in the world; that of the eternal people and that of the mission on the eternal way. Truth is consequently experienced in a dialogue between Jew and Christian. It does not reach a conclusion, but constitutes the very life of truth. The dialogue lives off its very openness, and the presence of the interlocutor. We are far from the medieval disputations that sought to provide conclusions. In spite of the impossibility of concluding it is, all the same, better this way! Perhaps it is in this perspective of friendly dialogue, which is aware of all the possible uncompromising differences, that we should place the brilliant thought of André Néher, whose very language seems a moving echo of dramatic Christian thought. The venerable Martin Buber, taking his cue from the mystical elements of Jewish Hassidism, went even further down the path of dialogue. Robert Aron also represents this tendency. But it is still only a tendency.

III

Zionism and the creation of the State of Israel mean for Jewish thought a return to oneself in every sense of the term, and the end of an alienation that lasted a thousand years.

Rationalism and the historical methods of Israeli scholars, the cult of nature and the earth, the scientific socialism of its builders, are just some of the new themes to be found in Israel's thought and literature. The people of the book are forced to become a people of the earth. But the religious essence of Israel and its thought is ill-concealed behind this denial of God. The State of Israel has become the place where man is sacrificed, where he is uprooted from his recent past for the sake of an ancient and prophetic past, where he seeks his authenticity. It is in order to revive this prophetic past that André Chouraqui 'went up into Israel'. And a whole generation of intellectuals, of whom I have spoken above and who were uprooted by National Socialism, regard the road to Israel as just such a going-up.

While the spiritual personality of Israel was for centuries excused its lack of participation in the history of the world on the grounds that it was a persecuted minority – not everyone has the chance to have pure hands because he is persecuted! – the State of Israel is the first opportunity to move into history by bringing about a just world. It is therefore a search for the absolute and for purity. The sacrifices and works which the realization of this justice invites men to make give body once more to the spirit that animated the prophets and the Talmud. The socialist dreams of Israel's builders do not become entangled in world circumstances. Socialism in one country? The collectivist society of the kibbutz attempts socialism in one village! 'The four cubits of the Law' in which God took refuge, according to the Doctors of the Talmud, become the four hectares of the collective farm. We must not lose sight of the universal meaning that this work assumes in the eyes of the Israelis themselves, who believe they are working for humanity.

Jewish universalism has always revealed itself in particularism. But for the first time in its history, Israeli Judaism gauges its task only by its own teachings, which in some way have been freed from an obsession with the Western, Christian world, towards which it moves fraternally but without any feelings of inferiority or timidity.

IV

But it will move further in the direction of this world than it thinks. Surely the rise of the countless masses of Asiatic and under-developed peoples threatens this new-found authenticity? On to the world stage come peoples and civilizations who no longer refer to our Sacred History, for whom Abraham, Isaac and Jacob no longer mean anything. As at the beginning of Exodus, a new king arises who does not know Joseph.

I do not in any way want to qualify this rise in materialism because we hear in it the cry of a frustrated humanity, and while one certainly has the right to denounce one's own hunger as materialist, one never has the right to denounce the hunger of others. But under the greedy eyes of these countless hordes who wish to hope and live, we, the Jews and Christians are pushed to the margins of history, and soon no one will bother any more to differentiate between a Catholic and a Protestant or a Jew and a Christian, sects that devour one another because they cannot agree on the inter-pretation of a few obscure books. They are a religious collectivity that has lost all political cohesion in a universe that is henceforth built around different structures.

Perhaps, in this enormous world now rising up before us, Marxism still unites us in an immediate and unique way, as a doctrine in which we can glimpse its Judaeo-Christian legacy. But surely these Marxist infiltrations will themselves be lost in the vastness of these foreign civilizations and impenetrable pasts. Is it not the case that evolving beneath such a gaze helps Jews and Christians to rediscover a forgotten kinship? It is not a kinship that leads to some syncretism or other, or a few common abstractions. Instead, a new feeling of fraternity is born in our childhood return from the depth of ages. And the current concerns of Christian ecumenism will surely go further than wherever their first steps take them? The dialogue this time will go beyond the level of the Graeco-Roman ideas common to Jews and Christians in the nations where until now they have lived on.

V

Is there a revival in Jewish thought? I think that in the brief inventory I have just given, the great traditional themes of this thought can be found. Is not authentic thought simultaneously an endless renewal, an attentiveness to the world's youth and a fidelity to its first enlightenment? Is a renewal of thought not both a pleonasm and a contradiction in terms? It is perhaps the consciousness of its permanence, its topicality and the still unexhausted character of its message which most strongly characterizes Jewish thought in 1961.

At the dawning of the new world, Judaism has the consciousness to possess, through its permanence, a function in the general economy of Being. No one can replace it. Someone has to exist in the world who is as old as the world. For Judaism, the great migrations of the people, the migration among people and the upheavals of history have never presented a deadly threat. It always found what remained to it. It has a painful experience of living on; its performance accustomed it to judging history and refusing to accept the verdict of a History that proclaimed itself judge. Perhaps Jewish thought in general consists today in holding on more firmly than ever to this permanence and this eternity. Judaism has traversed history without taking up history's causes. It has the power to judge, alone against all, the victory of visible and organized forces – if need be in order to reject them. Its head may be held high or its head may be down, but it is always stiff-necked. This temerity and this patience, which are as long as eternity itself, will perhaps be more necessary to humanity tomorrow or the day after tomorrow than they were yesterday or the day before.

Jacob Gordin

Twenty-five years ago, on 23 August 1947, 7 Eloul 5707, the philosopher Jacob Gordin died at the age of fifty. He died in Lisbon, where his family had taken him in the hope that a specialist might cure him of the grave illness which was eating away at him. On the eve of his death, he said only one thing to whoever approached his bed: 'I am a Jew'. And, as if Italian somehow sounded more Portuguese than French, he added proudly: '*Sono hebreo*'.

Who was Gordin? He came to Paris from Berlin with one of the first waves of *émigrés* to leave Hitler's Germany. He was one of those who, by their teaching and their presence, determined the direction taken by the spiritual and intellectual life of French Jews after the Liberation. Through their influence, the youth of the day moved towards an integral Judaism, a universal Judaism and culture, a Judaism that stood as interlocuter for the modern world, a Judaism that was 'unsurpassable'. He was a typical example of the glorious Russian intelligentsia, brought up as a Jew and educated as a Westerner. Born in Dunaburg in 1896 and nurtured on Hebrew from an early age, he was a graduate by the time he was fifteen. By the age of nineteen he had completed his cycle of studies in the Semitic section of the Faculty of Oriental Languages, and five years later his studies in the Philosophy Department in the Faculty of Human Sciences, both at the University of Petrograd – which was no longer St Petersburg but was not yet Leningrad.

Germany represented his first exile, but it was an exile in which he blossomed – an ambiguity that exists in many Jewish destinies. His Berlin years ended with the rise of the Nazis. But they were fruitful years for Jacob Gordin in terms of study and research: his infatuation with Marbourg's neo-Kantianism went hand in hand, despite the difference in register, with his exploration of Israel's mystical heritage, to be found in its kabbalistic literature. This double curiosity about the concept and the Mystery was to merge into one at a later stage where, in his teaching, the solid Cohenian *logos* was used to support the bold touch of a visionary. In Germany he began to publish texts in journals; fundamental articles on theology and philosophy were printed in the Jewish Encyclopaedia edited at that time by the Spinozist Jacob Klatzkine. Attached to the Hermann Cohen-Stiftung school, near the famous *Akademie für Wissenschaft des Judentums*, he brought out in 1929, a vigorous book entitled *The Infinite Judgement* [*Das unendliche Urteil*], which was published by this Foundation. The book displayed a relentless rigour in its logical analysis, and concluded by contrasting Hegel and Hermann Cohen, bringing out the barely perceptible incompatibilities that existed between the two dialectics: the reciprocity of antithetical terms without any priority in Hegel; the primacy of one of the two terms, which is revealed in this way to be the *origin* in Cohen.

Does this reveal a possible Judaic influence on the great neo-Kantian? The question is never raised. But the way in which he opens us up to rich tradition by exploiting a crack in the cast-iron rational system perhaps marks the difference between thought and folklore, philosophy and rhetoric. That was Gordin's style. He knew that the simple declaration of dramatic oppositions – a sign of the amateur – never helps us to isolate the originality of a great culture, and that only those changes of accent that can be picked up by sensitive ears explain that the Spirit varies. Jacob Gordin's teaching derived much of its power from this finely tuned ear.

On arriving in France, he immediately set to work. Let us imagine the apocalyptic atmosphere of the period 1933 to 1939! War is coming, and the crowds cheer the swastika, while the ancient wisdom of the West persists in seeing victory and reason. European Jews battle with problems that had been resolved over a century before. The Jewish question takes on metaphysical dimensions. It excludes those solutions that would avoid catastrophe. Without credo or worship, Judaism is lived out in a religious or apocalyptic way. This unique destiny, beyond the misery of a people, shows us the fundamental incompatability between the spiritual and the idyllic. The history of Judaism perhaps signifies no more than this. Gordin will see in it the very opening up of human history, the entry of Meaning into Being.

In 1934 Gordin gave a series of lectures at the Ecole Rabbinique de France[1] on medieval Jewish philosophy: a university lecture on a university theme. But his thoughts poured forth and communicated along another wavelength during the war, in occupied France, where daily life was dangerous. He had been in contact with the

French Jewish Scouts, founded by Robert Gamzon, the unforgettable Castor, since the First World War (which itself played an important part in the rebirth of Jewish consciousness in France) and he now participated in the Resistance, saving Jewish children threatened with deportation. But even in this semi-clandestine existence he revealed, to those of the younger generation who recognized him as a master, the high significance of Judaism, and so, in the words of Pirkeh-Aboth, 'established numerous disciples'.

After the war his teaching became a meditation that took place in the presence of friends and admirers, and there were many among the young generation. He also taught at a school, but one 'unlike the others', the *Ecole des Cadres*, part of the French Jewish Scouts – the famous school at Orsay, also founded by Castor, that dominated for almost twenty years the spiritual life of the young generation of French Jews devoted to an ambitious Judaism. Between 1946 and 1947 the school was the centre of Gordin's influence. Drawing on the riches of the *Midrash* and Jewish mysticism, but sustained by a remarkable philosophical culture, his classes founded a tradition in the school that was brilliantly carried on by Leon Askenazi and his disciples, and determined a whole style of Jewish studies – recognized, even in Israel, as due to the spiritual contribution of French immigration. Perhaps the studies themselves were responsible in large measure for that immigration.

Jacob Gordin possessed a highly speculative mind, but he never lost himself in abstractions. He had a particularly lively curiosity about human beings. During his illness, the presence of pupils, who surrounded him with an attentiveness that sometimes noted his sayings more than his hidden suffering, brought the greatest assuagement to this suffering. His openness towards human beings surpassed his taste for books and documents, and that is saying a great deal. From 1936, at the Alliance Library (the greatest collection of Judaica and Hebraica in Europe), from the time of the Liberation until he became the sectional head of the Centre for Contemporary Documentation, this librarian and archivist was as much a user of the library as an administrator.

He was a great polyglot reader, a lover of the written sign, attentive to faces, with a gift for human encounters, conversation, the famous 'Razgovar' of the Russian intelligentsia. As a result, he did not always find the time he needed in order to write. Apart from *The Infinite Judgement*, he left behind only articles (notably those published in the *Cahiers Juifs* edited by Piha). A philosophical biography of Maimonides which should have been ready for the

800th anniversary of the 'Eagle of the Synagogue' remained un-finished. But his words were heard by an age that craved living words.

Searching for reasons besides those of the heart, Gordin the philosopher bravely looked for answers to contemporary problems in the Jewish thinkers of the Middle Ages, who were nevertheless extremely faithful to those pagan masters who supported and articulated their monotheist theology. And it is in the gaps between the body of the ancient systems and the Jewish form with which it is dressed that Gordin's keen ear hears the essential difference. He extracts a philosophy from it, a philosophy of history that provides neither complacency nor consolation, but is experienced with the strange happiness that comes from being a Jew and the avowal that one has had the best share of things, as in the '*Sono Hebreo*' repeated on his deathbed.

Going back through liberalism and its precarious preservation of the West's great principles to Israel's religious and ethical sources, Jacob Gordin sees the existence of the Jewish people and its unique particularism not as something that offers must one more national-ism, but as something that opens up the historical perspective of humanity. The unique singularity of the destinies of the Jewish people which, in spite of every natural law and so-called historical law, maintained its individual existence as 'a people dwelling alone, and not reckoning itself among the nations' (Numbers 23:9), while remaining, for all time and in all places, the eternal companion of history – this singularity bears witness to the fact that here, and only here, we touch on the true spirit of history.

The martyrology of this people becomes a palpable example, a concrete projection of calvary and all suffering humanity. This pain-racked 'Slave of God' who condenses the world's tortures in his destiny becomes a concrete symbol of the humanity that learns to know itself, and a providential prefiguration of the future messianic humanity.

Nothing, perhaps, is more contemporary than the problems to which this vision responds. Written by the victors, and meditating on the victories, our Western history and our philosophy of history announce the realization of a humanist ideal while ignoring the vanquished, the victims and the persecuted, as if they were of no significance. They denounce the violence through which this his-tory was none the less achieved without being concerned by this contradiction. This is a humanism for the arrogant! The denuncia-tion of violence risks turning into the installation of a violence and an arrogance: an alienation a Stalinism. The war against war perpetuates war by ridding itself of all bad conscience. Our age certainly no longer needs to be convinced of the value of non-violence. But it perhaps lacks a new reflection on passivity, and a certain weakness that is not cowardice, a certain patience that we must not preach to others, in which the ego [*le Moi*] must be held, one which cannot be treated in negative terms as though it were just the other side of finitude. Enough of Nietszcheanism, even when purged of its Hitlerian deformations! But who will dare to say such a thing? The humanism of the suffering servant – the History of Israel – invites us to create a new anthropology, a new historiography, and perhaps, by bringing about the end of Western 'triumphalism', a new history.

Religion and Tolerance

At the triumphant conference held in the UNESCO palace in Paris between 21 and 23 June 1960 to celebrate one hundred years of the Universal Jewish Alliance, Professor Vladimir Jankélévitch gave a dazzling talk, full of wit and wisdom, on the philosophy of tolerance. He showed that this virtue assumed as many absolutes as there were persons (however paradoxical this plural form of the absolute may seem); that the rational truth which may join these separated beings does not engage their whole being; that the residue remaining outside unanimity was neither insignificant nor negligible, but was precisely absolute, and original for all eternity, like each individual self, which is taught through a direct and irrefutable experience of our irreducible uniqueness. These many different persons remain separate even in the truths in which they commune, but separation is not a last resort which we simply put up with. It opens up the path to another form of communication, that of love, which is inconceivable without the separation of beings. Tolerance paves the way to this love, when it does not already proceed from it.

An eminent scholar, who specialized in the study of a great monotheist civilization, found himself that day in the conference hall. He experienced a doubt. Does this multiplicity of irreducible absolutes still leave a place for the pre-eminent absolute of faith? Is it certain that religious intolerance does not merely reflect the barbarism of the Dark Ages? Is it not the case that the link between faith and the sword defines religious truth as such? While faith is distinct from rational evidence, in which tolerance and intolerance lose all meaning, does it not all the same belong to opinions in which tolerance is easy? Would faith benefit from the multiplicity of religions, as Her most gracious British Majesty benefits from the enlightened opinion of the Opposition whose leader is appointed by her? By placing confession in the realm of private opinions as though it resembled aesthetic taste and a preference for a political slant, is it not the case that the modern world here again attests to the death of God?

These are far-reaching reflections. They denounce an old prejudice, which is all the more serious for being one held by philosophers. In discovering the dignity of rational knowledge, they relegated all other forms of knowledge to the realm of opinion. They ignored the privileged domain of faith. Opinion knows that it is variable and multiple; it already foresees the profits to be gained from conflicting opinions. Religious certainty shields conscience from history's changing fortunes. Like the universal truth of philosophers, the believer's truth tolerates no limits. But it turns not only against every proposal that contradicts it, but also against every man who turns his back on it. Its fervour is rekindled by the burning stake. The most serene truth is already a crusade.

How then can we choose between religion and tolerance?

To find a way out of this dilemma, we should perhaps recognize that the modern age is defined precisely by the end of the wars of religion. For we all too easily give the term 'crusades' to the ideological wars of our day, which are in reality kept alive by a conflict of interests. But the imperishable aspect of religion is not sustained by a confession that is reduced to the realm of a private life. The fact that tolerance can be inherent in religion without religion losing its exclusivity is perhaps the meaning of Judaism, which is a religion of tolerance.

It retains the bitter taste of the absolute. It is not experienced – when it is experienced – as a unique but transitory moment through which eternity realizes a plan that escapes the individual. 'I will not fail you or forsake you', says the Lord to Joshua (Joshua 1:5), so marking the irremissible character of divine emotion.

But this emotion is experienced by Israel in the ethical life whose ritual law itself guarantees discipline and culture. The welcome given to the Stranger which the Bible tirelessly asks of us does not constitute a corollary of Judaism and its love of God (as Néher eloquently demonstrated during the same session in which Jankélévitch spoke), but it is the very content of faith. It is an undeclinable responsibility. 'The tomb is not a refuge, for despite yourself you were created, and despite yourself you were born and lived, and despite yourself you die, and despite yourself you will have to account for yourself before the King of Kings', says Rabbi Eliezer Hakappar. Before appearing to the Jews as a fellow creature with convictions to be recognized or opposed, the Stranger is one towards whom one is obligated. *The Jewish faith involves tolerance because, from the beginning, it bears the entire weight of all other men.* The way in which it seems to block off the outside world and to display indifference towards the idea of a mission, together with the religious war lurking within that mission, results not from a sense of pride but from the demands that one has to make on oneself. The intolerance this entails is directed not against doctrines but against the immorality that can disfigure the human face of my neighbour. The 'religious wars' of the Bible are waged against the evil that the earth itself, vomiting up its perverse elements – Nature – cannot endure. Idolatry is fought not on account of its errors, but on account of the moral degeneracy that accompanies it. In the words of Rab Yehouda (Sanhedrin 63b) the absurdity of idolatry is strikingly apparent, but people indulge in it because 'it justifies public debauchery'.

It has never been stated that the idea of Israel as a chosen people, which seems to contradict the idea of universality, is in reality the founding of tolerance. This idea is prolonged in Judaism to the point where we reach an ultimate intimacy with the Stranger, since 'the just of every nation have a share of the future world'; it leads to the affirmation that the world was created for 'the paths of peace'. It is conclusions such as these that reveal the sense of being chosen, which expresses less the pride of someone who has been called than the humility of someone who serves. Being chosen is no more appalling as a condition than being the place for all moral consciousness. Better than doctrinal unanimity, it guarantees peace. It is the arrogance of a gratuitous duty that scorns reciprocity.

In Judaism, the certainty of the absolute's hold over man – or religion – does not turn into an imperialist expansion that devours all those who deny it. It burns *inwards*, as an infinite demand made on oneself, an infinite responsibility. It is experienced as something for which we are chosen. As the Book of Amos states: 'You only have I known of all the families of the earth,' adding: 'therefore I will punish you for all your iniquities' (Amos 3:2). But this fact transforms Judaism into a modern religion, a religion of tolerance. In this sense it has not been surpassed by the religions that have evolved from it, nor even reduced to inaction by them. For by stubbornly surviving it has certainly contributed to the rehabilitation of tolerance in Christian and Islamic thought, and has brought such a message to the whole of the modern world.

Israel and Universalism[1]

Father Daniélou's brilliant exposition cannot be discussed – at any rate, a Jew cannot contradict its main thesis. A Mediterranean society comprised of Christians, Muslims and Jews, a civilization based on the principal values of the three monotheist religions, is a vision that is both familiar and dear to Jewish consciousness and thought. I can only bear witness to it here, in the hope that you will excuse the plodding nature of my remarks, a telling result of the rapid notes I have made in listening just now to Father Daniélou.

The good news, which I had already received during my stay at Tioumliline Abbey, seems to me to consist in the following: Catholicism offers the idea of a community that surpasses the limits of confession. I had thought up until then that charity was the only area into which a Catholic ventured, magnificently moreover, in order to meet those who do not believe as he does. To focus on a common civilization is to recommend institutions and, beyond the generosity of individual hearts, an objective terrain of coexistence and collaboration. This is very new and very comforting. For this comfort I thank Father Daniélou.

There are certain points in his exposition on which we do not agree. When he described the gestation and the birth of the three monotheisms and their reciprocal collaboration, Father Daniélou completely left out the element that remains essential to those of us who are Jews: the constitution of the Talmud. Rabbinical Judaism, in the centuries that preceded and followed the destruction of the Second Temple, is the primordial event in Hebraic spirituality. If there had been no Talmud, there would have been no Jews today. (It certainly would have saved the world a lot of problems!) Or else, we would have been the survivors of a finished world. This is the suggestion that, in spite of everything, persists in Catholic thought. We reject, as you know, the honour of being a relic. Was Father Daniélou's discourse entirely free from this suggestion? In order to demonstrate Judaism's contribution to the legacy of humanity, it confined itself to Jews without Judaism. He quoted only descendants of Jews. We cannot admit that the essential Jewish message is preserved in blood and transmitted via the obscure path of atavism.

Father Daniélou spoke movingly of the dramatic fate of every religion which, when confronted with others, is torn between charity and truth. It was in order to find a way out of this dilemma that he recommended the civilization that is founded on the values and beliefs common to monotheisms. Like him, I believe that we must take our conscience from this common civilization and that we must take conscience in common, in order to understand one another. But from this point on, I am convinced that we must have recourse to the medium of full understanding and comprehension, in which all truth is reflected – that is, to the Greek civilization and what it engendered: *logos*, the coherent discourse of reason, life in a reasonable State. That is the true terrain of all understanding. The civilization created by such a life permits an accord to be established between truth that can neither be reduced to their 'spiritual minimum' nor juxtaposed into a syncretism which we Jews regard with as much horror as you do.

Finally, I must confess that the drama spoken of by Father Daniélou is one we feel much less acutely. This is not because Jews are indifferent or egoists, or because they content themselves with one truth, their own, which must belong only to the Jews. The reason is that the truth – the knowledge of God – is not a question of dogma for them, but one of action, as in Jeremiah 22, and that a Jew can communicate just as intimately with a non-Jew who portrays morality – in other words, with the Noachide – as with another Jew. The rabbinic principle by which the just of every nation participate in the future world expresses not only an eschatological view. It affirms the possibility of that ultimate intimacy, beyond the dogma affirmed by the one or the other, an intimacy without reserve.

That is our universalism. In the cave that represents the resting-place of the patriarchs and our mothers, the Talmud also lays Adam and Eve to rest: it is for the whole of humanity that Judaism came into the world.

We have the reputation of considering ourselves to be a chosen people, and this reputation greatly wrongs this universalism. The idea of a chosen people must not be taken as a sign of pride. It does not involve being aware of exceptional rights, but of exceptional duties. It is the prerogative of a moral consciousness itself. It knows itself at the centre of the world and for it the world is not homogeneous: for I am always alone in being able to answer the call, I am irreplaceable in my assumption of responsibility. Being chosen involves a surplus of obligations for which the 'I' of moral consciousness utters.

This is what is represented by the Jewish concept of Israel and the sense that it is a chosen people. It is not 'still anterior' to the universalism of a homogeneous society in which the differences between Jew, Greek and barbarian are abolished. It already includes this abolition but remains, for a Jew, a condition that is at any moment still indispensable to such an abolition, which in turn at any moment is still about to commence.

Jews also think that historically they have been faithful to this notion of Israel, but that is another (hi)story.

Monotheism and Language

The long historical collaboration between Jews, Christians and Muslims, their geographical proximity as Mediterranean neighbours, the way in which they intermingle throughout in our world of homogeneous structures, the real world that mocks anachronisms, creates, whether we like it or not, a *de facto* community between Jews, Muslims and Christians – even if serious misunderstandings separate them and even if they are opposed to one another.

Whether we like it or not! Why should we not? Why should this community exist against the wishes of its members?

Each of these spiritual families taught universalism to the world, even if they did not always agree on matters of pedagogy. Our essential fates look kindly on one another.

Monotheism is not an arithmetics of the Divine. It is the perhaps supernatural gift of seeing that one man is absolutely like another man beneath the variety of historical traditions kept alive in each case. It is a school of xenophilia and anti-racism.

But it is more than that: *it obliges the other to enter into a discourse that unites him with me*. This is a point of the utmost importance. The logic of the Greeks established, as we know, harmony between men, but there is one condition: our interlocutor must agree to speak, and be brought into discourse. And Plato, at the beginning of the *Republic*, tells us that no one can oblige an Other to enter into a discourse. Aristotle tells us that the man who remains silent can indefinitely refuse to give himself over to the logic of non-contradiction. Monotheism, the word of the one and only God, is precisely the word that one cannot help but hear, and cannot help but answer. It is the word that obliges us to enter into discourse. It is because the monotheists have enabled the world to hear the word of the one and only God that Greek universalism can separate in humanity and slowly unify that humanity. This homogeneous humanity gradually forming before our eyes, which lives in fear and anguish but already achieves solidarity by collaborating economically, has been created by those of us who are monotheists! It is not the play of economic forces that has created the solidarity which is in fact uniting races and states around the world. The opposite is the case: the power of monotheism to make one man tolerate another and bring him to reply has made possible the entire economy of solidarity.

Islam is above all one of the principal factors involved in this constitution of humanity. Its struggle has been arduous and magnificent. It long ago surpassed the tribes that gave birth to it. It swarmed across three continents. It united innumerable peoples and races. It understood better than anyone that a universal truth is worth more than local particularisms. It is not by chance that a talmudic apologue cites Ishmael, the symbol of Islam, among the rare sons of Sacred History, whose name was formulated and announced before their birth. It is as if their task in the world had for all eternity already been foreseen in the economy of Creation.

Faced with the grandeur of this realization, and this sovereign collaboration with the work of unification – the end point and justification of every particular unification – Judaism has always paid homage. One of its greatest poets and theologians, Jehouda Halévy, who, as a Jew, certainly could not have denied a birthright to Judaism in this domain, writing in Arabic, exalted the mission of Islam.

This acknowledgement is strongly made by any Jew worthy of the name. For the Jew – and this is perhaps one of his definitions – is the man whom the worries and struggles of the moment leave open at any time to a lofty dialogue – that is to say, the word that passes from one man to another. Above all, the Jew is someone for whom lofty dialogue has at least the same determining importance as the worries and struggles of the day. It is inconceivable that such a disposition would not find an echo in those very people who have so magnificently achieved the task whose message was first borne by Judaism.

It is this that I should like to say, by way of explaining Judaism's attitude to Islam, to a meeting of Jewish students – that is to say, clerics and a people of clerics. The memory of a common contribution to European civilization in the course of the Middle Ages, when Greek texts entered Europe via the Jewish translators who had translated Arab translations, can be exalting only if we still manage today to believe in the power of words devoid of rhetoric or diplomacy. Without reneging on any of his undertakings, the Jew is open to the word and believes in the efficacity of truth.

Pious thoughts and generous words, I hear you say! I know that we can no longer believe in words, for we can no longer speak in this tormented world. We can no longer speak, for no one can begin his discourse without immediately bearing witness to something other than what he says. By denouncing mystification, they already seem to remystify.

But we who are Jews, Muslims and Christians, we, the monotheists, we break the spell, we speak words that shake themselves free of their distorting context, we speak words that begin in the person who utters them, we rediscover the word that penetrates, the word that unties, the prophetic word.

'Between Two Worlds'
(The Way of Franz Rosenzweig)

I have been asked to give not an exposé of Rosenzweig's philosophy, but his spiritual biography. I shall speak of his life in so far as it revealed his thinking, for the thought of Rosenzweig is the essential element in this significant life.

I shall speak of his thought, without turning it into psychoanalysis. I shall present it as a testimony, without being shocked by elements that are not systematized in this thought. I shall not turn his work into a philosophical or historical exegesis. The most interesting part of Rosenzweig's thinking lies in the questions it ultimately poses, rather than the influences it may have undergone.

I shall resist the temptation to present this life as an edifying one. It would none the less be tempting to a hagiographer. This German Jew, who died in Frankfurt in 1929 at the age of forty-three – thirty years ago next 10 December – was born in Kassel, into an assimilated family of the German upper middleclass. His best friends during his childhood and student days were his own first cousins, who were Jewish converts. In 1913 he found himself on the brink of conversion. He did not take the final step, illustrating, once again, Vladimir Jankélévitch's remark about the miracle of the Jewish destiny, happening at the eleventh hour, at the last moment, in an 'almost' no bigger than a pinhead, but big enough none the less for a voice to speak and arrest the hand stretched out to do the irreparable.

This 'No' to conversion is the great daring gesture (since we should wholeheartedly place my talk under the title 'Daring and Timidity'). From this point on begins the path of return and reconquest.

This bold and vigorous thinker, who came to history and philosophy after three years of medical studies, was trained by the most exacting disciplines to be found in a German university. His first publication as a philosopher was a critical study of a Hegel manuscript which he identified as being the work of Schelling; as a Hegelian, he published in 1920 the monumental *Hegel and the*

State, rich in insights and daring ideas that are still always steeped in erudition. The work was a product of his pre-1914 studies, yet from the moment of its publication he called it *A Debt Paid to the German Spirit*. He felt a stranger to the spirit that sheltered him. In reality he was already learning Hebrew from 1912 on, going back to the sources and entering into contact with Hermann Cohen, whom he admired for his Jewish writings prior even to knowing the rest.

This German Jew of old stock, who came from an environment that nurtured the prejudices that a Western Jew entertained with regard to the Jews of Eastern Europe, marvelled at the young Polish Jews he encountered during the war. At the end of hostilities, he found himself for some months in Warsaw and admired the young Jews he saw there, even their physical appearance. With the coming of peace, he gave up his university career, which had promised to be a brilliant one, in order to devote himself to the Free House of Jewish Studies [*Freies jüdisches Lehrhaus*]. He founded it in Frankfurt, working in close harmony with Rabbi Nobel, an influential figure of whom, as of Hermann Cohen, he spoke with great admiration and whom he acknowledged as a master. This is what all those brilliant university studies led to – a centre for Jewish studies, the sort we now found every year in Paris!

Another act of daring! Influenced by his training, which recognized the spiritual importance of the State and politics, by his Hegelian studies, and by his mentor at Freiburg, Professor Meinecke, he turned to Christianity in search of the foundations to being. This search through Christianity revealed Judaism to him, precisely the thing his family was forgetting in the opulence and quietude of bourgeois life in Kassel and imperial Germany, a life that was extremely comfortable for Jews before 1914.

This double movement, towards Christianity and then Judaism, is not of interest to us only as a phychological curiosity. It bears witness to the destiny of modern European Judaism, which can no longer ignore the fact that for two thousand years now Christianity has been a determining force in Western life. I even think that this understanding attitude with regard to Christianity also bears witness to the fact that, contrary to what was said this morning, Christianity no longer poses a danger for Judaism: it is no longer a temptation for us.

Rosenzweig's main book, the book of his life, published in 1921 under the title *The Star of Redemption* [*Stern der Erlösung*], was conceived in 1917 on the Balkan Front and written down on postcards, which were sent back to the family home. It is a general system of philosophy that heralds a new way of thinking. Rosenzweig recognized that it was new. His influence on the non-Jewish philosophers in Germany has perhaps been greater than they care to admit. They never cite him.

Yet this book of general philosophy is a Jewish book, which founds Judaism in a new way. Judaism is no longer just a teaching whose theses can be true or false; *Jewish existence* (and I write existence as one word) *itself is an essential event of being; Jewish existence is a category of being.*

And so, in the life as in the work of Rosenzweig, there is a movement that always follows the same itinerary, and it is one that makes him so close to us: he moves to Judaism from the universal and the human.

At the time of his death, Rosenzweig appeared in Germany to be the master and inspiration behind a Jewish revival.

This path to truth – which took no account of success, as we have seen – was one taken by a refined and penetrating intelligence (in spite of the critics of our day who recommend him only to a few young men) and by a sensibility which he sought to disguise through humour. This life was interrupted after eight years of illness. Rosenzweig's illness, which was diagnosed almost the day after his marriage, was at once recognized as fatal, yet he lasted eight years. These eight years of illness – and it is here that hagiography is most obviously in evidence – were eight years of intellectual effort, study and even joy, in spite of the immediate and almost total separation of the soul from the body. His soul remained trapped in a body that suffered creeping paralysis.

I should add that contact with Rosenzweig – which is largely possible not only thanks to his work, in which his life is reflected, but also thanks to the memories retained of him by friends and disciples who are still alive – can above all be achieved through his correspondence, which must first be translated into French. It possesses an incomparable charm and sincerity. Our contact with this dead man becomes one full of tenderness and affection. In spite of the years of terrible experiences that already separate us from his day, and in spite of the German landscapes that are the backdrop to his life, we recognize Rosenzweig as a contemporary and a brother.

My intention, however, is not to move you, or to commemorate, with an academic funeral oration, the thirtieth anniversary of the death of Rosenzweig. Through this authentic personality I want to search out, as we say today, one of the access points to Judaism and even to religion, such as was possible for a Jew of our day who, like all of you here, had read philosophy and history, knew sociology, biblical criticism and Spinoza, and was aware of all the doubts they cast on the naive realism of the believer. I also want to show how today's Jew accedes to Judaism, when he is recognized as a citizen of a modern State and is tempted, as you all are, as we all are, to view his participation in this life of the State as the accomplishment of his very vocation to be a human being. And finally, I want to show how a man accedes to Judaism when, in all these circumstances, he is also a man sound in spirit.

For this, we have to turn to *The Star of Redemption*. We are not going to speak of it as a system, nor gauge its influences, nor make an inventory of the variations on classical themes to be found in it, although it is a book that is perfectly worthy of a university-style exegesis, for it emanates from a thought that is rigorous and always admirably informed.

For this book is more than all that. It is a life's work, not only as the masterpiece that in a creator's life represents the fulfilment of his creative activity – though this was certainly also the meaning it held for Rosenzweig, who was delighted, relatively speaking, to have paid off, at the age of thirty-two a lifetime's debt that Goethe had not managed to pay off before the age of eighty-two, when he finally finished *Faust*. But *The Star of Redemption* is a life's work in another sense. Rosenzweig felt it to be *an essential moment in his relations with life*, a book that opened up the gates of life. Life extends beyond the book, but assumes a passage through it.

This curious relation, to my mind, characterizes the modern aspect of Rosenzweig's thought. It brings his situation close to us.

Rosenzweig felt the book coming, first of all, and there was a true sense of waiting for it to come, but he was not a sentimental person. In 1916 he wrote to one of his close friends, Eugen Rosenstock, who had of course converted from Judaism, on the subject of this coming book and of *Hegel and the State*, which was all ready:

> You must have seen that the book on Hegel did not owe its existence to any personal interest in Hegel, but to the desire to write a book, an urge to *produce* something in itself. That is over now. Having been a man who wanted only to produce, I am now a man who has no plan, only vague projects, without knowing what will emerge, or even wanting anything to emerge. (*Letters*, p. 647)

Once the book was written, he said he would not write another

(*Letters*, p. 371). Real life begins, and *this real life involves precisely no longer being a book. Nicht-mehr-Buch sein*! But it is for that very reason a reference to the book. In *A New Way of Thinking* [*Neues Denken*], he writes:

> Each person must philosophize once, each must look around him once, from his own viewpoint and from the perspective of his own life. But this look is not an end in itself. The book is not a definitive goal, or even a provisional one, it must be justified, rather than put itself forward or be supported by other books. This justification is won in everyday life.

The relationship affirmed between philosophy and life is made possible only by the situation that many philosophers today designate as the end of philosophy. This end of philosophy is not only an event that touches a host of intellectuals and their scholarly quarrels. It is perhaps the very meaning of our age.

The age of philosophy is one in which philosophy is revealed on the lips of philosophers. It can be freely practised by men, who are free to enter a coherent discourse, like the Aristotelian sage who contemplates pure essences and so crowns philosophy's ethical virtues, or like Descartes, who chooses the search for truth as the most worthy way to spend a life.

But it is also the age in which men are free to abstain from philosophy, to remain silent, like Thrasymachus, or bark like the cynics, or wage war, or indulge in the passions, or turn away, to use an expression from Goethe, 'from the dullness of theory towards the verdure of the golden tree of life'.

The end of philosophy is not the return to the age in which it has not begun, in which one was able not to philosophize; the end of philosophy is the beginning of an age in which everything is philosophy, because philosophy is not revealed through philosophers. This resembles a poem by Mayakovsky, in which everyday things and even emblems of signs begin to live on their own account among men, concepts go out into the street, arguments become events, and dilectical conflicts become wars. This is translated – and this is the concrete aspect of the situation – into the consciousness of each individual, however removed this individual is from what Judaism or Marxism openly professes, through *the anguished certainty of the inexorable march of history towards goals that surpass the intentions of men.*

The end of philosophy.... The movement that led to the liberation of man enslaves man within the system which he builds. In the State and nationalisms, in the socialist statism that emerges from philosophy, the individual experiences the necessity of philosophical totality as a totalitarian tyranny.

Rosenzweig knows that *'anthropos theoretikos* has definitively ceased to reign' (*Letters*, p. 635). He knows that Hegel spoke the truth when he affirmed that this was 'the end of philosophy and that philosophers have become superfluous, that is to say teachers' (*Letters*, p. 645).

But he also knows that the simple protestation of the individual consciousness, what he calls 'the individual all the same', cannot escape purely and simply from philosophy. A simple spontaneity is no longer possible after so much knowledge, and the anarchy of the individual protestations of subjective thinkers, as he calls them, such as Kierkegaard or Nietzsche, threatens us with every kind of *Schwärmerei* and every kind of cruelty in the world.

Liberation with regard to this philosophy without philosophers demands a philosophy, and Aristotle, in his famous formula 'one must philosophize in order not to philosophize', has basically defined the ultimate possibility of philosophy, the philosophy of the twentieth century.

The order, then, that allows us simultaneously to escape the totalitarianism of philosophy, that ignores the anxiety of 'the individual all the same', but also the anarchy of individual desires; this life that is beyond the book, this philosophy that becomes life instead of becoming politics, is religion. It does not precede philosophy, it follows it.

The word 'religion', rest assured, was avoided in *The Star of Redemption*. Rosenzweig congratulated himself on not having used it, for, he said, 'the good Lord did not create religion, he created the world'. Religion is not a separate reality that joins itself to reality. The first essence, for Rosenzweig, lies in *the very way in which being is*. Religion reflects an ontological plan that is as original as the one that, in the history of the West, gives rise to knowledge.

Rosenzweig therefore goes back to religion which is not a special institution among the human institutions (more or less in the sense given to it this morning), nor even a form of culture, nor even a collection of beliefs or opinions which are given by a special grace and run parallel to rational truths.

The separation of men into the religious and the non-religious does not get us very far. 'It is not at all a question of a special disposition which some possess and others lack', wrote Rosenzweig to his mother at the end of October 1913.

It has to do with questions that are put to every man and which one escapes, either by suspending action – an unsure course of action due to the eventual immortality – or by renouncing reason, and blindly subordinating oneself either to man, or to a mode, or to the passions, etc.

And ten years later, in his famous article 'A New Way of Thinking' he wrote:

The exceptional position of Judaism and Christianity consists precisely in the fact that, even when they become religious, they retain within themselves the power to free themselves from the *nature* of this religion, and rediscover themselves in order to return to the open field of reality. Every religion, other than Judaism and Christianity, is at its origin *founded* like a special institution. Only Judaism and Christianity have become only religious, in the special sense of the term, and moreover not for long; they were never founded: they were originally something totally nonreligious.

We therefore owe to Rosenzweig (I think this is self-evident, but the word 'religion' provokes so much violent reaction as soon as we utter it that it is best to recall the fact) the fact that he reminds us of a notion of religion that is totally different from the one that secularism combats and is put forth, as though emerging in the economy of being, at the very level on which philosophical thought emerges. No one is more hostile than Rosenzweig to the unctuous, mystical, pious, homiletic, clerical notion of religion and of a religious person, a notion that reformism, attacking the integral nature of the ritual, has never managed to surpass, and whose immodesty it even emphasized through its open display of the so-called religious soul.

But how can one challenge, with the same claim to truth, the structure of the real – as isolated by the European philosophy that runs 'from the Ionian Islands to Iena' – with an ontology of religious truth, a new thought that can be as sovereignly thought as the thought that runs from Thales to Hegel? This is precisely what is undertaken in *The Star of Redemption*.

Thale's assertion that 'everything is water' is, according to Rosenzweig, the prototype of philosophical truth. It denies the truth of experience, reducing dissimilarities, saying what all reality encountered *is fundamentally*, and incorporating all phenomenal truth into this Whole.

Everything, in fact, for ancient cosmology is reduced to the world; for medieval theology, to God; for modern idealism, to man. This totalization culminates in Hegel: beings acquire meaning only from the Whole of history, which measures their reality and encapsulates men, states, civilizations, thought itself and thinkers. The person of the philosopher is reduced to the system of truth of which the person is but a moment.

This totality, and this way of seeking to achieve totality through a process of reduction are denounced by Rosenzweig. Totality in fact gives no meaning to death, which each person experiences for himself. Death is irreducible. We must therefore turn back from philosophy which reduces things to experience – that is to say, to irreducibility; an empiricism that contains nothing positivist.

Through experience we must come to understand the profusion of facts, but equally ideas and values, at the heart of which flows a human existence: nature, facts both aesthetic and moral, others, myself, God. . . . Religious or atheist humanity has, in this sense, an experience of God, given the very fact that it understands this term, even if only to deny, reduce or explain its object.

Three great irreducible realities are constituted, and isolated within the totality, in this pure experience: Man, God and the World. The effort does not consist in reducing this God of experience to what He is *fundamentally* but in describing how He appears, behind the concepts, the most pious of which have already deformed and betrayed Him.

We must proceed in the same way with regard to Man and the World. Each of these realities, without anything linking them, exists for itself and conceives of itself on the basis of self. (*Per se sunt et per se concipiuntur*, as Spinoza puts it.) Man is not a simple singularization of man in general, for he lies for himself. As a part of nature, a singularization of the concept 'man', as the bearer of a culture, as an ethical being, Man can despise death, but not as 'ipseity', in which he is 'meta-ethical'.

Behind a God Who is efficient cause of the World, behind the World, which is the very order of logical thought, there is a metaphysical God, a meta-logical world. Beings isolated and closed in on themselves, existing on the basis of self, but precisely irreducible; separate because they are irreducible. And Rosenzweig identifies this notion with the experience of the ancient world, which would have had the plastic world of art, a mythical God, separate from the World, living like the Epicurean gods in the interstices of being; and the tragic Man, who would be precisely ipseity, closed in on himself, closed in on the World, not entering into relation with the World of God.

This, then, is the first effort involved in returning to an experience that is eternally true. The separation of beings is eternally true, because these irreducible realities are a stage of human experience.

But this brings us to the second moment in Rosenzweig's thought: this isolation is not the world of our concrete experience, for in our experience God, the World, and Man are not separate, but linked. They are not linked by the theory that embraces them panoramically, at the cost of a reduction. This is, in my opinion, the essential point: in the general economy of being, a union can take place between irreducible and absolutely heterogeneous elements, a union of what could not be united, because of *life* and *time*.

In place of the totalization of elements, produced under the synoptic gaze of the philosopher, Rosenzweig uncovers the way in which time itself, and life, are put into motion. This life is the one that comes after the book. Totalization is achieved not through the philosopher's gaze but through beings themselves, who are totalized and united. This achieved unification – like time – constitutes the original fact of religion. Religion, before being a confession, is the very pulsation of life in which God enters into a relationship with Man, and Man with the World. Religion, like the web of life, is anterior to the philosopher's totality.

Life or religion is simultaneously posterior and anterior to philosophy and reason, reason itself appearing as a moment in life. I insist on this fact: unity is not here the formal unity of God, Man and the World, which would be produced beneath the gaze that adds something even as it reduces, through the synthetic thought of a philosopher who remains outside the elements. Unity exists in the sense that these terms have for one another, when one is placed within these very elements. The unity is the unity of a life. *The relations between the elements are relations that have been achieved, not specifications of a relation in general.* They are not the specifications of a category. Each relation is irreducible, unique, original. And this is still an example of that deformalization of notions that characterizes the whole of modern philosophy.

The link between God and the World cannot be thought of as a specification of the conjunction 'and'. It is Creation. The conjunction, in the case in point, is Creation. The relation between God and Man, in the same spirit, is Revelation. Between Man and the World (but already to the extent that Man himself is determined by the Revelation and the world by Creation) the relation is redemption.

Rosenzweig therefore takes up theological concepts and re-introduces them into philosophy as ontological categories. The conjunction 'and' is not a formal and empty category. God 'and' Man, for example, is not the union of two terms which we can perceive from outside. God 'and' Man is God for Man, or Man for God. The essential point is played out in this 'for', in which both God and Man live, not in this 'and', which is visible to the philosophers. Or, more exactly, the conjunction 'and' designates an attitude of junction, which is experienced in diverse ways, not the conjuncture that is statable by a third party.

As parts of the World, Man and the World entertain with God the relation of creature to Creator. The World is not self-sufficient, it is not its own reason, as the idealists maintain. It is no longer an idea, it refers to an origin, a past; and that is what creates the whole weight of reality, for Rosenzweig. If it distinguishes itself from an image, an unreal plastic world, if it is a real world, it is precisely by reference to Creation, to the absolute past of Creation. The Creation and the knowledge that Man has do not transform him into nothingness, as in certain forms of modern philosophy; on the contrary, they transform him into a being sure of its being. Creation is by no means the limitation of being, but its basis. This is the very opposite of Heideggerian *Geworfenheit*.

Let us note finally that the relation between God and the World is achieved as something that has always already come to pass. If the relation between the elements God, World and Man is constituted as time, this time is inseparable from the concrete event articulating it, from the qualification of the 'and'. It is because of Creation that time has the dimension of the past and not the other way round. Here there is something very similar to the Heideggerian theory of the 'ecstasies' of time.

God loves Man as an ipseity. Everything He is in His relation with Man is this love. And God can love Man only as a singularity. This love-relation running from God to singular Man is what Rosenzweig calls Revelation. It is not that there is love first and then Revelation, or Revelation first and then love. Revelation *is* this love.

Here, Rosenzweig, whose analysis is exactly similar to phenomenological analyses, stressed heavily that the relation is never

thought through, but realized. It results not in a system, but in a
life.

Finally, it is curious to note what is produced in response to this
love of God and how the Revelation is prolonged. The love of God
for ipseity is, *ipso facto*, a commandment to love. Rosenzweig
thinks that one can command love. Love is commanded, contrary to
what Kant thought. One can command love, but it is love that
commands love, and it commands it in the *now* of its love, in such a
way that the commandment to love is repeated and renewed
indefinitely in the repetition and renewal of the very love that
commands love.

Consequently, Judaism – in which the Revelation is, as you
know, inseparable from the commandment – does not in any way
signify the yoke of the Law, but signifies precisely love. The fact
that Judaism is woven from commandments attests to the renewal,
at every moment, of the love of God for Man, without which the
love commanded in the commandments could not have been
commanded. It therefore transpires that the eminent role of the
Mitzvah in Judaism signifies not a moral formalism, but the living
presence of divine love that is eternally renewed. And consequently,
through the commandment, it signifies the experience of an eternal
present.

The whole of Jewish Law is commanded *today*, even though
Mount Sinai belongs to the past. This reminds us precisely of
this week's sabbatical section (Nitzavim). Whatever it means to
Judaism, God's relation with man – the Revelation – is the very
present, the production of what Heidegger was to call 'the ecstasy
of the present'. The present exists only because there is Revelation.

But the response to the love of God, the response to the
Revelation, cannot be effected in an act that simply goes in an
opposite direction, but on the same route opened up by the love of
God for Man; the response to the love of God for Man is the love of
my neighbour. Through this, the Revelation is already the Revelation of Redemption. It is directed towards the future of the
Kingdom of God, and achieves it.

The future is consequently revealed in the present itself, since the
love of God for Man is the fact that Man loves his neighbour and
consequently prepares for the Kingdom of God. In this Revelation
therefore lies the future of Redemption. The future is not, for
Rosenzweig, a formal and abstract notion. One might say that the
dimension of the future indicates, for him, a relation with Redemption
or with Eternity. Eternity, in turn, is not the disappearance of the

'singular' into its general idea, but the possibility for every creature to say 'we' – or, more exactly, as Rosenzweig put it, it is 'the fact that the *me* learns to say *you* to a *him*'.

All the same, if the Revelation is the Revelation of Redemption, it is not that Revelation *announces* to man that he will be redeemed. The Revelation *provokes* Redemption. The Revelation of God to Man, which is the love of God for Man, provokes Man's response. Man's response to God's love is the love of one's neighbour. God's Revelation therefore begins the work of Redemption which is none the less Man's own work. Here we have a Jewish moment in the work of Rosenzweig: Redemption is the work of Man. Man is the intermediary necessary to the Redemption of the World. But for that to happen, this love must also be *enlightened* by a collective experience.

We cannot follow here the analyses that lead Rosenzweig to the existence of the religious collectivity as demanded by the work of Redemption. In them he successfully moves from a position that had been until then philosophical to a religious position, and the great revealed religions enter into the sphere of his meditation. Let us retain their theme: the web of reality is religious history. It commands political history. That is Rosenzweig's anti-Hegelian position.

Be that as it may, the relation between the elements God, World and Man is not only past and present, it is also future, a future that is deformalized, the future of Eternity. The philosophers will perhaps be interested in this deformalization of the notions of the present, the past and the future, which are inseparable from the ontological events whose ultimate meaning they formally represent, and in which one can see, as I was saying before, an enterprise similar to the famous Heideggerian theory of the 'ecstasies of time'.

What interests Rosenzweig himself is the discovery of being as life, of being as life-in-relation: the discovery of a thought which is the very life of this being. The person no longer goes back into the system he conceives, as in Hegel, in order to become fixed and renounce his singularity. Singularity is necessary to the exercise of this thought and this life precisely as an irreplaceable singularity, the only one capable of love, the only one that can be loved, that knows how to love, that can form a religious community.

In this way we have described the first movement in Rosenzweig's thought: the passage from idealist philosophy to religion, to the love that is religion, to the religion that is the very essence of being. Initially, it concerns religion in general; we still see neither Christianity or Judaism, but we already see the role of religious communities. Two typically Jewish elements have appeared: the idea of the commandment, as something essential to the love-relation; love is manifested in the commandment, it is alone in being able to command love; the idea of Man the redeemer and not of God the Redeemer. Although Redemption begins with God, it absolutely requires Man's intermediary role.

The second movement is the passage from religion to Judaism.

In order for love to be able to penetrate the World, which is Redemption, in order for Time to move to Eternity, Love must not remain at the state of individual enterprise, it must become the work of community, the time of a community. One must be able to say, from now on, 'We'. Christianity and Judaism – (Christianity is, moreover, the only pastoral religion besides Judaism which, according to Rosenzweig, concretely completes religion in the ontological sense of the term, which we have just described; he is severe on Islam, a founded religion) – Christianity and Judaism emerge in history not as contingent events, but as the very entry of Eternity into Time. Judaism is experienced as already being eternal life. The Eternity of the Christian is experienced as a march, a way. The Christian Church is essentially a mission. From the Incarnation to Parousia, Christianity crosses the world and transforms pagan society into Christian society. It is an eternal way, for it is not of this world either. It is suspended between the coming of Christ and his return above the concrete events, all of which the Church can indiscriminately incorporate and penetrate. It therefore lies outside history, but it can incorporate the whole of history. The world is transparent for it.

The Christian bears his Christian essense above his natural essence. He is always a convert struggling with nature. And the permanent character of this superimposing of Christianity on nature finds its expression in the dogma of original sin.

The Jewish community, on the other hand, is a community that bears Eternity in its very *nature*. It does not derive its being from a land, or a tongue, or a legislation subject to renewal and revolution. Its land is 'holy' and a term of nostalgia, its tongue is sacred and is not spoken. Its Law is holy and is not a temporary legislation, created at the time for the purposes of political mastery. But the Jew *is born* a Jew and is confident in the eternal life whose certainty he sees through the blood ties linking him to his ancestors and his descendants. Rosenzweig uses the dangerous term of an eternity of blood, which we must not take in the racist sense, for at no moment

193

does this term signify a naturalist concept, justifying a technique of racial discrimination; on the contrary, it signifies a strangeness throughout the course of history, a rootedness within oneself.

The Jews are strangers to the history that has no hold on them. They are also indifferent to it. The Jewish community already has Eternity. The Jew has already arrived. He has no need of State. He has no need of land, he has no need of laws, to be sure of his permanence within being. Nothing comes to him from outside. The State known by those who are open to Christianity seizes hold of people in evolution, and imposes its Law on them by violence. It lives only through wars and revolutions, in contrast to the true Eternity of the Jewish people, which experiences this Eternity through its immutable law and through mystical time, which is the very way in which Eternity manifests itself in time.

This experience is produced through the ritual life, which consequently takes on an ontological importance. The experience of the Jewish year is not 'subjective' but a new contradiction of time, seized upon by Eternity, the very anticipation of Eternity. The Jewish year repeats, on the different feasts, the different moments of the Cosmic Day – morning, noon, evening – Creation, Revelation, Redemption. It is an experience of time which, for Rosenzweig, is as fundamental as that of clocks or political history and should not be interpreted in terms of the latter. We must turn to the extremely beautiful and incisive analysis of 'The Jewish Ritual Life' made by Rosenzweig, translated in a special edition of the *Table Ronde*, a translation of an English translation which is therefore not up to the standard of the original.

Religion – the essence of being – must necessarily, according to Rosenzweig, manifest itself through Judaism and Christianity, and must necessarily pass through both. The truth of being is structured in such a way that the partial truth of Christianity presupposes the partial truth of Judaism, but each religion must be expressed in all its integrity as an absolute, and their dialogue cannot, short of falsifying absolute truth, surpass within men the essential separation of dialogue. The Jew must therefore remain a Jew, from the Christian point of view itself. And this is why Rosenzweig, on the point of converting, writes to the friend awaiting the good news: 'It is impossible and it is no longer necessary.' Rosenzweig's homage to Christianity is rendered through Rosenzweig the Jew's perseverance in Judaism. What now begins is the Jewish life of Rosenzweig.

Rosenzweig is one of the rare Jewish philosophers who has not only acknowledged Christianity's fundamental place in the spiritual evolution of humanity, but acknowledged it by refusing to become a Christian. To love the authentic Jewish life is to bear witness to absolute truth. 'Human truth is always my truth.' The truth, in which Judaism and Christianity are united, lies in God. The way in which Man possesses the truth does not consist in contemplating it in God, but in verifying it through his life. *Human truth, both Christian and Jewish, is verification.* It consists in risking one's life by living it in reply to the Revelation – that is to say, in reply to the Love of God. But Man can reply only by way of the eternal life, as a Jew, or the eternal path, as a Christian. The two ways are necessary. There are only two ways. Either religion must authentically live only its own way. *Human truth is a testimony offered by a life* of the divine truth of the end of time. Rosenzweig calls this theory of truth the 'theory of messianic knowledge'.

Once more, the love of God for Man, which provokes the love of Man for his neighbour, is Revelation – that is to say, a manifestation of the truth. The knowledge of this truth through Man is his redemptive love. But love is possible only for a unique – that is to say, mortal – being. It is as a mortal, precisely, that he participates in God's Eternity. 'The fact that each moment may be the last is precisely the thing that makes him eternal.'

Love stronger than death is the biblical formula that Rosenzweig takes up in order to reply to the law of death, on to which his book opens, a book which leads to life.

What sort of life emerges from such a book? You will perhaps be surprised by the apparent modesty of this life. Rosenzweig founds a hostel in Frankfurt and sets himself up there. He gives up a university career. The work to be undertaken comes down to bearing witness, as a Jew, to the truth, to remaining in the eternal life, to guaranteeing the maintenance of the Jewish community. Rosenzweig founds a house for Jewish studies at Frankfurt. It is a question of returning to the sources and relearning Hebrew, the Hebrew of which one knew only, in polite Judaeo-German society, that it was, to use the vivid expression coined by Dr Richard Koch, Rosenzweig's doctor, 'the original form of the bad German accent'. This house of study posed the problem of good lecturers and good students, and that could not be taken for granted in the middle-class society of Frankfurt; at least from the moment when Rosenzweig fell ill. For this life suddenly takes a fatal turn. If there are doctors in this room, they will be able to measure the gravity of the illness that struck Rosenzweig: at the age of thirty-four he contracted

amyotrophic lateral sclerosis with progressibe bulbarous paralysis –
a terrible illness, which quickly overcame him. Rosenzweig lived on
for eight years with this illness, but he very quickly became
immobilized and deprived of speech. To enable him to communicate and even to write, a special apparatus was constructed that
allowed him to indicate with a barely perceptible sign, which only
his wife could see, the letters that translated his thought.

It is precisely during this period that he undertakes to translate
the poems of Jehouda Halévy and, in collaboration with Buber, the
Bible, as well as to write several articles later collected in a special
volume.

His house becomes an open, welcoming Jewish house, but also a
house in which all the ritual prescriptions are gradually adopted and
take on their life and meaning once more. Numerous old and new
friends guarantee a link between this immured man and the world.
The state of strict orthodoxy which Rosenzweig had gradualy
reached remained liberal in essence. Professor Ernest Simon, a close
friend of Rosenzweig, bears witness to this in a volume devoted to
Rosenzweig published in Germany, to mark the first anniversary of
his death. Rosenzweig was liberal in his conception of the Scriptures. He did not believe, as does orthodoxy, in the Mosaic nature
of the Pentateuch, and admitted that there were problems in biblical
criticism. But he thought that his critique did not throw into
question the authenticity of the Jewish message, and the famous
R. by which the critics designate the presumed author of each
sacred text was read by him as the initial of the name Rabenou, our
master. Whatever the origin of these texts, they are authentic by
virtue of their internal significance. The convergence of these
supposedly disparate texts is surely more miraculous than their
Sinaic origin.

Rosenzweig was liberal in the practical sense. He said that it was
impossible to distinguish between what is divine in ritual, and what
is human. But he added that in spite of the explanation, from the
point of view of their work, given of them by sociologists and
ethnographers, the rituals, for whoever practises them, possess an
incommunicable truth – though this is no less true than sociological
truths. The integral nature of the tradition, which seemed to him
necessary for a Jewish life and offered an anticipation of Eternity,
was not something he demanded of each Jew in particular. He
demanded it of the whole of Israel, rather than Mr Israel. The
individual could choose what tradition was to contribute. Only,
according to Ernest Simon, Rosenzweig chose everything. He was

orthodox by way of liberalism. In the matter of liberalism, everything depends on the person choosing.

What can we say about the person of Rosenzweig during this period of maturity? Here is the testimony of his doctor, Richard Koch:

> Despite his fine culture and very penetrating thought, he was the first man I ever heard speak without embarrassment of God and his unity, and of the destiny of man. Yet he spoke without naivety and it is precisely that which raised him above the others. For me, he was also the first Jew to overcome all the ghetto 'complexes'. His Judaism was not gloomy, nor unsettling, nor the effect of some peculiar form of piety. This Judaism was free and virile, reassuring and beautiful. There was no special problematical nature that elsewhere constitutes the heart of every profession of Jewish faith.

Thus it is true that Judaism can be defined by a supreme quietude, even though it is defined for many modern people by heartbreak and anxiety. What, on the basis of the conception Rosenzweig offers of Judaism, is the position of the Jew in the City? The Jew is eternal, the Jew does not enter the world like other humans. How, concretely, can one live this separate life? It is up to each and every one to find his own solution! Rosenzweig does not envisage any comfortable path for the fulfilment of the Jewish destiny. 'The degree to which the Jew participates in the life of the peoples depends not on him, but on those peoples', he writes in a letter.

> For the individual, it is in large measure a question of tact and conscience. For my part, with regard to the State, I took a comfortable attitude to its legalist duties: I present no thesis for teaching in a university; I did not volunteer to take part in the war, but joined the International Red Brigade, which I left as soon as possible, once my class was recalled, since the State would have claimed me anyway, if I hadn't signed up for the Red Cross. As regards German culture, my attitude is one of profound gratitude. (*Letters*, pp. 692–3)

In the same letter he writes:

> It is inevitable that passively we participate in some way or another in the life of the peoples, in order for us to live at all ... and we do so not so much through appetite as through a duty to live. ... But alongside this life, which is external to morality, in the profound sense of the term, alongside this life which is turned outwards, there is a Jewish life that is turned inwards, towards everything that serves to maintain the people and its life: these forms of life do not slot in beside the visible forms of the world; but this maintenance of Jewish originality and interiority is the supreme action of the Jew in the ecumeny of the world.

A Jewish particularism? Rest assured: for Rosenzweig, Zionist nationalism no more attains the heights of this metaphysical particularism than does assimilation into the historical nations. But I am not going to speak about Zionism.

I should like to conclude now by showing you in what way the Rosenzweig phenomenon and Rosenzweig's thought are topical – not in the sense in which events are topical, but in the sense in which questions of life and death are topical; questions that the Jew has put to him and which are merely masked by events.

I have not tried to give a general philosophical exposé, despite the slightly difficult part of this talk. It was necessary in order to show that we can find in Rosenzweig, or on the basis of him seek, a reply to a major question: does Judaism still exist? This morning I had the impression, in spite of the keen interest with which I listened to the papers, that the great stumbling block Judaism encounters today has not been evoked. No Jew today can ignore that what is put in question by events and ideas is the very fact that he is a Jew.

Why? I do not believe that it is political and religious forces that are hostile to us. I said a short time ago that if Christianity is accepted by Rosenzweig it is because, basically, it is no longer capable of putting our Jewish existence in question.

This morning, moreover, we saw clearly that the revival of Christianity – the so-called revival of Christianity – looks like an encouragement to the Jews. It is not therefore Christianity that henceforth is going to threaten our existence, nor atheism, nor science, nor even the philosophical science which, at a certain moment, seemed to compromise the authenticity of the fundamental texts. Rather it is the childhood crisis, the childhood illness, the adolescent illness which was contracted in the course of a contact that was too frivolous and imprudent. To be or not to be, that is the question that comes at us today from a certain conception of history that contests Judaism's oldest claim. The disappearance of this charm in the Jewish mind would be tantamount to the end of Judaism.

This most ancient of claims is its claim to a separate existence in the political history of the world. It is the claim to judge history – that is to say, to remain free with regard to events, whatever the internal logic binding them. It is the claim to be an eternal people.

This eternity of Israel is not the inexplicable miracle of a survival. It is not because it miraculously survived that it assumed a freedom in the face of history. It is because, from the beginning, it managed to deny the jurisdiction of events which it maintained in itself as the unity of a consciousness throughout history.

Such is the ancient claim without which Judaism cannot even return to the status of a nation among nations, because it is too strongly bound to the great nations of the world and too mature, even among the popular levels of its society, to be sincere about wanting to create a new Luxembourg, or a new Libya, or a new Canaan. The thing that attacks this claim to be an eternal people is the exaltation of the judgement of history, as the ultimate jurisdiction of every being, and the affirmation that history is the measure of all things. The judgement passed by a conscience on events that succeed, that have an efficacity, an objective visibility, would, you know, according to the exaltation of history, be merely a subjective illusion that vanishes like smoke in the face of the judgement of history.

For this conception, there is no eternal people liable to live free in the face of history. Every people is part of history, bears within it its determined essence, and contributes in its way to the universal work that incorporates and surpasses it – into which, consequently, it is finally absorbed and disappears. What would be eternal is the universal history itself which inherits the heritage of dead peoples.

The particularity of a people is identical to its finitude. It is Hegelian logic that presides over this announcement of disappearance. The particularity of a thing has significance in fact only in relation to a whole; and from that point on, in the name of Hegelian logic, the necessary disappearance of a people is announced, for everything that is finished must finish.

The famous independence of the Jews in the face of history is equally presented as a subjective illusion. The Jewish people, we are told, in order to survive throughout history, has well and truly accepted the historical conditions of existence; the laws of economy have not been able to be invoked because the people believed it had a separate existence. The industrial society that is heralded, and in which all of humanity is going to be found, will incorporate the Jewish people. To believe that one is a separate reality would therefore be a subjective belief, and its purely subjective significance is denounced at the very moment at which the real curve of events is drawn.

This prestige enjoyed by history is experienced by each one of us in our preoccupation with not finding ourselves opposed to the meaning and direction [*sens*] of history, which ultimately comes down to demanding that events give our lives meaning and direction. Philosophy, as it is summed up and crowned by Hegel, would precisely end up by integrating the individual and collective wills to the extent that they are real – that is to say, effective – into a reasonably structured totality, in which these living totalities are represented by their works, but in which these works derive their true – that is to say visible – significance not from the subjective intentions of their authors but from the totality, the only one to have a real meaning [*sens*] and to be able to confer it. The intentions of the authors and, consequently, everything that – to return to Judaism – the Jews think themselves, the whole of our *Aggadah* and *Halakhah*, would be just an old wives' tale, a theme for a sociology or psychoanalysis of Judaism. Judaism would not be true in what it wished, but in the place where the universal history would have left it. To wish to be a Jew today is therefore, before believing in Moses and the prophets, to have the right to think that the significance of a work is truer in terms of the will that wished it into being than the totality into which it is inserted; and, even more brutally, that will in one's personal and subjective life is not a dream whose death will allow us to draw an inventory of the work and the truth, but that the living willing of will is indispensable to the truth and understanding of the work.

This is, in effect, the meaning of Rosenzweig's contribution – a fracturing of the totality through which his work began – the substitution of legislation for the totalizing thought of philosophers and industrial society, for attitudes to life that are a series of structures of the absolute.

There is yet another way for history to put in question the existence of the Jewish people. Alongside its Hegelian and Marxist interpretation, in which it appears to be ineluctably directed towards a goal, there is an interpretation which offers to go nowhere: all civilizations would be equal. Modern atheism is not the negation of God, it is the absolute indifferentism of *Tristes Tropiques*. I think that this is the most atheist book that has been written in our day, the most absolutely disorientated and disorientating book. It threatens Judaism as much as does the Hegelian and sociological vision of history. The threat, of course, touches only the consciousnesses it can trouble, Mr Israel rather than all of Israel. But in France, Mr Israel's Judaism is troubled by three Jews, three great works: Eric Weil, Raymond Aron and Lévi-Strauss.

Whatever one thinks of Rosenzweig's analysis of the Jewish conscience, the Jewish year, it allows us, in the very name of philosophy, to resist so-called historical necessity. What Rosenzweig teaches us is the notion that the ritual year and the awareness of the way its circularity anticipates Eternity is not only an experience that is as valuable as the time of history and universal history, but 'anterior' in *truth* to that time, and that the defiance shown to history can be as real as that of history; that the particularity of a people can be distinguished from the singularity of a perishable thing; that it can be the reference point of the absolute. Whatever you think of his reply, he raises the question that is the first question a Jew today should raise.

The idea that a Jewish people is an eternal people, defended by Rosenzweig with so much pathos, is the intimate experience of Judaism. The *Midrash* attests to this in a more calm and serene way, and perhaps provides its ultimate meaning. Banished from the house of Abraham, Hagar and Ishmael wander in the desert. Their water supply has run dry. God opens Hagar's eyes; she spots a well and gives water to her dying son. The angels protest to God: are You going to quench the thirst of someone who later will make Israel suffer? What does the end of History matter? says the Lord. I judge each person for what he is, not for what he will become. The eternity of the Jewish people is not the pride of a nationalism exacerbated by persecution. Independence in the face of history affirms the right possessed by human consciousness to judge a world that is ripe at every moment for judgement, before the end of history and independently of this end – that is to say, a world peopled by persons.

Judaeo–Christian Friendship

The totally improvised exchange of ideas which we had with Jacques Madaule during the fourth Colloquium of French-speaking Jewish Intellectuals for me marked the essential moment. Do not think that I am being merely polite in making this declaration: for a long time I have known and admired the intellectual daring of Jacques Madaule. But we had not really spoken before now. What he said to me during the Colloquium is worth repeating to you here. For Madaule, the Jews who wait for the messianic age do not wait in vain, as so many Christians still believe, for an event that has been coming now for more than twenty centuries. The Jewish waiting for the Messiah makes complete sense to the Christian waiting for the return of his Saviour, for Parousia. It is not, therefore, finished, even for a Christian. And Jews are necessary to the future of a humanity which, knowing it has been saved, has nothing more to wait for. The presence of the Jews reminds conformists of every kind that everything is not for the best in the best of all possible worlds.

Until this point, friendship between Jews and Christians seemed to be based on their both belonging to humanity, the modern world, the West. Of course, from the Jewish point of view, Christianity was justified: it brought monotheism to the Gentiles. But what, then, was Judaism in Christian eyes? A prophecy that outlived its fulfilment. The testimony incarnate of a failure. A blindfolded virgin. A residue. A remnant. An anachronism. A fossil. A relic. An exhibit. But now Madaule shows Christians that we are significant to the future and to life. This significance can transform the very meaning of Judaeo–Christian relations.

But Madaule also told us of the appeal to which his thought responded: Léon Algazi wanted his Christian friends to go beyond respect for Jews and one day come to respect Judaism itself. The unforgettable demand of a complete Jew is answered by the total acknowledgement of a Christian. Like Algazi, like Madaule!

V
DISTANCES

Let my lord pass on before his servant, and I will lead on slowly.
(Genesis 33:14)

Freedom of Speech

So Khrushchev has disowned the report on Stalin published in the press last year, which universal opinion had attributed to him, and which up until then he had never denied.

This text, relating many things that had been guessed, suspected or known, none the less left an invincible impression of strangeness. This was perhaps due to the way in which the facts denounced compromised the sincerity of the very words that, even as they condemned them, also prolonged them. Never again was this extreme situation, constructed by logicians, in an abstract sense, to be so fully incarnated in historical reality. The immensity of the reality that occurred – its haunting and central presence in man's thought – finally stripped heady intellectualism of all precious nuance. The uninterrupted growth of the Communist Party, its conquest of the world, which was more rapid than the spread of Christianity or Islam, its catholic range, the faith, heroism and purity of its youth, its attachment, on the level of theory, to the great humanist ideals which it ultimately claimed for itself – without ever attempting, like fascism, to pull off the philosophical masquerade of disguising good as evil and evil as good – have accustomed us to hearing in this movement the very footsteps of Destiny.

This myth created a cloud that enveloped and uplifted the brain, making it possible to see this irresistible progression clearly. Contradictions lost all sense of absurdity. Unbelievers, clear thinkers and scoffers became indignant and 'judged from on high' and laughed – albeit often with little self-confidence. And as a result, a religion lost both its mysteries and its infallibility. The revolutionary movement returned to the nature and human scale of things after thirty years of mythological grandeur. The struggle, which until then had been epic, was henceforth exposed to strategic and tactical uncertainty. Spiritual risks and perils were surely replacing the simple soul's conviction in the militant's heart.

Meanwhile those not involved – who, at least in Europe, felt ill at ease like people who, in the train of history, sit with their backs to the engine – surely felt they had their chance one more. The message for them was that history has no meaning. Those who held the key to its final enigma wandered about like uninitiated lost souls. Totality broke out. But already a vaster totality, which was destined to absorb even these shocks, was being heralded. The rehabilitation of the victims of Stalinism remained as strange as the Moscow or Prague show-trials which had condemned them. The quarrel and eventual reconciliation with Tito seemed of the same order of events. Togliatti, engaged in polemic with the Soviet heads of state, was as eerie as the forest at Dunsinane marching towards Macbeth and chilling his blood. Khrushchev's denial and the events that filled the rest of the year were to annul the breakdown in the system.

The most troubling circumstance of de-Stalinization is the way in which the language it revives at the level of collective experience is totally discredited. We can no longer believe in words, for we can no longer speak. It is not that freedom of speech still remains out of reach for most of the world, or that men use words to tell lies. We can no longer speak, because no one can begin his discourse without immediately bearing witness to something other than what is said. Psychoanalysis and sociology lie in wait for the speaker. Words are symptoms or superstructures, such that conscious cries and gestures form part of the nightmare they had to interrupt.

The famous and lucid Western consciousness is no more certain of remaining awake. Its doubts about the reality of the images it contemplates do not give it the power to escape from fiction. This doubt insinuates itself into its dreams and offers it neither the light nor the contours of true things. I think and perhaps I *am* not. Mystification is denounced, but in a new mystification, and the negation of negation is not an affirmation. One dream fits into another and is narrated to the characters of the second dream, which dissipates the first. As in Gogol's *Gamblers*, a work that is already truly Kafkaesque, all cards are marked, all the servants are bribed and every attempt to cut the knot of an inextricably tangled web serves only to reknot a horribly continuous thread. Through a thousand cracks, falsehood seeps into a world that cannot recover its self-control. In the inn, the swindlers have conned an arrant swindler by pretending to open play in an open way. Surpassing one falsehood does not mean that we enter the realm of truth, but that we lie beyond the previously established limits. There is always someone slicker than you!

We are powerless to break out of this infinity of falsehood. Political totalitarianism rests on an ontological totalitarianism.

Being is all, a Being in which nothing finishes and nothing begins. Nothing stands opposed to it, and no one judges it. It is an anonymous neuter, an impersonal universe, a universe without language. We can no longer speak, for how can we guarantee the value of a proposition, if not by offering another proposition which, however, no one can answer for?

In this world without speech, we recognize the West. From Socrates to Hegel, it moved towards the ideal of language, in which the word counts only because of the eternal order which it manages to bring to consciousness. At the end-point of this itinerary, the speaking man feels part of a discourse that speaks itself. The meaning of language no longer depends on the intentions placed on it, but on a coherent Discourse to which the speaker merely lends his tongue and lips. Not only Marxism, but the whole of sociology and psychoanalysis bear witness to a language whose principal feature lies not in what words teach us, but in what they hide from us. We have a closed language, and a civilization composed of aphasiacs. Words have once more become the mute signs of anonymous infrastructures, like the implements of dead civilizations or the abortive acts of our daily lives. By being coherent, speech has lost its speech. From this point on, there is no longer any word that has the authority necessary to announce to the world the end of its own decline.

The only believable word is the one that can lift itself out of its eternal contest and return to the human lips that speak it, in order to fly from man to man and judge history, instead of remaining a symptom or an effect or a ruse. This is the word of a discourse that begins *absolutely* in the person in possession of it, and moves towards another who is *absolutely* separate. It is a masterful word that Europe can no longer hear. It is a word that penetrates to the heart.

And in a precise sense, one that contains not a whiff of saintliness, it is a phophetic word.

Judaism and the Present

On the mean and petty level of day-to-day reality, a human community does not resemble its myth. It responds to a higher vocation, though, through its intellectuals (its elders), who are concerned with *raisons d'être*, and its youth, who are ready to sacrifice themselves for an idea – who are capable, in other words, of extremist ideas. Western Jews between 1945 and 1960 will not have displayed their essence by converting, changing their names, economizing or forging a career for themselves. What they did do was carry on the Resistance, in the absolute sense of the term. A career is not incompatible with a rigorous intellect or a sense of courage, something that is always difficult to display. The young uprooted themselves and went to live in Israel as they had done in Orsay or Aix or Fublaines; or else, in other ways, they accepted whatever inhuman dogmatism promised to free Man. To situate Jews in the present is something that leads us, therefore, into a radical mode of thinking, one whose language is not always a lie. I should like to undertake such an analysis with all the due modesty and prudence dictated by the writing of a mere article on the subject. For, without even this brief study, the position of Judaism, in the latter half of this century, would be further reduced to the interminable question of anti-Semitism.

A religious age or an atomic age – these characterizations of the modern world, whether slogans or imprecations, hide a deeper trend. In spite of the violence and madness we see every day, we live in the age of philosophy. Men are sustained in their activities by the certainty of *being right [avoir raison]*, of being in tune with the calculable forces that really move things along, of moving in the direction [*sens*] of history. That satisfies their conscience. Beyond the progress of science, which uncovers the predictable play of forces within matter, human freedoms themselves (including those thoughts which conceive of such a play) are regulated by a rational order. Hidden in the depths of Being, this order is gradually unveiled and revealed through the disorder of contemporary history, through the suffering and desire of individuals, their passions and their victories. A global industrial society is announced that will suppress every contradiction tormenting humanity. But it equally suppresses the hidden heart of man. Reason rises like a fantastic sun that makes the opacity of creatures transparent. Men have lost their shadows! Henceforth, nothing can absorb or reflect this light which abolishes even the interiority of beings.

This advent of reason as an offshoot of philosophy – and this is what is original about this age – is not the conquest of eternity promised to the *Logos* of ancient wisdom. Reason does not illuminate a thought which detaches itself from events in order to dominate them in a dialogue with a god – the only interlocutor of any work, according to Plato. There is nothing in reality that can be encountered in its wild or pure state; everything has already been formed, transformed or reflected by man, including nature, the sky and the forest. The elements show up on the surface through a civilization, a language, an industry, an art. Intelligibility is read in the mark left on things by the work of mortals, in the perspectives opened up by cities and empires that are doomed to fall. From that point, in the epic or drama of intelligence, man is an actor prior to being a thinker. Reality appears – that is to say, radiates intelligible light – within the history in which each human undertaking takes its place, a work of finite freedoms which, by virtue of being finite, betray their projects even as they carry them out, and do not dominate their work. The individual's destiny consists in playing a role (which has not yet been assigned him) in the drama of reason and not of embracing this drama.

What matters is to be authentic and not at all to be true [*dans le vrai*], to commit oneself rather than to know. Art, love, action are more important than theory. Talent is worth more than wisdom and self-possession. Is it not the case that, a few years ago, a British Jewish intellectual conducted a very successful lecture tour throughout England in which he measured the value of Judaism in terms of the talent and originality of de-Judaicized Jews?

Within the indulgent attitude towards mortality which we call the historical conscience, each of us has to wait for that unique, if perishable, moment in which it falls to our lot to rise to the occasion and recognize the call addressed to us. To respond to the call of the perishable instant! It must not come too late. Such was the case of the Angel who, according to the *Midrash*, had only one song to sing before the Throne of the Lord, at one single moment, which was his and his alone, in the whole of God's eternity. But this Angel, who was an antagonist of Israel, had a bad encounter, and his story took place on the night before the unique instant of his destiny.

In the wake of the Liberation, Jews are grappling with the Angel of Reason who often solicited them and who for two centuries now has refused to let go. Despite the experience of Hitler and the failure of assimilation, *the great vocation in life resounds like the call of a universal and homogeneous society*. We do not have to decide here if the nature of modern life is compatible with respect for the Sabbath and rituals concerning food, or if we should lighten the yoke of the Law. These important questions are put to men who have already chosen Judaism. They choose between orthodoxy and reform depending on their idea of rigour, courage and duty. Some are not necessarily hypocrites, others do not always take the easy way out. But it is really a domestic quarrel.

Jewish consciousness is no longer contained within these questions of choice. Like a house without a *mezuzah*, it exists as an abstract space traversed by the ideas and hopes of the world. Nothing can halt them, for nothing hails them. Interiority's act of withdrawal is undone before their unstoppable force. The Judaism of the Diaspora no longer has an interior. It enters deeply into a world to which it is none the less opposed. Or is it?

For the reason that shines forth from the Angel (or the Seducer) frees Judaism from all particularisms. Visions of ancient, crumbling things trouble our hazy dreams. Surely a greater, virile dream is born in this way. The cheap optimism of the nineteenth century, whose idealism was produced by isolated and ineffectual beings who had little grasp of reality, gives way to a transformation of being that derives its nobility from the attention it pays to reality. It becomes an uncompromising logic that tolerates no exceptions and is universal like a religion. Our age is defined by the major importance which this transformation of things and societies takes on in the eyes of men and the attention that established religions pay to the transformations of life here below. The religious and the profane have perhaps never been so close. So how can one withstand the winds of change which threaten to sweep the Jewish personality away? When Reason tolls the knell for privileged revelations, isn't the sound as seductive as the song of the Sirens? Will Judaism raise the banner against what we tautologically term free thought, and the achievements of the concrete world? Is it not different from the religions it has spawned in that it questions whether personal salvation can be something distinct from the redemption of the visible world? And yet those other religions have every opportunity of doing the same. They offer supernatural truths and sacraments and consolations that no science can dispense. The reason that conquers the world leaves them with an extraterritoriality. Judaism unites men in an ideal of terrestrial justice in which the Messiah represents a promise and a fulfilment. Ethics is its primordial religious emotion. It does not found any church for transethical ends. It insists on distinguishing between 'messianism' and a 'future world'. Every prophet has only ever announced the coming of the messianic age; as for the future world, 'no eye has seen it outside of You; God will bring it to those who wait' (Sanhedrin 99a).

This struggle with the Angel is therefore strange and ambiguous. Isn't the adversary a double? Isn't this wrestling a twisting back on oneself, one that may be either a struggle or an embrace? Even in the most impressive struggle that Israel undertakes for the sake of its personality, even in the building of the State of Israel, even in the prestige it holds for souls everywhere, this sublime ambiguity remains: is one trying to preserve oneself within the modern world, or to drown one's eternity in it?

For what is at stake is Israel's eternity, without which there can be no Israel. The combat is a very real one. The modern reason which transforms the world threatens Judaism to an unparalleled degree, though Judaism has been threatened before. Cosmology and scientific history in their time had compromised the Bible's wisdom, while philololgy had questioned the special character of the Bible itself, dissolved in a sea of texts, pitching and rolling through its infinite undulations. Apologetics chose to reply to these attacks by discussing the arguments put forward. But believers have above all resisted them by interiorizing certain religious truths. Why worry about science's refutation of biblical cosmology, when the Bible contains not cosmology but images necessary to an unshakable internal certainty, figures that speak to the religious soul that already dwells in the absolute? Why worry about philology and history challenging the supposed date and origin of the sacred texts, if these texts are intrinsically rich in value? The sacred sparks of individual revelations have produced the light needed, even if they were thrown up at different points in history. The miracle of their convergence is no less marvellous than the miracle of a unique source. Eternity was rediscovered within the fortress-like inner life which Israel built on an unshakable rock.

At this point, modern thought denounces the eternity of Israel by questioning whether the inner life itself is a site of truth. Truth is henceforth manifested in the development of a society, which is the condition for every idea that arises in an individual brain. Only pipe dreams and ideologies have no social founding. Those elements in the Jewish Revelation open to reason are obtained from economic and social determinism. Those ideas imbued with the force of inner conviction emerge as an impersonal and anonymous destiny that holds men in its grip. Reason just toys with them. They imagine they are thinking for themselves when they are really carrying out its plans. Prophecies are produced by the play of historical forces in the same way as synthetic oil and rubber are manufactured in the laboratory.

This time, the blades of reasonable History erode the very rock of Israel. This is what causes the erosion of the Absolute.

But this eternity of Israel is not the privilege of a nation that is proud or carried away by illusions. It has a function in the economy of being. It is indispensable to the work of reason itself. In a world that has become historical, shouldn't a person be as old as the world? Deprived of any fixed point, the modern world feels frustrated. It invoked reason in order to have justice, and the latter surely needs a stable base, an interiority, or a person, on which to rest. A person is indispensable to justice before being indispensable to himself. Eternity is necessary to a person, and even in our own day it has been sought by the most lucid thinkers. Those who stress commitment [*engagement*] in Sartre's work forget that his main concern is to guarantee disengagement [*dégagement*] in the midst of engagement [*engagement*]. This results in a nihilism that is given its most noble expression – a negation of the supreme commitment which in man's case is his own essence.

But dumping ballast in the face of the problems posed by existence, in order to gain even greater height over reality, leads ultimately to the impossibility of sacrifice – that is to say, to the annihilation of self. Here, Judaism filters into the modern world. It does so by disengaging itself, and it disengages itself by affirming the intangibility of an essence, the fidelity to a law, a rigid moral standard. This is not a return to the status of thing, for such fidelity breaks the facile enchantment of cause and effect and allows it to be judged.

Judaism is a non-coincidence with its time, within coincidence: in the radical sense of the term it is an *anachronism*, the simultaneous presence of a youth that is attentive to reality and impatient to change it, and an old age that has seen it all and is returning to the origin of things. The desire to conform to one's time is not the supreme imperative for a human, but is already a characteristic expression of modernism itself; it involves renouncing interiority and truth, resigning oneself to death and, in base souls, being satisfied with *jouissance*. Monotheism and its moral revelation constitute the concrete fulfilment, beyond all mythology, of the primordial anachronism of the human.

It lies deeper than history, neither receiving its meaning from the latter, nor becoming its prey. This is why it does not seek its liberation with respect to time, where time has the status of dead civilizations such as ancient Greece or Rome. Even in the grave, these do not escape the influence of events. When he lay dying, Rabbi Jose b. Kisma said to his disciples: 'Place my coffin deep (in the earth), for there is not one palm-tree in Babylon to which a Persian horse will not be tethered, nor one coffin in Palestine out of which a Median horse will not eat straw.'

Judaism, disdaining this false eternity, has always wished to be a simultaneous engagement and disengagement. The most deeply committed [*engagé*] man, one who can never be silent, the prophet, is also the most separate being, and the person least capable of becoming an institution. Only the false prophet has an official function. The *midrash* likes to recount how Samuel refused every invitation he received in the course of his travels throughout Israel. He carried his own tent and utensils with him. And the Bible pushes this idea of independence, even in the economic sense, to the point of imagining the prophet Eli being fed by crows.

But this essential content, which history cannot touch, cannot be learned like a catechism or summarized like a credo. Nor is it restricted to the negative and formal statement of a categorical imperative. It cannot be replaced by Kantianism, nor, to an even lesser degree, can it be obtained from some particular privilege or racial miracle. It is acquired through a way of living that is a ritual and a heartfelt generosity, wherein a human fraternity and an attention to the present are reconciled with an eternal distance in relation to the contemporary world. It is an asceticism, like the training of a fighter. It is acquired and held, finally, in the particular type of intellectual life known as the study of the Torah, that permanent revision and updating of the content of the Revelation where every situation within the human adventure can be judged. And it is here precisely that the Revelation is to be found: the die is not cast, the prophets or wise men of the Talmud know nothing about antibiotics or nuclear energy; but the categories needed to understand these novelties are already available to monotheism. It is the eternal anteriority of wisdom with respect to science and history. Without it, success would equal reason and reason would be merely the necessity of living in one's own time. Does this sovereign refusal of fashion and success come from the monks who render unto Caesar the things that are Caesar's? Or from the Left who dare not carry through their political thought to its logical extremes, but are seized with an attack of vertigo and grind to a senseless halt at the edge of their own conclusions?

It is not messianism that is lacking in a humanity which is quick to hope and to recognize its hopes in everything that promises, builds and brings victory and presents itself as the fulfilment of a dream. Seen in this light, every nationalism carries a messianic message and every nation is chosen. Monotheism has not only a horror of idols, but a nose for false prophecy. A special patience – Judaism – is required to refuse all premature messianic claims.

These young people, who are eager to behave reasonably and turn their backs on Judaism because like a waking dream, it does not offer them sufficient enlightenment concerning contemporary problems, that 'vast reality taking place outside Judaism', forget that the strength needed to resist the importance that high society places on itself is the privilege of Judaism and the absolutely pure teaching that it offers man; they forget that the Revelation offers clarification but not a formula; they forget that commitment alone – commitment at any price, headlong commitment that burns its bridges behind it, even the commitment that ought to permit withdrawal into the self – is no less inhuman than the disengagement dictated by the desire to be comfortable which ossifies a society that has transformed the difficult task of Judaism into a mere confession, an accessory of bourgeois comfort.

No doubt the advocates of commitment resemble those disciples of Rabbi Jose b. Kisma who asked the Master: 'When will the Master come?' They were already probably denouncing the sterility of Halakhah-style discussions, which remain aloof from the burning issues of messianism, of the meaning and end of history. Rabbi Jose shied away from the question: 'I fear lest ye demand a sign of me.' The disciples will continue to find the Master's wisdom too general and abstract. Already they are thinking that the messianic age is heralded by the events of history as the fruit is by the seed, and that the blossoming of deliverance is as predictable as the harvest of ripe plums. Will the Master speak?

The disciples will not ask for a sign. Rabbi Jose then speaks of the periodic structure of history, the alternating periods of greatness and decline from which the messianic age will ensue neither logically nor dialectically, but will enter from the outside: 'When this gate falls down, is rebuilt, falls again, and is again rebuilt, and then falls a third time, before it can be rebuilt the son of David will come.'

Does the Master perhaps bury himself in generalities in order to evade the issues? History is separated off from its achievements, as is politics from morality. The rigorous chain of events offers no guarantee of a happy outcome. No sign is inscribed here. So be it. But can the Master withhold the signs necessary to those who reject the good if false news, and from which the Jew would derive the strength of his rejection, and the certainty of his *raison d'être*, in a world crossed by currents of energy and life in which he is nothing, overflowing with joyful waters which rise from the depths of the elements and joyously sweep up the builders of states, regimes and churches? A *No* demands a criterion. Rabbi Jose gives the required sign: '"let the waters of the grotto of Paneas turn into blood"; and they turned into blood'.

Paneas, the source of the Jordan, and one of the three legendary sources that remained open at the end of the Flood. The waters from all the ends of history and from every nationalism (even the Jewish one) gushing forth like the irrepressible force of nature, the waters of every baptism and every effacement, the waters of every messianism! Those men who can see cannot turn their gaze from the innocent blood which these waters dilute.

The State of Israel and the Religion of Israel

The idea that Israel has a religious privilege is one that ultimately exasperates everyone. Some see it as an unjustifiable pride, while to others it looks like an intolerable mystification which, in the name of a sublime destiny, robs us of earthly joys. To live like every other people on earth, with police and cinemas and cafés and newspapers – what a glorious destiny! Despite being scarcely established on our own land we are happy to emulate all the 'modern nations' and have our own little problem of the relationship between State and Church to resolve.

The satisfaction we can experience when, like a tourist, we can see a Jewish uniform or a Jewish stamp, is certainly one of our lesser delights. But it is difficult to resist. It imposes itself by way of contrast. It reveals both the obsessions of the traditional Jewish ideal and everything that is phoney about its by now literary perfection. It also reveals the prestige that men, whether or not they are Jews, attach today to anything bearing the stamp of the State.

The point is not that people are free to denounce such idolatry. We need to reflect on the nature of the modern State. The State is not an idol because it precisely permits full self-consciousness. Human will is derisory. It wishes to be of value but cannot evaluate the universe it repulses. The sovereignty of the State incorporates the universe. In the sovereign State, the citizen may finally exercise a will. It acts absolutely. Leisure, security, democracy: these mark the return of a condition, the beginning of a free being.

This is why man recognizes his spiritual nature in the dignity he achieves as a citizen or, even more so, when acting in the service of the State. The State represents the highest human achievement in the lives of Western peoples. The coincidence of the political and the spiritual marks man's maturity, for spiritual life, like political life, purges itself of all the private, individual, sentimental chiaroscuro on which religions still nurture themselves. Elevation to the spiritual no longer equals possession by the Sacred. A spiritual life with no sacred dimension! Only a superficial analysis could claim that when men forget God, they are merely changing gods. The decline of Church-constituted religions is an undeniable historical phenomenon. It stems not from man's mendacity but from the advent of states. When set against the universality of the political order, the religious order inevitably taken on a disordered or clerical air. Modern humanist man is a man in a State. Such a man is not merely vulgar; he is religion's true antagonist within the State of Israel itself.

But is it enough to restore the State of Israel in order to have a political life? And even if it were a life of the spirit, could it contain Judaism? A small state – what a contradiction! Could its sovereignty, which, like the light of satellites, is merely borrowed, ever raise the soul to a state of full self-possesion? It is obvious that Israel asserts itself in a different way.

Like an empire on which the sun never sets, a religious history extends the size of its modest territory, even to the point where it absorbs a breathtaking past. But, contrary to national histories, this past, like an ancient civilization, places itself above nations, like a fixed star. And yet we are the living ladder that reaches up to the sky. Doesn't Israel's particular past consist in something both eternal and ours? This peculiar right, revealed by an undeniable Jewish experience, to call our own a doctrine that is none the less offered to everyone, marks the true sovereignty of Israel. It is not its political genius nor its artistic genius nor even its scientific genius (despite all they promise) that forms the basis of its majority, but its religious genius! The Jewish people therefore achieves a State whose prestige none the less stems from the religion which modern political life supplants.

The paradox would be insoluble if this religious genius did not consist entirely in struggling against the intoxication of individual forms of enthusiasm for the sake of a difficult and erudite work of justice. This religion, in which God is freed from the Sacred, this modern religion was already established by the Pharisees through their meditations on the Bible at the end of the Second Temple. It is placed above the State, but has already achieved the very notion of the spirit announced by the modern State.

In an anthology of essays written in Hebrew which appeared in New York, Chaim Grinberg, head of the Cultural Section of the Jewish Agency, brought together articles by several Israeli authors on the relation between religion and State. Reading these texts, which are above all eye-witness accounts, one is struck by the ease with which the move from religion to ethics is carried out. We do not get the impression of a morality being added to the dogma, but of a 'dogma' that is morality itself. The grand terms 'love' or 'the presence of God' achieve a true grandeur even as they are given concrete expression in the sordid questions of food, work and shelter. Contrary to all the fervent mysticism that overexcites the othodox or liberal tendencies of the Diaspora living alongside Christianity, an Israeli experiences the famous touch of God in his social dealings. Not that belief in God *incites* one to justice – it *is* the institution of that justice. Moreover, is this justice just an abstract principle? Doesn't religious inspiration ultimately aim to bring about the very possibility of Society, the possibility for a man to see the face of an Other?

The thing that is special about the State of Israel is not that it fulfils an ancient promise, or heralds a new age of material security (one that is unfortunately problematic), but that it finally offers the opportunity to carry out the social law of Judaism. The Jewish people craved their own land and their own State not because of the abstract independence which they desired, but because they could then finally begin the work of their lives. Up until now they had obeyed the commandments, and later on they fashioned an art and a literature for themselves, but all these works of self-expression are merely the early attempts of an overlong adolescence. The master-piece has now finally come. All the same, it was horrible to be both the only people to define itself with a doctrine of justice, and to be the meaning incapable of applying it. The heartbreak and the meaning of the Diaspora. The subordination of the State to its social promises articulates the significance of the resurrection of Israel as, in ancient times, the execution of justice justified one's presence on the land.

It is in this way that the political event is already outstripped. And ultimately, it is in this way that we can distinguish those Jews who are religious from those who are not. The contrast is between those who seek to have a State in order to have justice and those who seek justice in order to ensure the survival of the State.

But surely the religious Jews are those who practise their faith, while the irreligious Jews are those who do not? Such a distinction was valid during the Diaspora, when religious rites, isolated from the work sustaining them, miraculously preserved Judaism, but is it still valid at this dawning of a new age? Is it not the case that a revolt against ritualism stems from a rejection of any magical residue it may still possess, and so opens up the way to its real essence? We cannot doubt the absolute link that exists between justice and the fully developed civilization of Jewish ritualism, which represents the extreme conscience of such justice. It is in the justice of the kibbutz that the nostalgia for ritual is once again to be felt. This is provided that we wish to think of this sort of justice, because of our suspicions regarding any unconscious fervour. Religious liberalism moved back from ritual to a feeling of vague religiosity, hoping to move History back. It happens in the best of families. But if ritual is valuable, it will be reborn only in the virility of action and thought.

Religion and religious parties do not necessarily coincide. Justice as the *raison d'être* of the State: that is religion. It presupposes the high science of justice. The State of Israel will be religious because of the intelligence of its great books which it is not free to forget. It will be religious through the very action that establishes it as a State. It will be religious or it will not be at all.

But how are we to read these books? The studies collected by Chaim Grinberg in the aforementioned volume show that the spirit of the Torah proclaims the essential values of democracy and socialism and can inspire an avant-garde State. We had had slight misgivings. But why, after all, should we get lumbered with the Torah? And how can we apply it to a contemporary situation that is so different politically, socially and economically from the order envisaged by the Law? This is a question put by one of the contributors, Dr Leibovitz, in an article entitled 'Religion and State'. Carrying out the Law does not involve the precondition of restoring outmoded institutions; nor does it allow you to ignore the modern forms of life that exist outside Judaism. The social and political situation described by the Bible and the Talmud is the example of a given situation that is rendered human by the Law. From it we can deduce the justice required for any and every situation.

This is an idea which we consider fundamental. The great books of Judaism do not in fact express themselves as parables that are open to the whims of a poetic imagination or as concepts that are always schematic, but as examples that betray nothing of the infinite relations that make up the fabric of the social being. They offer themselves up as an interpretation that is as rigorous as parables are vague and as rich as concepts are poor. Whosoever has encountered the Talmud, especially if the encounter is with a real master, notices this immediately. Others call this splitting hairs! We must isolate the ancient examples and extend them to the new situations, principles and categories which they contain. This means that between the Jewish State and the doctrine which should inspire it, we must establish a science, a formidable one. The relationship between the Jewish State and the Jewish religion – we do not dare to say Church – is that of study.

The progressive drying-up of talmudic and Hebraic studies in the West in the course of the nineteenth century broke just such a secular contact between Judaism and this prophetic morality to which Judaism claimed an exclusive right. Separated from the rabbinic tradition which already guaranteed this contact through the miracle of its very continuity, and then absorbed into the so-called scientific mechanisms of the prestigious Western universities, through the philosophies and philologies of the day, this morality, like a translated poem, certainly lost its most typical and perhaps its most virile features. By reducing it to what everyone knows, we lost what it had to teach us.

Henceforth we must return to what was strongest in rabbinical exegesis. This exegesis made the text speak; while critical philology speaks *of* this text.

The one takes the text to be a source of teaching, the other treats it as a thing. Despite its method an its apparent modesty, critical history already claims to have gone beyond the archaeological curiosities which have been exhumed, and no more invites us to use these ancient truths than it asks us to cut wood with a Stone Age axe. On the other hand, the apparent artifice and ingeniousness of the other method consists in saving the text from being turned into a mere book – that is to say, just a thing – and in once more allowing it to resonate with the great and living voice of teaching.

From the Rise of Nihilism to the Carnal Jew

To have been an adult between 1939 and 1945 and to survive the end of the war by twenty years is certainly to witness the rise of a new human wave. A change [relève] of generation is not necessarily expressed through an antagonism, but the action of moving back changes one's perspective. In history, we are supposed to see things better from afar. Change lies precisely in this affirmation of the rights of history. The Nazi persecution and, following the exterminations, the extraordinary fulfilment of the Zionist dreams of a State in which to live in peace is to live dangerously, gradually become history. This passion in which it was finished[1] and this bold new beginning, in spite of the conflicting signs affecting them, were felt, even yesterday, to be signs of the same notion of having being chosen or damned – that is to say, of the same exceptional fate. Contemporaries retained a burn on their sides, as though they had seen too much of the Forbidden, and as though they had to bear for ever the shame of having survived. Elie Wiesel has spoken well of this. Whatever the thought of this generation, be it rebellion, negation, doubt or a gloriously confirmed certainty, in the midst of humiliation, such thought bore the seal of the supreme test.

For Christians themselves, after twenty centuries of anachronic existence, Judaism once more became the theatre of the Divine Comedy. It is at this level that the State of Israel was founded. It was revived in 1948 in a challenge made to every sociological, political and historical probability. The Zionist dream, which evolved from the most faithful, durable and implausible of nostalgias, returned to the very sources of the Revelation and echoed the highest expectations. It took shape at the price of the labours and sacrifices provoked by the splendour, invisible to those whom this dream had not haunted and who had managed to discern, beside their tumbledown houses, only the most miserable of Eastern lands in which, by way of milk and honey, they saw only alternating desert and swamp.

Western Judaism found itself abruptly in proximity to its

forgotten tradition which it thought had been emptied of its meaning after a century of philosophy, spiritualization and inevitable critique. But here were its basic experiences also putting themselves forward as the very lessons that for a moment they bring back on to the scene.

Our enemies began. They cast doubt on the facts and figures. This continued among ourselves. The unsayable which had to be made word without being turned into literature through the mouth of those who remain in the background in the face of what is true – a Leon Poliakov, or Lucien Steinberg, or Joseph Billig, a whole team initiated into the spirt of *Yad Vashem* – was laid open to the lurid imagination of pulp novelists. They manufactured drama, turning everything into a spectacle. Such shamelessness and sacrilege were justified by talent, as though true Art could find, in forms of life that were still hot-blooded, the expression for this value and this blood. Ideologies were invented. That of the martyrdom of survival replaced that – which had already served its purpose – of the martyrdom of a justice in the process of disappearing. We have reached the stage where Jews are the authors of their own extermination. Soon to be deprived of any real mystery, this mystery of paper and letters, in which we will cease to believe, will gradually be eaten up by social, economic and political necessities. There will be an end to the meaning that, in spite of one's knowledge of the cause involved, casts light on an event and calls people and nations into being. Already one successful young author has brought the genocide of the camps down to the problems posed by the workers' conditions in the Renault factory. A religious conformism and a dull atheism are simultaneously reborn. The prescriptions of the ineffable seems to them the supreme work of Time and Spirit. And, at each successive session of the Council, have we not heard the echoes of the storm gradually die away, a storm that Cardinal Bea tried in vain to recall, in the midst of a general contrition and apocalyptic rumblings?

As for Israel, by dint of insisting on its significance as a State, it has been entirely reduced to political categories. But its builders found themselves abruptly on the side of the colonialists. Israel's independence was called imperialism, the oppression of native peoples, racism. Fact became separate from the Ideal. The eschatological dream was substituted by the seduction of tourism, and eighteen years after the creation of the State of Israel, glossy brochures still feed their readers an implausible and invariable visual diet of athletic young girls striding joyfully towards the rising sun.

In this world there are no more problems than in the publicity-image world of a modern electrical appliance. For the first time perhaps in their history, Jews see themselves rejected on the side of Reaction and their hearts are torn between the instinctive certainty of what they adhere to, and their equally irremissible progression. Doubt gnaws at the soul of the young generation, the progressivist language of traitors deceives the traitors themselves.

What is proclaimed at the end of this twenty-year evolution is the return of the forces to which in reality we have been exposed since our Emancipation. They are not the forces of Evil. The danger of assimilation – if it retains some meaning – does not stem from the value inherent in any nationalism. It comes from the essential ambiguity of an admirably free thought to which we cannot refuse to give ourselves, but which is not protected against tyranny – that is to say, against nihilism. For throughout its entire exercise it questions the victors of today, tomorow or the day after. It is so respectful of the fact that it risks falling into the trap of the *fait accompli*. It is at the price of faults, crimes, wars and revolutions that amends are made for its errors. Woe betide the person who makes a decision while its harsh truth is still being forged. The freest form of thought in the world is also the most subservient.

The prophets of Judaism do not philosophize within the traces or the predictions of the conquerors. They separate victory from truth. They designate good and evil without worrying about the meaning of history. To be an eternal people is perhaps this: not to prophesize after the event like dialectic, to tell one's right from one's left and, in this way, tell the Right from the Left; not to admit that the disciples of Rabbi Akiba can take lessons in humanity and humanism from violent people, or that survivors can be substituted for victims in order to absolve the killers; to contest the validity of concepts like National Socialism or a single party, which are contradictions in terms; not to believe that, after Hitler, one can shelter Nazis while still embracing the suffering of his people and representing the avant-garde of the Revolution. Even Jean-Paul Sartre himself, whom we admire and like enormously, cannot persuade us of that.

When the dialectic reaches this point, we must resist total assimilation. Without abjuring logic, we can recall that besides the Israel that is interpreted spiritually, where there is an obvious equation between Israel and the Universal, there exists an Israel of Fact, a particular reality that has traversed history as a victim, bearing a tradition and certainties that did not wait to win acclaim from the end of History. Israel equals humanity, but humanity includes the Inhuman, and Israel then refers to Israel, to the Jewish people, its tongue, books, Law, earth. After the daring exploits of an existence freed of all constraint and criteria, its essence calls and calms us; after the inner and unformed adventures, after the nationless humanism and the occasional danger-free idealism, we must, beyond all confrontations with the theories that claim to be the latest, most up-to-date view, hear a sure vocation that has crossed the centuries, 'reviving the soul', 'making wise the simple', 'rejoicing the heart', 'enlightening the eyes' and teaching ordinances that are 'righteous together' (Psalms 19:7–9).

To be conscious of being a nation implies being conscious of an exceptional destiny. Every nation worthy of the name is chosen. But to the extent that we articulate such a proposition without contradicting ourselves, we already belong to a supranational order. The choosing of each people henceforth mingles with its ability to carry out the common task, which it derives from its youth or its long past, the latter bearing a universal meaning that prohibits the peoples from growing old.

But the choosing takes on a stronger meaning, when it expresses in addition *the responsibility which a nation cannot shirk*. Each nation must behave as though it alone had to answer for all. This is a moral sovereignty which the great peoples retain in a world that henceforth can submit only if political sovereignties are limited. But, for nations as for people, moral sovereignty is experienced as the faculty of dying for an idea. As long as truths remain inseparable from the symbols that give them expression and the rituals that celebrate them, the limit to concessions beyond which man sees himself as a renegade and a traitor is clearly and vigorously drawn for all to see. For a forbidden gesture, a modified formula, a profaned tradition, we accept martyrdom.

But no abandon can wear down the principles confessed – as it is flippantly put – 'in spirit and in truth'. Nothing can arrest the soul's movement as it folds back inward. The essential element finds the time to take deeper and deeper refuge: the moment of confrontation never comes, the day of glory never arrives. These are the infinite resources of the dialectic and of mental reserves! The world without ceremony in which everything is spiritualized, if it does not concern the end of time, is a world in which no one dies a violent death any more, apart from mountaineers and saints. But in the Jewish life in the West which tried to be completely inner, the State of Israel achieves the return of the possibility of an abnegation: as in the period when people went to the stake rather than be baptized, we once again have a Jewish value that, to those most assimilated into it, appears worthy of an ultimate sacrifice. The State of Israel, in this sense, constitutes the greatest event in modern Judaism.

But the destiny of a Jew who is not one only according to spirit, who remains the detestable carnal Jew vomited forth by Pascal, is still more mysterious. Since the Emancipation, he has increasingly freed himself in Europe from the letter of the texts. He has regarded as outmoded everything that was seemingly contingent in the traditions he inherited. Everything in its texts that could separate him from others, and everything in its rituals that seemed unique, no longer provoked any passion capable of generating anger. A Jewish heart and a Jewish soul hid their identity deep within and showed only a sceptical smile. Only world struggles were worth fighting to the death. At which point the most blind, brutal force history has known with an iron hand traced the line – mythical and invented, but not chosen or willed – behind which no denial can go.

Of course, we do not owe Judaism to anti-semitism, no matter what Sartre may say. But perhaps the ultimate essence of Israel, its carnal essence prior to the freedom that will mark its history, this manifestly universal history, this history *for all*, visible to all, perhaps the ultimate essence of Israel, derives from its innate predisposition to involuntary sacrifice, its exposure to persecution. Not that we need think of the mystical expiation that it would fulfil like a host. To be persecuted, to be guilty without having committed any crime, is not an original sin, but the obverse of a universal responsibility – a responsibility for the Other [*l'Autre*] – that is more ancient than any sin. It is an invisible universality! It is the reverse of a choosing that puts forward the *self* [*moi*] before it is even free to accept being chosen. It is *for the others* to see if they wish to take advantage of it. It is for the free *self* to fix the limits of this responsibility or to claim entire responsibility. But it can do so only in the name of that original responsibility, in the name of this Judaism.

The Meaning of History

Philosophers have ended up worrying about the meaning of history in a way a shipping company worries about weather forecasts. Thought no longer dares take flight unless it can fly straight to the haven of victory. After the ancillary duties exercised for theology, would philosophy seve politics? To be sure of our certainties, we have to think of the industrial potential of people and the government's audacity: 'Never to take something to be true unless I absolutely know it to be so' – we have changed all that. Evidence shines in all its glory only on success. Regiments on the march scan our truths and launching pads crush, before their missiles, the will that should adhere to a clear and distinct idea.

This ill thinking is already devouring the Jewish soul. 'Are we following the line?' is the only question. The guides of our conscience are set back. So many apolitical subtleties are lost for nothing in discussing Christianity's theses or in reconciling Sciences and the Bible. The spirit no longer risks its salvation with such dangers, in these happy ahistorical times.

The fact that nothing great can emerge in the world without changing, that a Kingdom of God that is not of this world takes advantage of men, was the great lesson of Judaism, the one best understood by the political people. But it made them violent with messianism. They renounced their reason and sought it in the events that bore a messianic meaning and in which intelligence was born from the bloody confrontation of our human follies and of the gentleness, as in the enigma of Samson, of a cruel and devouring force. Cruelty is taken to be the rigour of logic, and crimes to be works of justice. This was the tragic error of an interrupted lesson – the master was too hastily given leave for rambling on aimlessly. He taught action in history but, for the Jews, men can live nineteen centuries against it.

Such was its long patience, its high passion, its tough apprenticeship. Such is its old doctrine. Think of Hillel contemplating the skull of the assassin floating along in the current. The grand Doctor denies the assassins of the assassin the dignity of judges. Crimes are often paid for in history, but one is wrong to expect justice from history. Its anonymous unfolding, when morality does not come along to guide it, is a series of crimes that are set off like a chain reaction. Think of that strange and ironic pasage of 'Roch Hachane' in which Cyrus is none other than Darius. What scandalous ignorance of modern erudition! Or what sovereignty! The great moments in history offer no criteria to judgement. They are judged.

Not to submit the Law of justice to the implacable course of events, to denounce them if necessary as counter-sense [*contre-sens*] or madness, is to be a Jew. A completely negative definition. One does not yet in any way belong to Israel in deciding one day to retain one's *sang-froid* in the face of wars and rioting. One must keep one foot in the Eternal. A tough discipline of knowledge, exercises carried out every day in order to cling to the steep rock that juts out – the Torah is, perhaps, all that. Only in this way is there fulfilled on earth and for men a privileged possibility: a free being who judges history instead of letting himself be judged by it.

For 150 years now, Judaism has been on the point of losing this freedom. This is its real crisis. For 150 years, in every one of the forms in which it has existed, the Zionist one included, it has believed in the messianic age. No one has been stupid enough to denounce the necessary and loyal pacts concluded with specific periods in history. But is one right to lose one's head and fling oneself into history, looking for directives and leaving behind, never to be recovered, a soul that is stronger than the perils of the hour?

To hasten the end is a major danger whose treacherous and tempting nature is foreseen by the Talmud. The Ephraimides in Egypt wanted to be free without waiting for Moses and his Law; having set off for the Promised Land, they ran into the Philistines and were exterminated. Here the Talmud teaches neither the superstition of lucky and unlucky days, nor the Hölderlinian doctrine of the maturation of time, nor the sterile passivity of so-called orthodox piety lying in wait for a miraculous Messiah, but paralysing the efforts demanded by our ordeals and indignities. The good news of failure, or suffering for suffering, of resignation, is not very talmudic. Here the book narrates a perilous impatience that holds for all times. It is perhaps beautiful in its youth, courage and faith. But it consists in effacing at every moment, even the ultimate moment of history, the interval that enables us to differentiate between model and work. Let us learn how to keep our distance, in our indispenable commitments, in the face of what is presented, imposed and pressed upon us as a glorious fulfilment. It is not 'at hand'! Patience!

The Light and the Dark

The lights of Hanukkah shone in Jewish homes for a week. The light spread slowly, like the rhythm of a musical phrase reaching crescendo. One light the first evening, two the following day, three the day after, and so on up until the triumphant blaze of light on the final evening – up until the strange and mysterious night that will surround the candelabra after this final illumination. But this growing, expanding light is different from the flame that burns in the hearth. The latter provides light and heat for the family circle. The heat of the hearth, even when it offers hospitality to the passer-by, is a promise of pleasures enjoyed at home, behind closed doors; the lights of Hanukkah gleam outside. The Law tells us to place them in a part of the house open to the street, where life inside rubs shoulders with public life. These lights do not shine for a family, or for a people; they bring a message to everyone. They do not invite us to intimacy, they broadcast a miracle. What is this message? What is this miracle?

Does it have to do with the heroic military deeds of Judas Maccabaeus in the second century BCE? Does it concern his victory over Antiochos Epiphanus, the invader of Judaea, persecutor of the religion and profaner of the Temple? The heroism of a handful of idealists defying a world political power has always excited the popular Jewish imagination. The memory of this struggle and this victory flattered our national pride; but it also confirmed our faith in the superiority of the weak, strong in their justice, over the strong, who rely on their force alone. This memory did not only comfort a persecuted Judaism for centuries. No doubt even today, it sustains the magnificent combatants of the young State of Israel. And certainly it merits being broadcast. But if it contains the essential point in our message, does it none the less contain the whole point?

For the fable, throwing itself into the violence of combat, risks becoming accustomed to this violence which momentarily it has had to accept. Will it one day abandon the political and warlike paths it has chosen for a time? It finds itself caught up in a world it wanted to destroy. To engage unequivocally one's absolute principles in a war or a political struggle is to betray those principles in some way. One should keep a part, the best part of oneself, of the highest form of combat. Israel's religious thought dares to judge these warriors victorious. The Hasmoneans dangerously accumulated priesthood and political sovereignty. The Doctors of the Talmud acknowledge and denounce the perils that await even just violence.

The doctors of the Talmud, who introduced the festival of Hanukkah into the Jewish liturgical year and to whom we owe the annual ceremony of the kindling of lights, do not narrate the history of the Hasmoneans. They refer to it only in passing. The Talmud is silent on the national liberation of Israel during the reign of Judas Maccabaeus. It retains one legendary episode from the period. This is the story narrated on page 21b of Tractate Shabbath:

> What is [the reason of] Hanukkah? For our Rabbis taught: On the twenty-fifth of Kislew [commence] the days of Hanukkah, which are eight on which a lamentation for the dead and fasting are forbidden. For when the Greeks entered the Temple, they defiled all the oils therein, and when the Hasmonean dynasty prevailed against and defeated them, they made search and found only one cruse of oil which lay with the seal of the High Prest, but which contained sufficient for one day's lighting only; yet a miracle was wrought therein and they lit [the lamp] therewith for eight days. The following year these [days] were appointed a Festival with [the recital of] Hallel and thanksgiving.

Hanukkah is therefore for us the miracle of a light richer than the energies feeding it, the miracle of 'more' from 'less', the miracle of surpassing. The Hasmonean resistance is also this light detached from its material sources. But the talmudic text restores to a national war, a war defending a culture, the permanent horizon of marvel. It is the daily marvel of the spirit that precedes culture. It is a flame that burns with its own fervour: the genius that invents the previously unheard-of, even though everything has already been said; the love that is inflamed even though the loved one is not perfect; the will that undertakes to do something despite the paralysing obstacles in its way; the hope that lights up a life in the absence of reasons for hope; the patience that bears what can kill it.

It concerns the infinite resources of the spirit that, as a creator, surpasses the prudence of techniques; without calculation, without past, it joyfully pours forth its feelings in space, freely and prodigiously entering into the cause of the Other.

But the text I have just cited corrects this audacious wisdom with a further wisdom. Creation, freedom, permanent renewal. Does this revolutionary essence of the spirit tell us everything of its mystery? It blows where it will. But is every wind that blows in this way already a spirit, by virtue of this simple contempt for frontiers? Is to transgress already to surpass? Our own lights cannot burn in a simply gratuitous manner. Before the miracle of generous light, and as a condition of this miracle, another miracle took place: a dark miracle that one forgets. One forgets it in the blaze of lights triumphantly burning brighter. But if, in the Temple ravaged and profaned by the infidels, one had not found in a little flask of pure oil bearing the seal of the High Priest, which, ignored by everyone but unchanging, had remained there throughout the years while the candelabra remained empty, there would have been no Hanukkah miracle. There had to be preserved somewhere a transparent oil kept intact.

Oh! nocturnal existence turned in on itself within the narrow confines of a forgotten phial. Oh! existence sheltered from all uncertain contact with the outside, a lethargic existence traversing duration, a liquid lying dormant on the edge of life like a doctrine preserved in some lost yeshiva, a clandestine existence, isolated, in its subterranean refuge, from time and events, an eternal existence, a coded message addressed by one scholar to another, a derisory purity in a world given over to mixing! Oh! miracle of tradition, conditions and promise of a thought without restraint that does not want to remain an echo, or brief stir of the day.

Oh! generous light flooding the universe, you drink our subterranean life, our life that is eternal and equal to itself. You celebrate those admirable hours, which are dark and secret.

Heidegger, Gagarin and Us

We must urgently defend man against this century's technology. Man will lose his identity and become a cog in a vast machine that chews up both things and beings. In the future, *to exist* will mean to *exploit* nature; but in the vortex of this self-devouring enterprise there will be no fixed point. The solitary stroller in the country, who is certain of belonging, will in fact be no more than the client of a hotel tourist chain, unknowingly manipulated by calculations, statistics and planning. No one will exist for himself [*pour soi*].

There is some truth in this declamation. Technical things are dangerous. They not only threaten a person's identity, they risk blowing up the planet. But the enemies of industrial society are in most cases reactionary. They forget or detest the great hopes of our age. For faith in man's liberation has never been stronger in human souls. This faith is not placed in the facilities that machines and the new sources of energy offer the childish instinct for speed; it is not attached to the pretty mechanical toys that entice the perpetually puerile adult. It identifies only with shaking up sleepy civilizations, eroding the heavy dullness of the past, fading local colour with the fissures that crack all these cumbersome and obtuse things that burden human particularisms. One has to be underdeveloped to claim these as reasons for being, and struggle in their name for a place in the modern world. The development of technical progress is not the cause – it is already the effect of this lightening of human substance, emptying itself of its nocturnal sluggishness.

I am thinking of one prestigious current in modern thought, which emerged from Germany to flood the pagan recesses of our Western souls. I am thinking of Heidegger and Heideggarians. One would like man to rediscover the *world*. Men will lose the world. They will know only matter that stands before them, put forward in some way as *an object* to their freedom. They will know only *objects*.

To rediscover the world means to rediscover a childhood mysteriously snuggled up inside the Place, to open up to the light of

231

great landscapes, the fascination of nature, and the delight of camping in the mountains. It means to follow a path that winds its way through fields, to feel the unity created by the bridge that links the two river banks and by the architecture of buildings, the presence of the tree, the chiaroscuro of the forests, the mystery of things, of a jug, of the worn-down shoes of a peasant girl, the gleam from a carafe of wine sitting on a white tablecloth. The very *Being* of reality will reveal itself behind these privileged experiences, giving and trusting itself into man's keeping. And man, the keeper of Being, will derive from this grace his existence and his truth.

The doctrine is subtle and new. Everything that, for centuries, seemed to us to be added to nature by man, was already shining forth in the splendours of the world. A work of art, a blazing forth of Being and not a human invention, makes his anti-human splendour glow. Myth announces itself within nature. Nature is implanted in that first language which hails us only to found human language. Man must be able to listen and hear and reply. But to hear this language and reply to it consists not in giving oneself over to logical thoughts raised into a system of knowledge, but in living in the place, in being-there. Enrootedness. We should like to take up this term; but the plant is not enough of a plant to define an intimacy with the world. A little humanity distances us from nature, a great deal of humanity brings us back. Man inhabits the earth more radically than the plant, which merely takes nourishment from it. The fable spoken by the first language of the world presupposes links that are more subtle, numerous and profound.

This, then, is the eternal seductiveness of paganism, beyond the infantilism of idolatry, which long ago was surpassed. *The Sacred filtering into the world* – Judaism is perhaps no more than the negation of all that. To destroy the sacred groves – we understand now the purity of this apparent vandalism. The mystery of things is the source of all cruelty towards men.

One's implementation in a landscape, one's attachment to *Place*, without which the universe would become insignificant and would scarcely exist, is the very splitting of humanity into natives and strangers. And in this light technology is less dangerous than the spirits [*génies*] of the *Place*.

Technology does away with the privileges of this enrootedness and the related sense of exile. It goes beyond this alternative. It is not a question of returning to the nomadism that is as incapable as sedentary existence of leaving behind a landscape and a climate. Technology wrenches us out of the Heideggerian world and the superstitions surrounding *Place*. From this point on, an opportunity appears to us: to perceive men outside the situation in which they are placed, and let the human face shine in all its nudity. Socrates preferred the town, in which one meets people, to the countryside and trees. Judaism is the brother of the Socratic message.

What is admirable about Gagarin's feat is certainly not his magnificent performance at Luna Park which impresses the crowds; it is not the sporting achievement of having gone further than the others and broken the world records for height and speed. What counts more is the probable opening up of new forms of knowledge and new technological possibilities, Gagarin's personal courage and virtues, the science that made the feat possible, and everything which that in turn assumes in the way of abnegation and sacrifice. But what perhaps counts most of all is that he left the Place. For one hour, man existed beyond any horizon – everything around him was sky or, more exactly, everything was geometrical space. A man existed in the absolute of homogeneous space.

Judaism has always been free with regard to place. It remained faithful in this way to the highest value. The Bible knows only a Holy Land, a fabulous land that spews forth the unjust, a land in which one does not put down roots without certain conditions. The Book of Books is sober in its descriptions of nature! 'A land flowing with milk and honey' – the landscape is described in terms of food. In a parenthetical phrase: 'Now the time was the season of the first ripe grapes' (Numbers 13:20), we see the grape ripen in the heat of a generous sun.

Oh! tamarisk planted by Abraham at Beer-sheba! One of the rare 'individual' trees planted in the Bible, which appears in all its freshness and colour to charm the imagination in the midst of so much peregrination, across so much desert. But take care! The Talmud is perhaps afraid that we will let ourselves be carried away by the song, in the southern breeze, and not look for the meaning of Being. It wrests us from our dreams: Tamarisk is an acronym; the three letters needed to write the word in Hebrew are the initials used for Food, Drink and Shelter, three things necessary to man which man offers to man. The earth is for that. Man is his own master, in order to serve man. Let us remain masters of the mystery that the earth breathes. It is perhaps on this point that Judaism is most distant from Christianity. The catholicity of Christianity integrates the small and touching household gods into the worship of saints, and local cults. Through sublimation, Christianity continues to give piety roots, nurturing itself on landscapes and memories culled from family, tribe and nation. This is why it conquered humanity. Judaism has not sublimated idols – on the contrary, it has demanded that they be destroyed. Like technology, it has demystified the universe. It has freed Nature from a spell. Because of its abstract universalism, it runs up against imaginations and passions. But it has discovered man in the nudity of his face.

Hegel and the Jews

Professor Bourgeois, from Lyons, analyses Hegel's meditations on Judaism and Christianity as presented in his Frankfurt writings.[1] With a few modifications, they were destined to be integrated into the system which Hegal fully grasped at Iena. In order for us to understand their significance, let me first offer a few pedantic propositions.

The Hegelian system represents the fulfilment of the West's thought and history, understood as the turning back of a destiny into freedom, Reason penetrating all reality or appearing in it. An unforgettable enterprise! Universal thought must no longer be separated, in the heads of some intellectuals, from the individual whom it renders intelligible. A *separate* universal is no longer universal but has once again become something particular. It must be separated from its separation; the universal, identified from the different, must remain *in* the different from which it had been taken, whether it be, according to the famous formulae, *identity of identity and of non-identity* or *concrete universal* or *Spirit*. This sort of terminology, of course, frightens the honest man! But it announces a form of knowledge that does not get bogged down in specialization, an Idea that does not remain an abstraction, which animates in its form – in its *entelechy* – Reality itself. *The fulfilment of an idea still belongs to its intelligibility!* The history of humanity, throughout religions, civilizations, states, wars and revolutions, is nothing but this penetration, or this revelation, of reason within Being, long before the philosopher's thought has become aware of it in formulating the System.

This is what leads to Hegel's efforts at Frankfurt to situate Judaism and Christianity, to adjust them into the System, while adjusting the System to Reality and History. The System proceeds from an exaltation of the Greek spirit: the particular feeling 'at home' in the City. This harmony is still particular; the modern world fulfils it in the universal. Judaism and Christianity mark important stages along the way. The ultimate meaning of modernity will therefore be essentially Greek. Professor Bourgeois exposes with complete mastery all these perspectives and every movement of the Hegelian sovereign reason in these perspectives.

Neither Judaism nor Christianity is therefore at the end of its course; they simultaneously contribute to the definitive truth and include aspects that are outmoded. These aspects are revealed in Hegel's critical discourse. Christianity, the penultimate stage of History, is presented in formulae in which today's Christian will perhaps not always recognize himself, but in which nothing will wound him, above all if the Old Testament no longer calls upon him to witness anything. As for Judaism, the critical discourse is translated – both in Hegel's writings and in the account Bourgeois gives of it – by a whole doctrine that corroborates (is it its source, or is it, despite all Hegel's greatness, a consequence?) the argument that, up to the present day, has nurtured anti-semitism. Certainly, in Hegel, it would have acted from a *particular* anticipation of the *universal* critique of political naturalism, or nationalism, which will be developed into the mature Hegelian system' (p. 117); it concerns Judaism only to the extent that it represents in the life of the Spirit the stage in which '[*spiritual*] universality and [natural] particularity are separate' (p. 54). But what ensues from this, first, is that 'the Judaic spirit is the negation of spirit' (ibid.). And from this point on, we get virulent formulae in which the enemy of the Jew will neither bother to understand nor, above all, make understood the ambiguity of terms. Anti-Semitism is based within the System, which amounts to saying within the absolute. What a godsend!

When we let go of the dialectical pegs of deduction – otherness, nature, negativity, etc. – we find well-known themes, the ancient ones and a few more recent examples, presented quite starkly. The separation of the universal and the particular in which Judaism would be maintained would signify *domination*, 'for what is hostile can only enter into the relation of domination' (pp. 36–7). 'The act by which Abraham founds the Jewish people is an act of separation, the breaking of all ties with the surroundings' (p. 38): 'Cadmus, Danaüs, etc., had also abandoned their fatherland, but in combat; they would search for a soil on which they would be free to love; Abraham did *not* want to love and to be free for that' (ibid., footnote). And Bourgeois comments (p. 39):

> Judaism is in this sense the absolute antithesis of the Hegelian ideal of freedom, the fulfilment of ugliness as Hellenism was the fulfilment of beauty. ... *Abraham's*

existence is therefore that of a being who separates himself from nature as the object of love and fixes it as the object of need ... the Jew is not attached to an idea 'but to an animal existence'. In a word, both Abraham and Judaism at bottom involve a fall back into bestiality.

And later, on p. 40:

To live, to preserve oneself through the satisfaction of one's needs, therefore, remains the essential thing for Abraham. ... Thus Abraham's existence was completely dominated by an exclusive concern for his own preservation, his own security in the midst of natural vicissitudes. ... Abraham – a thinking animal – thinks precisely like an animal.

The God of Abraham is merely 'the absolutization of his lazy bestiality, his passive materialism' (p. 43).

This is a position held against nature, full of contradictions. It grants Judaism a tragic destiny which Hegel recognizes. But 'the great tragedy of the Jewish people is not a Greek tragedy, it can awaken neither fear, nor pity, for both are born only from destiny, the necessary false step taken by a wonderful being; the Jewish tragedy can awaken only horror' (pp. 53–4).

One wonders on reading this catalogue, which we abridge in order not to copy out whole pages of the book, if Marx's essay 'About the Jewish Question', which Lenin never cited, reflects only an ignorance of the real structures of the nineteenth-century Jewish masses, if it is not due to a knowledge, transmited by osmosis, of Hegel's Frankfurt philosophy and of the impossible pity it teaches; if Hitler's propaganda itself did not draw heavily on this store which, *without adopting the slightest distance from it*, a high-class French university lecturer opens up for us again in 1970. We understand the concern for objectivity that motivates the scholar, but does he even know that if Judaism is a movement of ideas incorporated (perhaps) into Christianity, 'suppressed' and 'preserved' (perhaps) in Hegelianism, it also remains, rightly or wrongly (but certainly), a credo or a spirituality or a principle of solidarity or a reason for living and, in any case, the cause of death for millions of his contemporaries? Would the historians of philosophy lack to such a degree an immediate memory and pay so little attention to the present? As for the monotheisms which evolved from Abraham and were reconciled within his paternal breast, they are in a fine pickle indeed!

Certainly, when faced with the Hegelian saying [*le dire*], one cannot easily raise one's voice – not only because thought becomes timid, but because language seems lacking. There is nothing more derisory than 'putting forward an opinion' on Hegel – classing him, either in order to reduce him in stature or to glorify him, as a mystic or romantic or anti-Semite or atheist. It is not by means of the approximate terms of our daily language, even that of the university, that we can understand someone who allows us only to lend a worthy meaning to terms. We speak a poor language! It has no beginning. No word is first. Each one, in order to be defined, appeals to others that have yet to be defined. We express ourselves in a language that has not established its grounding. We are content to speak in the air. A great philosophy is perhaps only a language that miraculously found in Greece – or somehow gave itself – a justified point of departure. Its discourse is, from that point on, able to articulate the truth of all the other discourses. This is the West's miracle – or mirage. Is it the source of its science? I do not know. But since Hegel we use a new figure of speech; philosophy *speaks the truth* of ... an art, or a politics, or a religion. Hegel, like Marx at a later date and Freud today, *speak the truth* of the attachments and certainties deep within the innermost recesses of our conscience.

This is true unless, in the face of the obvious ramblings, undertaken in the name of his sublime schemes, of someone who is probably the greatest thinker of all time, we ask ourselves whether language does not hold another secret to the one brought to it by the Greek tradition, and another source of meaning; whether the apparent and so-called 'non-thought' 'representations' of the Bible do not hold more possibilities than the philosophy that 'rationalizes' them, but cannot let them go free; whether the meaning does not stem from the Scriptures that renew it; whether absolute thought is capable of encompassing Moses and the prophets – that is to say, whether we should not leave the System, even if we do so by moving backwards, through the very door by which Hegel thinks we enter it.

Exclusive Rights

To free oneself from particularisms signifies for the heirs to the Graeco-Roman world to confront, in discussion or war, one's certainties with the certainties of others.

The dawn of truth comes up, and the first gesture of universalization is made, when I become aware of the coherent discourses that are different from mine and stand alongside my own, and when I search for a common language. The life of truth and its expansion can thus be conceived as a life in the City, like a politics. To respect the Other is, before all else, to refer to the Other's opinions.

Each discourse on contact with each other becomes larger. As the various affirmations get jostled about, they lose their harshness. War itself still attests to this passion for confrontation. It demands recognition and accord from the vanquished party. There are only religious wars. Imperialism is a universalism.

Between the wars which emerged from particularisms and the violence of those which seek to reduce them to a State, is there not a place for an absolutely pacifist and apolitical universalism? It would perhaps consist in loving men rather than being concerned about their discourse; in not constructing one's truth from the shavings of the opinions one has come up against; in not recognizing the progress of Reason in successive examples of human madness, or eternal structures in the fragile institutions of ephemeral states. 'To mistrust every thing and love every man' was a motto chosen by Léon Brunschvicg in his early notebook; are opinions not *the thing* in man?

A dissident of Judaism one day asked Rabbi Abbahu, with an irony one can imagine: 'When will the Messiah come?' To which Rabbi Abbahu replied: 'When darkness covers those people who are with you.' At the beginning of the fourth century BCE this must have represented a deplorable lapse in the universalist spirit. 'You have condemned me!' Rabbi Abbahu's interlocutor indeed cried. But the Doctor invoked a verse from Isaiah (Isaiah 60:2): 'For, behold, darkness shall cover the earth, and gross darkness the

239

people: but the Lord shall shine upon thee, and his glory shall be seen upon thee.'

The truth taught by Judaism is not propagated by encapsulating in its catholicity little packets of truth that are disseminated to all the human civilizations. Perhaps it is even for that reason that it is so little propagated.

The very idea of a fraternal humanity united in the same destiny is a Mosaic revelation that, flying the Christian flag, was imposed on the most distant shores. But – why deny it? – the form in which this original universalism emerges in Jewish thought and sensibility does not resemble that vast process of assimilation, concession and mutual compromise – even if they are syntheses – which unfold like a political evolution, rather than like the progress of a truth rallying every reasonable being. This is no doubt the meaning of the mysterious apologue in which Moses claims for Israel exclusive rights to the divine history or comparative ethnography.

Rest assured that the light is not reserved for Israel alone, and darkness for the rest of humanity. Moses was as convinced of this as we are. Rabbi Abbahu, who quotes Isaiah, chapter 60, verse 2, is not unaware of verse 3, which precisely promises the light of Israel to every nation and State on earth. But for him, this light cannot shine in such a way that the products of political determinism will seem seductive and attractive, as though they were the very illumination of reality. The prestige must cease. The prophetic struggle against idolatry does not attack the statues of stone and wood, but this mirage of lights that are infinitely repeated. Perhaps Israel in the first place signifies all men together freed from this fascinating hallucination.

Not to impose its thought through war, but not to seek, in its contact with different civilizations, the shocks from which clarity leaps, earns prophetic Judaism a solid reputation as a particularism that cannot be shaken. It frightens the modern Jew. The universality of influence that is none the less claimed by prophetic truth thus remains unknown. Contempt for the burgeoning of opinions and the political fanaticism from which they proceed (or which they inspire) rests on the love of men to whom truth is sometimes offered in exhortation and even in invective, but never the violence, and never by mixing up ideas.

This stubborn refusal to ignore historical circumstances can none the less feel itself to be [*s'éprouver*] and prove itself to be [*se prouver*] authentic only in the courage of renunciation and total disengagement. In concrete terms, this signifies insecurity and the condition of being a victim. Such was the destiny of Judaism before the Emancipation. The Emancipation brought it back to history. It recognized reason in the discourses of this world and renounced the insecurity of its condition. It left the interstices of Being. This unquestionably heralded the most important resolution ever in its inner life. The attention paid to the world, and to its political evolution, was certainly due in large measure to the new spirit that began in 1789 to blow across the Europe in which the prophecies were to be fulfilled. But the history this assumed through the Emancipation immediately surpassed, in the Jewish soul, the meaning it took from these achievements. Henceforth history seemed to be given a meaning in all of its manifestations; henceforth the Jew participated in events, aspired to responsibilities and, on the vulgar level, to the 'benefits of civilization'. Henceforth *confrontation* imposed itself on all his beliefs.

Against all the folklores of the world the Jew will measure his certainties. In this way prophetic universalism dies. How can we judge a history with which we commit and compromise ourselves? How can we belong to the world and reject, without madness, the two alternative terms that events impose on us?

To reject current events without accepting exile, which henceforth becomes hateful, sounds false, like an impotent and verbal moralism. There is nothing more derisory than the Jew who is nicely set up and attached to all the vanities of the world, forgetting the difficult teaching yet taking himself all the time to be a prophetic consciousness. How much more serious seems a will that renounces both these measureless perils and this state of being chosen, for the perils of history and the political act!

Only there is this: from time to time strange dusks interrupt the clear light of History, the light splits up into unnumerable tiny trembling ambiguous flames, the earth is pulled away from under your feet, and events begin to turn, in a whirling infernal vortex, around a conscience that once again no longer feels at home. And certainties that make a mockery of confrontation float back up to greet you from forgotten depths.

VI
HIC ET NUNC

Since the destruction of the temple, the Lord God has devoted a quarter of his day to teaching children
(Abodah Zarah 3b)

How is Judaism Possible?

Some weeks ago, before the most illustrious company to be found in this country, we were given a brilliant reminder of the clear and distinct idea on which Jewish consciousness rests in France. The difference between nation and religion, universal and particular, public and private, political life and inner life, places within its just limits the Jewish destiny and stems the potential overflowing of the Jewish soul.

The venerable institutions that form the framework of the Jewish community bear witness to the solidarity of this idea. This Spinozist idea admirably regulates our duty towards the nation. It guarantees our rights as citizens. It is the citadel that protects us against injustice. We must beware of tampering with it!

But we must also recognize the lesson learned from facts in order to give this luminous and incontestable formula its best content. Unequal consideration has been given to the Jewish spiritual energy that embodied itself in the forms taken by the French nation, as opposed to intimate matters. A citizen's life was the great event in our modern history. These descendants of prophets certainly showed themselves to have little talent for the inner life! Jewish intelligence shone ever more brightly at the Bar, at university, in the arts and humanity, in Parliament, in constituent bodies, in industry and commerce; intrepid in arms, and daring in power. The influence of the synagogue and the community was gradually lost, in spite of the number of remarkable people who devoted themselves to it and the names that one can evoke with pride. Practices were forgotten, and Jews, in increasingly small numbers, entered the temple like cold and abstract beings. Judaism not only vows with the unbelieving manner of the unfaithful faithful. It preserved – or perhaps acquired because of the external brilliance, by way of contrast – a certain exotic, fusty and narrow image. Charities, schools and assemblies lack a brilliance, lack horizons, and become outmoded as soon as they are inaugurated. Real events and real things are to be found outside. 'Everything Jewish is disgraceful', said the influential boss of a Jewish charitable organization quite recently, and in the version reported to me the adjective was even more vernacular, cruel and offensive.

Why is there this disgrace? It emanates from a very common perception from the old days, in which religion means a liturgical relation with God. The interiority in which Israel's destiny had henceforth to be written was reduced to the interiority of a house of prayer. Charitable works were an extension of this piety. The rabbis became servants of worship. These scholars, thinkers or saints came to resemble ecclesiastics. School henceforth signified the rabbinic seminary. The other school had the mission of opening up for latecomers or the backward the way through to national life. As a private community deep within the nation, Judaism transformed its spiritual life into a *privatissime* business. Such a life fell to specialists in spiritual matters, and was celebrated in special places on special days at special times and, soon, in the presence of a clientele of specialists and often even of paid specialists.

Such a style of life not only leads Judaism prematurely to the status of museum, but betrays its profound essence. The conception that locks it into this status makes it prey to the religions it resembles in appearance. It is also anachronistic and no longer corresponds to the religious demands of its peers. Finally, it is particularly unjust for Judaism, which is ill at ease and feels stifled within the walls of a church. To criticize the thought that sees in worship the supreme expression of religious life is not to be opposed to this worship. The criticism is easy, but cruel to the critic who would like this worship not to die for lack of faithful worshippers, and a silence on their part; who postulates a whole mode of existence without which he is nothing. A Synagogue without foundation could not survive. We must seek out the conditions that make it possible. For it is a certain fact that reduced to itself, in these tempestuous modern times, the Synagogue has emptied the synagogues.

There is in fact a sense of inequality between Christianity – which, even in the secular state, is present everywhere – and Judaism, which does not dare to show its face out of doors, held back as it is by scruples about being indiscreet enough to break the pact created by the Emancipation. The non-religious City incorporated into its secularized substance the forms of Catholic life. Between the strictly rational order of political existence and the mystical order of belief are realities intermediary to the diffuse state, realities that are half-rational, half-religious. They permeate this political life. They float around in it like lymphatic matter. The churches are integrated into landscapes that always seem to be waiting for them and to sustain them. We give no more thought to this Christian atmosphere than to the air we breathe. The juridical separation of Church from State did nothing to dispel it. The rhythm of legal time is scanned by Catholic feast days, cathedrals determine towns and sites. Art, literature and morality whose basis classically lives off Christian themes are still nurtured by these themes.

A Fénelon, Bossuet, a Pascal and the divine Racine are not for the young generation only models of style. They are princes! And who would dare to ignore them? But our adolescents receive them into the secular culture in which these kings can no longer reign. And our adolescents, brought up in Hebraic syllables so as to drone out prayers they do not understand, will bow, if they are intelligent, before the sovereign thought of these masters.

The subsistence of this religious and Christian atmosphere beneath a national life that purports to be religiously neutral explains, for example, the phenomenon – which at first glance is surprising – of the reappearance on the political scene in Europe of parties that are openly Christian. The churches do not draw their influence from the catechism, but from all these realities which Christianity provoked in the course of history and on which it is nurtured. It is the spread of Christian culture everywhere that gives Christianity its impact, not the pious sermons and the parish bulletin. We are the only ones in the world to want a religion without culture.

The entry of Jews into the national life of European states led them to breathe an atmosphere completely impregnated with Christian essence, and that heralded the baptisms. It is not the local church priest who has converted our children and brothers, it is Pascal, Bossuet and Racine; it is the people who built Chartres Cathedral with them. Judaism understood as a Synagogue is reduced to an abstract confession that does not even earn a civil status. We were limited to it only by moving family memories, popular melodies and a few recipes.

The reduction of religion to private worship is anachronistic, and this is the second reason for our difficulties. It is not that in itself worship seems to us a outmoded formula; but when it is jealously private, it lives and breathes in a hothouse, communicates no vital energy and does not project itself into life. The inner life, reduced to being present at temple, interrupting a man's daily activities, before he returns to serious things, is perhaps enough in a world free of rifts in which eternal and daily matters each remain peacefully in their proper place. The Christian churches set themselves up within this distinction and inaugurated an academism of the spiritual in which the inner life frees itself of all responsibility. Today the churches themselves do not feel at ease in the niche they have created. They are returning to the life that the greatest of their believers illustrate by their will and their courage.

For Judaism, such a situation is a defect. It is intolerable that life in 1959, in the twentieth century, no longer permits this peaceful distinction and this taming of the Eternal. There is no longer, properly speaking, any private life. And conversely, all the questions that call for decisions on our part and put us in touch with our contemporaries engage our most intimate particularity. Moral purity, moral dignity are no longer played out in a *tête-à-tête* with God, but are sorted out between men. The Jewish God has never tolerated these *tête-à-tête*s. He was always the God of the multitudes. The Judaism in us should not be aroused on Yom Kippur, at the hour of prayer for the dead, but every day, and for the living. So we are the ones who have remained most faithful to this religion of comfortable hours and have forgotten the expansiveness of a God whom a temple could in no sense contain. The dishonour into which our religion falls stems not from the devaluation of the Divine, but from its domestication. We delight in the possibilities it offers us of a good conscience that is not disturbed. One is spiritualist like one is a pharmacist.

The present disaffection of Jews with regard to their worship therefore stems largely from the fact that the absolute is reduced to this very worship. Between a thousand-year-old existence in which attachment to the truth remains the great affair of a life, and one's place in the synagogue where one listens to the organ, the gap is, after all, considerable. To live dangerously for twenty centuries as Jews or as Marranos, only to end up attending pretty ceremonies! Savouring metaphysical anxiety and the presence of the Sacred in social quietude has, after all, been done better elsewhere. But as soon as a great Jewish cause offers itself up to the human appetite for the absolute, fidelity is affirmed. Building a just State on an arid and dangerous land brings back to Israel the Jews who left the synagogues. Not because this work accords with agnosticism and demands no ritual – although no doubt there is a little of that – but because of the scope of the enterprise, its effect on the whole of a man's life.

And that brings me to my third point. Judaism feels cramped

within the concept of religion as defined by sociology, and does not limit itself to the procedures which religious psychology assumes operate in the believer's soul. Here I call on testimony that others will find suspect, but which in my view must be treated seriously and with respect. Judaism is to be adhered to with particular tenacity by those very people who attach no religious meaning to their adherence and sometimes attach no meaning to it at all – that is to say, those very people who, in the words of Jerome Lindon, have no comment to make about the matter apart from: I am a Jew.

Mysterious returns after long departures occur in the toughest consciousness. It confesses its Judaism while remaining hostile to any demonstration of confession. It equally refuses to equate Judaism with a Jewish nationality, or the Jewish state, and even less with an apparent Jewish race. It tries to provide its adherence with many excuses, but in fact lives off the heart's dark reasoning in which reasons, starved of nourishment, take refuge and become anxious. It comes from further back than these excuses. It is the last cold spark of an ancient flame which, for 150 years, has not been fed. All that burns is a strange reflection, lighting nothing and unable to transmit itself: a fire that devours nothing and burns without consuming anything. *But it attests to a spirituality that is foreign to the received category of religion.*

The classical schema of an all-powerful God helping or crushing men who place their confidence in Him or quake before Him does not express the essence of the phenomenon of Judaism. To gauge the elevation that falls under the common term of religion, listen to the forms of atheism: 'The empty sky' or 'waiting in vain for Godot', or 'God is dead'. What childish nonsense do these puerile remarks hope to counterbalance? The word is no longer governed by witchcraft. Splendid philosophy! For ages now the Jew who has preserved or renewed contact with Judaism has no longer dared to reply that he believes when his sympathetic friends quiz him. He feels that they want to pass him off for a magician of some kind.

Judaism as a form of worship that does not extend into other forms of spiritual life, a confession composed of a single institution, an academic Judaism that commits itself to no exploits, abusing the supernatural like all the others ... can such a thing survive? Is Judaism still possible? The blindfold statue that stands by the side door of Strasbourg Cathedral cannot see its own splendour.

The years preceding and following the Second World War have already shattered the limits whose narrowness I have shown. The chants of Edmond Fleg allowed this to be foreseen. Three new facts

Difficult Freedom

appeared in Jewish life in France; and the catastrophe that fell on us with the rise of National Socialism gave them full weight. These three facts, in reality intermingled, are: the constitution of the State of Israel and the presence of this State to a consciousness; the appearance and development of youth movements; and the renewal of Jewish studies within these very movements and in the full-time Jewish schools which emerged from 1935 on. The house of prayer coming out into the world is their common significance. A search for space!

The State of Israel, whatever the ephemeral political philosophy of its greatest workers, is not for us a State like any other. It has a density and depth that greatly surpass its scope and its political possibilities; it is like a protest against the world. And it reflects our thoughts in the vast culture of the visible, which until then had been subjective thoughts.

The youth movements transport into day-to-day life the merely weekly or autumnal Judaism of their elders. In its teaching they look for the meaning of the concrete commitment that a modern man is called to make, and our avant-garde rabbis welcome and support these novelties. Right in the heart of the Latin Quarter in Paris, there is a hostel that is too small for the youth who flock to it.

The return to texts puts us on the level of our real essence, which the 'concept of Mosaic confession' had impoverished and falsified. Judaism's great books finally carry with them the decor that had disappeared ever since everything was reduced to an incomprehensible liturgy. They restore the equivalent of the perspectives and dimensions that the cathedral builders had opened up within the Christian space. The builders of Judaism had chiselled out in their books a minute and precise architecture. It is time, in fact, to bring once more to the surface, to the clarity of modern intelligence, the submerged cathedrals in these texts.

Jewish wisdom is inseparable from a knowledge of the biblical and rabbinical texts; the Hebrew language directs the reader's attention towards the true level of these texts, which is the most profound level of Being. In an increasingly homogeneous world nothing can oppose the pressure on us to be brought outside, out of our knowledge; knowledge as a unique power of reversion. Judaism can survive only if it is recognized and propagated by lay people who, outside all Judaism, are the promoters of the common life of men.

The new type of Jewish school – a school that does not prepare you for any ecclesiastical role – must assume a place at the forefront

250

of the community. A full-time school in which the teaching of the Hebrew language and the basic texts would be conducted by highly qualified teachers; in which the Jewish humanities would not be taught with a view to promoting historical criticism or cheap piety but for their intrinsic truth, whatever the path of their marvellous confluence. Teaching texts, not relics or alluvial deposits from the past.

But to make this school fully effective, we must not leave it isolated. We must rethink the whole structure into which it has to be woven and envisage setting up new institutions alongside the synagogue, perhaps to the latter's greater glory.

At the centre, the secondary school, whose aims differed from those of a charitable organization. We must attract pupils of the highest standard into them in order to make them prefer, by some miracle, the Jewish school to the private school. Consequently, this school must offer them superior material conditions and intellectual standing. We are in open competition here. In the final-year classes, at least, we should recruit pupils by the most rigorous selection procedures. The style of a Jewish school must not resemble that of a state school, ready to take in hundreds of pupils, but rather that of a hotel for intense work, a fervent workshop.

But the Jewish school, in which professional teaching staff can also be trained, must on the one hand rely on a superior Jewish education, both traditional and modern, on research and scientific publications; and on the other on a Jewish intelligentsia, in possession of Jewish knowledge and nurturing that knowledge, whose pupils, on leaving the school, would expand such knowledge. The community must therefore take an interest in the Jewish studies being pursued in the faculties at Paris and Strasbourg, where they are taught so magnificently.

Even when directed by Jews, these studies retain a philosophical and historical character. The community needs truths that generate life. It needs a doctrinal and philosophical teaching that can be given on the level of cultivated minds. This teaching, in a lay country, can be created only by the community itself. It must be sustained, if need be provoked, at all events co-ordinated and unified. Pluralist tendencies do not exclude the unity of the institution in which they might be grouped. A Jewish higher education will address itself to the student youth that had been prepared to receive it in the Jewish school or in its previous Jewish studies. This education will try to attain in another form, adapted to the pastimes and tastes of a young generation that has not up until now received a Jewish education, the future elite of French Jewish society. Finaly, the yeshivoth must be integrated into the Jewish higher-education system and a collaboration with them must be pursued and demanded.

Around the Jewish high school or the Jewish institution of higher education we should bring together, in a group that is conscious of its existence and it numerical importance, those Jewish intellectuals who know Hebrew and the basic Jewish texts, and attach vital importance to these texts. This intelligence already exists in scattered form – we must gather it together.

In the provincial towns in which the existence of a full-time Jewish school is impossible, a Jewish education should be guaranteed in the form of complementary classes on Sundays and Thursdays.[1] The community houses or centres in which lessons could be given would take on a role of primary importance both through this teaching and through this gathering together of all the Jewish energies which they put into operation, and of which they become the living and visible expression. We must recognize an educational value in the simple fact of *bringing together* a Jewish youth, under whatever pretext.

But the Jewish school cannot claim, in a free country like France, to embrace most of the Jewish youth. Its work is therefore extended to those Jewish children attending state schools, through complementary classes, youth clubs and movements, the organization of vacation courses and activities, and the Community House.

These are the outlines of a plan that can serve as the basis of a Jewish cultural politics in France, and would lead to new institutions. We do not so much need to create all that at once – less still to destroy something – as to have a line of conduct, an orientation, the criteria for a choice.

I have said nothing about the content. When speaking of a true science one can only speak that science itself. There is no royal way in either mathematics or Judaism. Formulae are empty or unintelligible without the science they come out of. In exchange for an act of allegiance to Judaism, we cannot immediately be presented with the dossier of every value to which we subscribe. Those famous Jewish values! It is all right to call them values, for they are only actions and obligations. But we must credit their substance to some degree at least, even if we are no longer capable of faith.

A true culture cannot be summed up, for it resides in the very effort to cultivate it. That is the whole meaning of my proposals. To demand a digest of culture is a new way of showing impatience with those who, during Yom Kippur, at the hour of the *Kol Nidre*, acquit themselves of all duties and claim Judaism's conclusions without having put forward the premises. Ah! the eternal repugnance towards the efforts and hours of boredom that go to make up culture! When a Roman, some twenty centuries ago, asked Hillel what the essence of Judaism was, the Roman did not even offer him a chair so that he could expand on the subject. He made him stand on one foot in order to dissuade a drawn-out reply. It is this detail that gives the whole apologue its spice. Hillel's response is worth repeating for its final point: 'Do not do to the Other what you would not wish him to do to you – that is the whole of the Torah and, for the rest, go and learn.'

But if the effort demanded is disproportionate to the results promised; if, by some miracle, life without Judaism and without Jews can still attract the Jewish spirit in 1959, let me conclude by telling you this tale.

The second Psalm includes a vese which greatly impressed Saint Paul and modern thinkers. I shall take the precaution of reading it out, since for a long time now we have shown little consideration for our texts unless they appear as quotations in now-Jewish books. This is the verse: 'Serve the Lord with fear, with trembling kiss his feet'[2] (Psalms 2:11). This phrase became extremely popular. Kierkegaard's famous 'fear and trembling' is a paraphrase of it. It served as an analysis of the religious feeling in which the presence of God to the believer provokes a tension between the contradictory emotions of joy and trembling. What a magnificent dialectic this is for those souls that are brought to liturgy! Something in it shocked me, though, perhaps because of an innate mistrust of feelings being confused. The translation has always seemed to me not so much un-catholic as un-jewish. One day I saw the commentary on it in Tractate Berakoth in which the commentator, referring to the Jerusalem Talmud, read the verse as: 'Serve God with fear – and with the trembling of all, you will rejoice.' The grammar is remarkable: the subject who trembles is not the subject who rejoices. This time the translation seemed to me not only shocking, but dull and scandalous. It seemed dull set alongside the dialectic of the first version, which still engages your imagination. It seemed to me scandalous, for what we had was a Jewish particularism that dooms the world to trembling and keeps the joy for itself!

We must nevertheless ask ourselves what this trembling consists of. We must discover, on the basis of the nature of this trembling, the meaning of the 'Serve the Lord with fear' which opens our verse and is the 'essence of Judaism'. The trembling is not simple fear or anguish, something dear to our contemporaries. Trembling is when the foundations of the world are rocked, when the identity of things, ideas and beings is abruptly alienated, when A is no longer A, when B is no longer B, when Mr B is no longer Mr B but a traitor and a lecherous viper, while Mr K is no longer Mr K. Trembling is when the newspaper you buy buys you, when the word you hear signifies neither what it signifies nor what it refutes, when the lie that exposes itself lies as it exposes itself, without the negation of negation becoming an affirmation. Trembling is the whole modern world on both sides of the Iron Curtain, when we see it without curtains or veils. Trembling is also when we still hesitate to judge this world because – and this is a supreme trembling – through my mouth there perhaps speaks another, an unknown person who has seduced me or bought me, someone I cannot get to coincide with myself.

Judaism promises a recovery, the joy of self-possession within universal trembling, a glimpse of eternity in the midst of corruption. Should we believe it? Up until now it has been the victim of history; it has not taken on its cruelty. It once knew how to speak a word that stands apart from these swarming insinuations, a word that breaks and unties, a prophetic word. Should we credit it? Nothing is certain, but the opportunity presents itself.

Take the opportunity!

Credit it! The signature is not false!

Assimilation Today

The Dreyfus Affair and the twenty years of National Socialism tragically shook the material and philosophical foundations on which European Judaism had rested for 150 years. These two crises did not mark a definitive break between Jews and the Western world. The creation of the State of Israel revealed to Jews themselves, to the great surprise of some of them, the depth of their enrootedness in Western countries.

From France, Italy, England and the United States, Israel received a lot of enthusiasm and precious few immigrants. This reserve is explained by economic reasons, of course. But the sense of roots also takes in the economy, and the economy is not summed up by sordid matter. It rests on a psychological and cultural behaviour which it in turn fashions. And why deny only Jews the right to love the soil that nurtures them, when every patriotism shamelessly exalts its attachment to the earth that produces man's bread? Moreover, economic reasons alone did not explain the fact that there was no new exodus. Western Judaism remained in the West because, for 150 years, it had received a Western education. The men, things and landscapes of the West are a substantially real world for Judaism. The successful creation of a State of Israel provided the opportunity to become conscious of the reality of assimilation.

And yet assimilation failed. It failed because it did not put an end to the anguish felt by the Jewish soul. Assimilation failed because it did not placate the non-Jews, or put an end to anti-Semitism; on certain points, it stirred up heated reactions and arguments once more. Anguish and anxiety still surreptitiously alter apparently free behaviour and every Jew remains, in the largest sense of the word, a Marrano. We can already glimpse new concessions to the surrounding world being made by the Jew, to the point where he abdicates completely. Assimilation seems to have a lead to dissolution. A strange apathy about Judaism has penetrated the innermost depths of the Jewish soul. To use a phrase from Chaim Grinberg; if the

Jews do not convert to Christianity, it is not because they believe in Judaism but because they no longer believe in anything religious. The fact that assimilation can succeed only in dissolution, and that only irreligiousness slows down this dissolution, is the most serious crisis of assimilation. We have in fact forgotten the ambitions of its promoters: they hoped to maintain Judaism. They wanted to reconcile a Jewish religious existence with a national existence at the heart of states more and more resembling spiritual communities, associations of free individuals, incarnating ideas. The failure of assimilation in the forms its success takes attests to the fragility of the philosophy guiding it and the lack of precision in that philosophy's concepts.

Yet what could have been clearer than the distinction between nationality, the realm of public life, and religion, the domain of private life? Is it not the case that freedom of conscience figures among the achievements of the French Revolution? Shall we say that the threat of dissolution hanging over Judaism stems from contemporary irreligiousness – a general phenomenon common to Jews and non-Jews alike? But we must ask ourselves if the disaffection of individuals with regard to religious beliefs has really worn down the Christian character of the society in which we live, and if the philosophy of assimilation that separated the religious from the political orders has not affected the Jewish religion more deeply than the general lack of belief in the modern world has hit the churches.

The irreligiousness of Christian individuals is played out at the very heart of a State that, even as a lay State, preserves within its secularized substance the forms of religious life. What makes irreligiousness irremediable in the Jews is that the collectivity no longer recognizes that it has any historical vocation, and that its religion merely totalizes the beliefs of individuals. Ignorance of the secularized forms of religious life at the heart of the secular states themselves was the fundamental vice of the philosophy of assimilation. The great theoreticians of Emancipation such as Joseph Salvador, for example, professed both a sincere attachment to Judaism and the conviction that the world which evolved from the French Revolution should free itself from the Christian structures that underpinned pre-revolutionary society.

There exists in fact an element of diffuse religion, halfway between the strictly rational order of political thought and the mystical order of belief, in which political life itself swims. One does not think of this religious atmosphere because one breathes it naturally. It does not simply vanish as a result of the juridical separation between Church and State. The national spirit is strongly marked by religious history which, throughout the centuries, has impregnated daily social customs. It gives the individual's religious life its most substantial nourishment. It is the reality of the half-rational, half-religious element in which political realities swim like lymphatic matter, realities which bring into the very State of Israel a guarantee of religious persistence for the Israeli population, even if individuals go beyond every ritual rule and every belief. For this time the element is Jewish. Herein lies the incalculable value of the young State, albeit secular, to the religious future of Judaism, independently of its significance for the political destiny of the Jewish people.

From this point on, the error of assimilation becomes visible. Jews' entry into the national life of European states has led them to breathe an atmosphere impregnated with Christian essence, and that prepares them for the religious life of these states and heralds their conversion. The strictly private Judaism that advocated assimilation did not escape this unconscious Christianization.

The national life that was accepted without precaution could not fail to lead to the abdication of Judaism. In a world which had evolved from the Christian past, the Jewish religion was trans-formed into an abstract confession.

And if we wish to remain citizens of the great Western nations, participate in their values, guarantee the resulting duties, but remain Jews, we have to resolve to follow a new discipline.

This would involve finding in something other than family memories those concrete realities that could counterbalance, in our daily lives, the imperceptible but real influence of the religions embodied in the life of the State. This requires cultural realities that could be used as substitutes, in order to guarantee the integration of Jews into Western countries against any dissolution. We must revive a Jewish science. This is impossible unless we return to Hebrew. The 'inner cathedrals', built four thousand years ago in the texts, must rise up again on the horizon. Rest assured that they will not ruin the great beauty of modern landscapes. These old texts teach precisely a universalism that is purged of any particularism tied to the land, or recollection held within the plant. It teaches the human solidarity of a nation united by ideas.

The existence of the State of Israel and the living interest in this State will certainly feed, within Judaism, those Jews living among the nations. But it is not enough for them only to keep alive a Jewish flame in those hostels submerged in the light of the West, which takes the shine off all borrowed lights. The curiosity which has been reawakened in the great books of Judaism, and the necessity of applying a thought to them that is not simply emotional but is a demanding one, is the principal condition for the survival of the Jews in the Diaspora. Everything finally comes down to the problem of Hebraic studies.

The effort such a discipline demands certainly poses a preliminary question: do we still want to be Jews? Do we still believe in the excellence of Judaism (a question that has infinitely more meaning for a modern person than the still abstract question: do you believe in God?)? But to this question, we can give a worthy reply only if we understand the reasons behind it. The resurrection and study of Hebraic civilization is therefore in turn presupposed by each and every examination of conscience. How can we break out of the circle without clinging to every last remnant of instinctive fidelity, however sentimental, that lingers in the Jewish soul, after the trials and tribulations of the twentieth century and of twenty centuries, in spite of a conscious apathy that grows ever more dangerous?

Space is not One-dimensional

Two hundred years after the French Revolution, despite all the freedoms the spirit has taken, all the concepts intelligence has enlarged, all the courage that reason has shown in thinking through the most irreconcilable contradictions, the dialectic was to find itself powerless on one point: the behaviour of French Jews in 1967. Unable to accept with an untroubled soul the possible disappearance of Israel and extermination of the Israelis, they were no longer to accord with the definition of a French person. Are we going to have to talk of 'double allegiance', therefore, recognizing that Jews accept a particularism when they speak (or whisper) among themselves, only to oppose it and become offended when non-Jews start to speak of it? Will we have to explain a contradiction in such basic terms? Does being French, short of Euclidean space, mean moving only in one dimension?

It is not pleasant to indulge in apologetics. Producing patriotic service records for a community to which one belongs, including (why not?) a certificate in recognition of bloodshed for the national cause, brings back sad memories. But the ordeal for one's modesty is greater than that of exhibiting (how can one avoid it?), beyond the dossiers and genealogies, certain secret recesses of the soul that up until then, in the land of human rights, we had thought were better protected than impregnable homes.

But how can we shirk it? Precocious problems, if left unanswered, can provide real dangers. The following lines, which reflect only the author's personal views, do not recoil from certain considerations which attest that, for this author, a sense of spirit [esprit] still inhabits the journal Esprit.

I

Has a new way of being a Jew in France come into existence since June 1967?

If allegiance is judged by respect for laws, I can see no breach of

259

rules to date to have put such allegiance in doubt. No French Jew has been allowed, or tempted, to fail in his obligations as a citizen. Not to share the government's opinion on a point of foreign policy, provided that one fulfils the duties demanded of a citizen and those entrusted to an official, does not exclude one from the national community. An avowal of active sympathy for the State of Israel does not stem from any duplicity or clandestine allegiance, and does not constitute treason. Nor is it the fiercest blow that an open opposition could deal to the country's interests. France, Israel: the disproportion between the two political terms when juxtaposed in this way removes from their potential antagonism any appreciable damage to France. How much weight can a disagreement of this kind carry, placed alongside the difficulties raised by other massive anti-government measures, both possible and real, undertaken by French citizens? The life of a great free nation like France is open to the winds of the spirit blowing over the world. Such a life must find expression in the possibility of disagreement between such and such a member of its spiritual families and the successive turns taken by its government's politics.

II

But one's attachment to a great modern nation, the love of one's country, cannot be reduced to mere obedience to the laws and to a professional conscience. We are being asked if, in spirit, Jews in France are not witnessing the beginning of a new way – a contradiction in terms – of being French. Do the people who ask us this know exactly what the old way is? Must we describe the moods of the Jewish groupings of various provenance as they threw themselves into the history of France? However long ago they came to this country, the moment during which they obtained citizenship was a solemn act that reverberated throughout their inner lives, in some way or other touching religion. This is scarcely surprising for a collectivity whose cohesion down the centuries was affirmed, beyond any type of ecclesiastical organization, by a feeling, whether open or not, of being part of the world in all its fundamental affairs; of being, from the momment of the world's creation, responsible for humanity and its sense of justice, in the image of Abraham interceding on behalf of Sodom. It is not because of a predilection for even numbers that one rabbinic apologue suggests that the tomb of Abraham, Isaac and Jacob should also preserve the bones of Adam. Adherence to France is a metaphysical act, of course; it had to be France, a country that expresses its political existence with a trinitarian emblem which is moral and philosophical, and is inscribed on the front of its public buildings.

Need we recall that the Jews from the South of France, emancipated before the Revolution, experienced this emancipation as a gentlemanly act? Need we recall what entry into the nation was like for the Jews of Alsace, the intensity with which they experienced their loss in 1870 of two sides of the 'green border' of the map of France? Need we recall what the Crémieux Decree represented for the Jews of Algeria and how, for every North African native, France represented the apogee of humanity? Finally, need we say how, among the Jewish peoples of Eastern Europe, France was the country in which prophecies came to pass?

It is on the basis of this exceptional essence epitomized by France, in which political and moral life came together, and on the basis of the ideals of the 1789 Revolution and the Declaration of the Rights of Man, through the literature and the institutions that gave it expression, that an attachment was formed with the history and the country that had generated these ideas, to the point where it became the conscience of a vegetable sense of roots in which many Jews could forget the religious source of their love, having become natives, children of the soil, as naturally French as fields are green and trees blossom. This spirit is one that is kept alive by family tradition. If certain changes have come about, it is only to the extent that family traditions have changed among all the French as they open up to new experiences, seek new *raisons d'être*, and shift everyone's sense of nationality. Attachment to the existence of the State of Israel is not the cause, but the effect of this change.

III

It was probably the Dreyfus Affair, not the creation of the State of Israel (although the Dreyfus Affair lay at the origins of political Zionism), that marked the great psychological turning point. Certainly, to the extent that justice triumphed in the Affair, and politics once more rejoined ethics, a new pride in being French could be added to the ancient one. But this was also an unforgettable experience of the fragility of Reason, the possibility of its failure, and the power of nihilism and its most hideous echoes in anti-Semitic abuse, in addition to what Madame Amado-Lévy-Valensi will one day outline for us in other terms – namely, the presence of anti-Semitism in every form of racial hatred, persecution of the weak, and human exploitation. The anti-Semitic remark is like no other. Is it therefore an insult like other insults? It is an exterminating word, through which the Good that glorifies Being sees itself brought to unreality and shrivels up in the deepest recesses of a subjectivity, like an idea transfixed and trembling deep within a cornered moral consciousness. It is a word that reveals to the whole of humanity, through a collectivity that is perhaps cruelly chosen to hear it, a nihilist howling that no other discourse can suggest.

It was perhaps the birth of a new sensibility within emancipated Judaism. It did not alter patriotic feeling but created a new vigilance, a new attention paid to the world, a new way of being stirred and tense in one's existence, a reunion with an old religious experience. This created the first indications of the revalorization of the religious message among the Western Jews who had forgotten it. This was a religious experience in a very broad sense, one that does not begin in practices or the liturgy and remains accessible to people who recognize no link with the transcendent, no theology, no attachment other than a national one.[1] It is also at this point that one begins in the West to suspect that the Jewish religious culture is something completely different from an empty or outmoded theology or simple folklore.[2]

IV

What happened in Europe between 1933 and 1945, culminating in the death camps, led this sensibility beyond the impossible. Religion certainly does not begin with a triumphant, irrefutable Religion, like a sunrise, and then go on to lock itself into forms of worship and priests' sermons, whatever we are told by people who consider themselves believers just as easily as freethinkers consider themselves thinkers. But there are human events which tear open their own envelope. There are events which burn up the concepts that express their substance. There are despairs that words cannot recount but which shatter the silence that holds them without breaking that silence, as though some god passing incognito stole their secret. Is the intolerable intensity of life the phantasm of this god or his light touch? Like the misdeed that was not confessed, the bite of remorse is *perhaps* already the knowing look that burns. Lived experience is too small for its meaning. The ambiguity or *enigma* of the situation is more religious than the solutions one brings to it. Does the true God ever cast off His incognito image? The essence in any case begins here below. There is in the Jewish liturgy a text (whose age and original version are borne out by Tractate Sotah) in which the faithful return grace not for what they receive, but for the very fact that they can return grace.

The Nazi persecution and, following the exterminations, the extraordinary fulfilment of the Zionist dream, are religious events outside any revelation, church, clergy, miracle, dogma or belief. It was as such that these events, too heavy for their frame, entered the consciousness of French Jews and non-French Jews, and non-Jewish Frenchmen and non-French and non-Jewish men. The Passion in which 'it was finished' [*tout fut consommé*] (John 19:30) and this daring task of recommencement – despite the conflicting signs affecting them – have been experienced as signs of the same sense of being chosen or damned – that is to say, of the same exceptional destiny. Contemporaries retained a burn mark on their sides. Had they been too close to the Forbidden and the Unsayable? Or were they wrong to survive? Whatever the thought of that generation – rebellion, negation, doubt or a gloriously confirmed certainty in the midst of humiliation – it bore the seal of the supreme ordeal. For all humanity, it took on a significance that lay outside all categories.

After twenty centuries of apparent anachronism, diasporic Judaism once more became, for the Christians themselves, the locus of the Divine Comedy. The creation of the State of Israel was produced at this level. It came alive once more in 1948, scorning all sociological, political or historical improbability. The Zionist dream, which had evolved from the most implausible nostalgia, going back to the very courses of Creation and echoing the highest expectation, took shape at the cost of labour and sacrifices inspired by the glory invisible to the eyes of those who had not been haunted by the Dream, and who have never been able to make out, in contrast to their own poor tumbledown dwellings, anything more than a miserable arid land in the East, half-swamp and half-desert pretending to be honey and milk.

It is not because the Holy Land takes the form of a State that it brings the Reign of the Messiah any closer, but because the men who inhabit it try to resist the temptations of politics; because this State, proclaimed in the aftermath of Auschwitz, embraces the teaching of the prophets; because it produces abnegation and self-sacrifice. And certainly, this identity, geographically localizable through all Sacred History and nearly all Western history, holds great power over failings and wills. But it lends this power to all the messianic institutions of Israel, all those that tear us out of our conformism and material comforts, dispersion and alienation, and reawaken in us a demand for the Absolute.

V

The resurrection of the State of Israel, its dangerous and pure life, can no longer be separated from its doubly religious origins: a Holy Land resuscitated by the State, in spite of the profane forms it assumes. To 'go up' into Israel for a French Jew is certainly not to change nationality, it is to respond to a vocation. Others make espousals of faith, enter religious orders, go on a mission or join a revolutionary party. Through the appeal of the Holy Land, Jews hear new truths in their ancient books and enter into a religious destiny that cannot be summed up in dogmatics, but in a history which its own limits canot define.

It explodes. Towards the heavens? What does it matter![3] This is the nature of Sacred History. It is a destiny confusedly felt by a great number of French Jews who will perhaps not go beyond these vague feelings and have certainly not thought of these new truths, and a great number of French Jews who could not explain the emotion that gripped them between May and June 1967.

This truth and this destiny are not contained within political and national categories. They no more threaten allegiance to France than they threaten other spiritual adventures, even if our own is one of the highest and most ancient. To be a fully conscious Jew, a fully conscious Christian, a fully conscious communist, is always to find yourself in an awkward position within Being. And you too, my Muslim friend, my unhated enemy of the Six-Day War! But it is from adventures such as these run by its citizens that a great modern State – that is to say, one that serves humanity – derives its greatness, the attention it pays to the present and its presence in the World.

Reflections on Jewish Education

I

The existence of Jews who wish to remain Jews – even apart from belonging to the State of Israel – depends on Jewish education. Only this can justify and nurture such existence. Yet religious instruction, in the sense in which it is understood by Catholics and Protestants, is insufficient as a formula for Jewish education.

To be convinced of this, we have no need to reopen a debate on the essence of Judaism. Religion, nation, a reality refractory to these categories – what does it matter? We can sidestep these metaphysical quotations and stick to the data of experience. Jewish education, reduced to religious instruction, does not include the effective lessons of the Catechism. Educators can testify to the fact, as can the lack of children attracted to those famous Thursday and Sunday classes, the dearth of ideas they take away with them, and the relatively small numbers that join cultural associations.

One essential reason – to stick to the strictly pedagogical plan we have set ourselves here – dictates this failure: the most ancient of the modern religions cannot be separated from a knowledge of an ancient language, Hebrew; and the knowledge of Hebrew is not easily acquired. Judaism is not inseparable from it only because its forms of worship are celebrated in Hebrew and because the faithful are its main actors. One could get away with using translations. Judaism is inseparable from the knowledge of Hebrew because the Jews everywhere constitute a religious minority. If we detach them from the deep and real life that animates these square letters with its precise rhythms, we reduce them to the poverty of a theoretical catchism.

In a world in which nothing is Jewish, only the text reverberates and echoes a teaching that no cathedral, no plastic form, no specific social structure can free from its abstract nature. Christian religious instruction can content itself with summary notions because Christian civilization is here and present, giving these notions a concrete meaning and confirming them every day.

The notions that a Jewish child picks up on Sundays and Thursdays from the synagogue are limited – without Hebrew – to schemes whose meaning is watered down or dispersed in the face of these Christian forms of Europe to which Western humanism itself has for so long been linked.

If emancipated Judaism has managed to survive as Judaism for more than 150 years, despite the progressive drying up of Hebrew studies, it is because this dryng up was only progressive and because, while one moved further away from the age in which moral and social structures of life were steeped in Jewish knowledge, this atmosphere had for a long time been transported within the family furniture. But family memories cannot ultimately take the place of a civilization.

II

These days we have come to understand the way in which Jewish education rigorously depends on Hebrew studies.

The creation of full-time Jewish schools in which the teaching of Hebrew occupies a prominent place as a language of general culture stems from a clear-sightedness that confers honour on the leaders of our communities.

In the Alliance schools in North Africa, in its teacher training college, this theoretical view has always been accepted.

In France, we certainly could not hope to welcome the whole of the young generation into our Jewish schools, but at least we have tried to train an important nucleus of Jews who have been taught about Judaism.

And yet, in these very schools, in which a large place was reserved in the programmes for Hebrew studies, we have not managed to make them fully effective. We believe that the difficulty does not stem only from the quality of the teachers, some of whom are excellent, nor from the uneven preparation of the pupils in Hebrew disciplines.

The problem of Jewish education poses in its turn a more general problem. Hebrew studies do not exert on the young generation the prestige that one would like to confer on them, as though the culture that Hebrew studies must convey had lost its human value and could not match the spiritual nourishment given by the surrounding civilization. There is a hint of sacrilege in this, but that is in fact what it signifies.

The history of Judaism during the last centuries has in effect led to a certain weakening of what we might call the potential of Jewish culture. As we know, a culture is not a collection of archaeological curiosities on which we confer value and appeal by virtue of a vague feeling of piety. It is a collection of truths and forms that respond to the demands of spiritual life and life in general. However, they can respond only if they envelop history and if they are present in intelligences. But modern Hebraic culture, in its deliberately secular forms, lives in a world of yesteryear. It has not yet achieved the level of the Western civilizations – a level that alone can give credit to the more modest, secondary education of adolescents who think and draw comparisons.

As for its religious form, Jewish culture has ceased to be – through the fault of certain generations which made no intellectual demands – that source of thought and life, that integral civilization that it so eminently is. It imposes itself only in the name of the tradition that is not a *raison d'être*; it imposes itself in the name of piety, which is not a reason. Traditionalism or pietism are orthodoxies, not doctrines.

In order for the permanent values of Judaism, contained in the great texts of the Bible, the Talmud and their commentators, to be able to nurture souls, they must once again be able to nurture brains. It is our trust in these values that invites us to look to them for our substantial sustenance. As long as the presence of a real Jewish civilization, whether secular or religious, is not felt behind the Hebrew classes given in our secondary and even primary schools, Hebrew, despite the amount of time spent on it, will remain an option for which we have simply suppressed the right to exercise an option.

III

We find, therefore, that religious instruction demands Hebrew studies and that the success of Hebrew studies in secondary, primary or higher education depends on the Advanced Studies whose promotion is perhaps the most urgent task faced by modern Judaism, even in Israel. The revision of forms that have been simply transmitted by Jewish culture is certainly necessary. But contrary to the aspirations of liberalism, it is not a question of sifting things or cutting down on overheads, as one does when trying to prevent the bankruptcy of an honourable estate.

On the contrary, we must enlarge the science of Judaism and, fundamentally, raise it only to the level of a science.

But let this be clearly understood: to raise Judaism to the level of a science does not involve submitting its sources to philosophy. For 150 years, we have done nothing else.

The nineteenth century wore itself out with the philology of Judaism. Fifty centuries were catalogued – an immense Jewish epigraphy, a collusion of epigraphs – for which historical accounts were important and which had to be placed at the crossroad of different influences. What a graveyard! A grave for 150 generations! The philologist who subjects texts to a critical apparatus may feel some tenderness for all this touching folklore, but for a moment he, the critical spirit, is more intelligent than his object. He risks eternalizing this moment. Only the handling of a card index scans the work of thought.

To raise Judaism into a science, to think Judaism, is to turn these texts back into teaching texts.

Until now, no one in the West has taken talmudic texts seriously. Their truths are acknowledged when they concur with the most basic common sense; we no longer see the still unfinished dialogue they open up with a world that has been once more put into question.

Pure philology, which is not enough for the understanding of Goethe, is not enough for the intellection of Rabbi Akiba or Rabbi Tarphon. It is finally time to allow Rabbi Akiba and Rabbi Tarphon to speak if we want to be Jews – that is to say, claim them for ourselves.

Pure piety is no longer enough. We can still pull off a pedagogy of exaltation, enthusiastically admit propositions that demand adherence to a reason at the expense of a total effort; but pure feelings which, even when they are pure feelings or hothouse feelings, pass for ideas, have no future. Nothing is really vital, we have to say, unless it bears the mark of intellect. No cheap acquiescence! Too many young people speak lightly of the crisis in intelligence. The sole honour of modern times consists in having become conscious of the reason in which Judaism recognizes itself. Alone, these advanced studies will make possible a secondary or primary education that will not feel refuted or forgotten on its first contact with the world in which we still try to live, work and create.

Education and Prayer

Prayer is one of the most difficult subjects for a philosopher, as it is for a believer.

Even if the philosopher, on his itinerary leading from one piece of evidence to another, were led to an evidence that went beyond evidence, we would still have to go much further in order to understand prayer. Is a discourse that begins in the here below and moves 'beyond language' possible? And when the possibility of such a discourse – an extravagent one, in the etymological sense of the term – had been established, one would still have to understand how this discourse could reasonably offer supplication when it addresses itself to Him Who knows all human suffering; how it could glorify Him Who is all glory, how it could sanctify Him Who is all-holy. For a descendant of the Greeks, such a thing is scandalous!

The simple believer, like the philosopher, runs the risk of scandal. He cannot confess his experience of prayer. The simple believer (in today's world, at all events) is already scandalous for espousing his belief: he seems to some a bourgeois conformist who entertains comfortable ideas that protect his comforts; to others a wizard, a strange man who entertains relations with a secret, magic world. But above all, how can one evoke prayer, which deals with the most intimate parts of our lives, without being shameless or indiscreet?

The eminent orators who have preceded me have avoided all these dangers by dealing with prayer as an already existing social reality and questioning its history and emotional effectiveness. Like them, I shall deny myself the difficult role of philosopher and witness. I know, certainly, that scandal often shelters difficult truths. I am persuaded that, finally, the philosopher and the believer are called to understand one another. But I also know that it requires a lot of philosophy and a lot of belief, and that neither the one nor the other can be exhibited in front of so many people.

I shall therefore confine myself to two reflections which are a great deal less ambitious: first to affirm that in Judaism the first place goes fully to prayer, which is not a pious thought pronounced at any meeting of the French Jewish Foundation; and then to grant prayer, in fact, only second place.

Whatever the ultimate meaning of prayer, whatever its heights or depths, it is collective prayer, familiar to us all, that opens up this ultimate meaning to the daring tenderness of a few. From this point on, what is the commonly known significance of this collective experience that can be confessed without shame? In it the individual renews his links – through the number, or *minyan* – with the community of Israel dispersed throughout space and time, and through this unity he renews his links with the highest Unity. His presence and participation in the office, for which the prayer of an isolated person is often merely a consolation, the act of embracing such ancient expressions, such primordial thoughts, all those verbal gestures in a language that thousands of years of history have not destroyed – all this makes one conscious of the presence, permanence and eternity of Israel. What in our prayers consequently passes, in the eyes of our reformed brothers, for sterile, formalist immobilism constitutes the force and grandeur of the Immutable. Through Him it is possible to have an elementary, massive and incomparable experience, one we must cultivate in this way: the experience of the reunion of Israel. It does not, for all that, represent a necessary collectivist substitute in the absence of any transcendent nourishment.

This emotion of the presence of Israel and of our participation in the collectivity of Israel, in spite of space and time, is a basic monotheist experience. The proximity of the Divine is inconceivable for a Jew without the presence of the people of Israel. Prayer rests unanswered in a windowless room. God is near to whoever invokes Him, but the invocation presupposes an opening up and a truth. A God Who leads Himself to a *tête-à-tête* outside of all Israel, without the certainty of the durability of Israel, of the continuity of its history; without solidarity, throughout this history, with the history of humanity, is a dangerous abstraction, and a source of suspect intoxication. According to one apologue in Berakoth, the Lord God Himself would put on His *tefillin* each morning. The 'Hear, O Israel: The Lord our God is one Lord' (Deuteronomy 6:4), written into our earthly *tefillin*, has as its celestial counterpart: 'Who is like you O Israel, a nation unique on the earth?' To adore the Lord God is not to shy away from humanity, a humanity that is unique and united, a humanity towards which eternal thought leans [*se penche*] and to which it pours out its heart [*s'épanche*].

In this sense the synagogue and the offices it celebrates and the verbal gestures of prayer, which together envelop all the other liturgical gestures, constitute the substance of Jewish life as a religious life. Better still, in this sense, prayer supports even the Judaism that no longer wishes to be religious. It is the synagogue and, consequently, prayer enveloping all the liturgical gestures of Israel, that has prepared for Jewish nationalists, in spite of the temptations of History, a nation to exalt.

So much for the impossibility of replacing prayer, if one does not wish to replace Judaism.

But a second remark, of a pedagogical nature, must be made, one that should make us more circumspect with regard to this priority of prayer. What has already been said by Chief Rabbi Schilli moves us in this direction. We live, in this century, in an open world. The Jewish collectivity is seduced by every worldly activity. And however paradoxical it may seem, the activities of the modern world have lost the world's profane character. Science on the one hand, and political and social activities on the other, claim to satisfy the whole of man's humanity. They present themselves as the roads to salvation. Thinking, active men – the best in our time, at any rate – hold to the idea that no religious salvation can be possible as long as reason and justice are left unsatisfied. The prayer that institutes Judaism, and confirms it, no longer opens itself up sufficiently to God and humanity to satisfy the contemporary Jewish consciousness in Europe.

For a whole generation that experiences its rational and political destiny religiously, prayer cannot link this religion of the world to the religion of the Bible. Perhaps it is the omega of Judaism, but it is not the alpha. The Judaism of the house of prayer has ceased to be transmittable. The old-fashioned Judaism is dying off, or is already dead. This is why we must return to Jewish wisdom; this is why in our recitation of this wisdom we must reawaken the reason that has gone to sleep; this is why the Judaism of reason must take precedence over the Judaism of prayer: the Jew of the Talmud must take precedence over the Jew of the Psalms.

But this is also why we must follow with more confidence everything that in our young generation is attracted to generous actions, even when this young generation no longer bears the label of Judaism or expressly rejects it. There are abnegations that atone for denial. By closing ourselves to the Jews who are without Judaism but who, without Judaism, act as Jews, we risk ending up with a Judaism without Jews.

It is not only by simplifying or modifying worship – I regret that I must disagree here with my eminent friend the Chief Rabbi of Paris – that we shall manage to transmit the gift of prayer which we must first acquire. Our collective prayer has, paradoxically, become the prayer of isolated people. The guardians of tradition, the guardians of the messianic institutions, have a sacred mission, built on tenacity, patience, and expectation. But to the multitudes, the reading of a newspaper has become – to use a famous phrase – their morning prayers. There is still a great deal to do if we are to bring this oration back to our venerable expressions which dominate time without ignoring it. There is still a great deal to do, but we must do something. At the synagogue, alongside the elite, there are many who continue in their inertia, and among those who have left the synagogue and been blown across the world there are many great souls in love with the absolute.

Let us be frank. We for whom the walls of the synagogue are familiar, and our friends – where do we find the most dazzling confirmation of our truth? Where do we look for the signs that believers do not speak about, but which even the most committed believers need in order to confirm their beliefs? Is it the synagogues, even at *Yom Kippur*, when they are full and vibrant with people? Does our quest for signs not move in the direction of less familiar thoughts, less consecrated places, less assured people? Our state of being chosen – that is to say, our irremissible reponsibility – pierces and marks us, not so much in the solemnity of offices as in the flash of talmudic genius, when we are still capable of perceiving it. And according to another order, the certainty of being chosen comes to us each time the Jewish presence is manifested in those men who struggle and die for a just cause; as well as each time the ancient message guiding these just struggles – in a vocabulary that threatens to render it unrecognizable, unaware even of the features of its typical physiognomy, as though by a miracle – shines. But we must open up to yet other signs. The builders of a better world – who, in the name of Reason, ignore the Judgement – are enclosing and walling up our sons like the living bricks of biblical Egypt spoken of by the Talmud; and in these uniform bricks, which should prefigure a humanity based on equality, we can see a strange germination in such a homogeneous matter. That germination is *Difference*, within which we find the stirrings of a stubborn and difficult freedom.

For a Jewish Humanism

At this halfway point in our century, alongside the State of Israel which is struggling for its existence, the Judaism of dispersion searches for a content. Limited groups have ties with the synagogue, but they are not always sure that their sons will have the same ties. In every social class the piety that once bonded communities together has become weaker. The surrounding civilizations exert an irresistible seductive power on the younger generation through their artistic values, social experiences and political ideals. The conscious and unconscious adherence to the great historical nations of the West is scarcely coloured by a Jewish sentimentalism. Judaism is no longer either a religion or a separate nation. An existence cannot really be deduced from such an inconsistent essence.

Those who do not resign themselves to this end turn to Hebrew and the Jewish school where their children are taught. Here again, they are not spared heartbreak. Is Hebrew one more living language to learn? And does the Jewish school not represent a return to the confessional school?

We should like to show that, without prejudicing the religious orders, the teaching of Hebrew and the Jewish school that ought to see such teaching as its principal vocation in no way betray the ideals of the secular school, and that the study of Hebrew itself lends support to what can today give a meaning to Judaism. It lends support to the Jewish humanism which cannot remain indifferent to the modern world in which it seeks a whole humanity.

A Jewish humanism: the phrase seems as suspect for its noun as for its adjective! Humanism, a much-used, misused and ambiguous word, can none the less designate a system of principles and disciplines that free human life from the prestige of myths, the discord they introduce into ideas and the cruelty they perpetuate in social customs. But in that case, we have already defined not just humanism, but Jewish humanism. Its notion remains secular. It does not exhaust the essence of all the forms that Judaism adopted throughout the ages, but is not absent from any one of them. It is all too true that Judaism is still to be found at the crossroads of faith and logic.

Mendelssohn put to the moderns a view that Spinoza had borrowed from Maimonides: the most ancient monotheism is not a revealed religion, but a revealed Law. Its truth is universal like reason; its rule and moral institutions, Judaism's particular support, preserve this truth from corruption. Judaism's excellence already consists in not substituting itself for reason, and not doing violence to the spirit. But its genius is a practical one: it seems to avoid, in its conquest of the intellect, the doctrine in man's thought. There is therefore an erosion of the values preserved or transmitted in a state of abstraction. There is a remarkable relation between the spiritual nature of ideas and the carnal nature of social habits, an element in which the final truths are preserved unaltered and from which they draw their power.

The eighteenth century, in love with eternal truths to the point of believing them to be active and effective even in a state of pale abstractions, did not therefore completely ignore the dangers presented by the way in which social customs do not keep up with ideas and, in short, the inconsistency of truths when separated from conduct, ideas without culture. This is why universal ideas spread everywhere, even beyond Europe, and preserve their true face nowhere! The bare intellect can scale great heights, but cannot endure there. Reason, sovereign and subject to the truth, succumbs to the idolatry of myths that tempt, betray and shackle it. Truth according to Judaism finds a faithful symbolism that preserves it from the imagination only in practical attitudes, in a Law. The great texts of rabbinic Judaism, which are inseparable from the Bible, expose this law which supports the great truths. Certainly, they do not expose it as a code, nor as a dogmatic treatise, nor as a collection of quotations to be used by theologians or as recipes for spirituality. They reflect an entire world which must be entered patiently – like the Greek world, for example – at the cost of discipline, toil, method, and grammar, but also with an acute sense of the spiritual, and not only the philological, problem: with the intrepid nature of the enquiring spirit. It is before all else, in the superior sense of the term, a literature and a civilization.

The monotheism that brings it to life, which is the most dangerous of abstractions since it is the highest, does not consist in preparing man, with all his weak imperfections, for a private meeting with a consoling God; but in bringing the divine presence to just and human effort, as one brings the light of day to the human eye, the only organ capable of seeing it. The vision of God is a moral act. This optics is an ethics. Let us be wary of direct contacts which are a process of trial and error.

The Bible clarified and accentuated by the commentaries from the great age that precedes and follows the destruction of the Second Temple, when an ancient and uninterrupted tradition finally blossoms, is a book that leads us not towards the mystery of God, but towards the human tasks of man. Monotheism is a humanism. Only simpletons made it into a theological arithmetic. The books in which this humanism is inscribed await their humanists. The task for those who wish to continue Judaism consists in having these books opened. This is the monotheist mission of Israel – if one can still derive any pride from it after all those who, ignoring sources, the books and virtues of Judaism, boast of teaching the oneness of God to the peoples of the earth who, better than us, know this abstraction.

The *no* with which the Jews, so dangerously over the centuries, replied to the calls of the Church does not express an absurd stubbornness, but the conviction that important human truths in the Old Testament were being lost in the theology of the New. But without the Talmud, we should be able to offer only the alternative of our own hesitant reading, an individual wisdom, to the Christian tradition (albeit one more recent than that of our Doctors). Taking refuge in our old folios, the truths of Jewish humanism became the thought of an isolated people. The passion for justice that aroused the West after the Renaissance broke this isolation but made Jews lose the secret of their science, which they did not suspect beyond a few memories taken from translated writings.

The Hebrew language and the texts, to which it is substantially linked and which are revealed only through it, is the vehicle for a difficult wisdom concerned with truths that correlate to virtues. This wisdom is as necessary as the Graeco-Roman legacy. Laid down in the Hebrew Bible, the Mishnah and the Gemara, this civilization built on justice unfolds in science. It is as inept to reproach this science for its meticulousness and fine distinctions as it would be stupid to denounce these in mathematics. The emergence of this science is a school.

Marc Cohn recently recalled Rabelais's desire to see a culture that included, alongside Greek and Latin, both 'the Arabic language and the Hebrew language'. Alcofribas Nasier, an abstractor of quintessence, isolated the elements of the new world. The Jewish school of the Diaspora can serve this ideal, by instituting Hebrew studies that do not bring man to an exotic wisdom, but reawaken one of the souls of his soul. They herald a man freed from myths and identify spirit with justice.

The rare privilege of the Jewish religion consists in promoting as one of the highest virtues the knowledge of its own sources. This knowledge can lead pious souls to forms of life that demand ulterior options. It does not impose the sacrifice of a cockerel at Esculape. The terrain remains neutral. From this point on, is it not the terrain on which a Jewish Alliance should continue today? This Alliance would seek neither to demand an impossible denial of national belonging nor to prejudice religious commitment. The discovery and preservation of Jewish humanism would already be one sufficient *raison d'être* for the Jewish school, in a world in which we want above all to see an education that does not separate men. It in no way involves maintaining divisive beliefs; rather it seeks to save from oblivion the notes that over the centuries have stirred these very beliefs, notes that are indispensable to human harmony.

Antihumanism and Education

Until the fairly recent past, Western humanity looked to humanism for its *raison d'être*.

In a wide sense, humanism signified the recognition of an invariable essence named 'Man', the affirmation of this central place in the economy of the Real and of his value which engendered all values. This created respect for the person, both in itself and in the Other, which made it necessary to safeguard his freedom; a blossoming of human nature, of intelligence in Science, creativity in Art, and pleasure in daily life; the satisfaction of desires without prejudice for the freedom and pleasures of other men and, consequently, the institution of a just law – that is to say, a reasonable and liberal State or, in other words, a State at peace with other states and – an important point – above all opening up for individuals as broad as possible a domain for private life, on the threshold of which the law stops. A limit to law is necessary to humanism, for humanism can perhaps see no laws other than those of the State and of nature.

In a narrow sense, humanism signifies the worship accorded to these very principles. The inner flame of humanism is rekindled on contact with certain work and by the study of certain books in which these principles, these humanities, were expressed for the first time, and through which they were transmitted.

But from this point on also, as if the human had to realize itself through the human world and as if man were not only to realize but were already at the nexus in which all causes were assembled, humanism wishes to become an action in the guise of beautiful language. It adopts a certain style, half-artistic, half-preacher, wholly generous, the language of *belles-lettres* which states these values. Through this it becomes indulgent in these statements, as though they were acts, and from this point on it progressively forgets these noble principles which are lost in rhetoric and ideology.

277

II

There can be no doubt that between humanist values and the biblical ideal there are certain analogies, even certain analogies between the worship of *belles-lettres* and an attachment to books, an attachment off which Judaism lives; just as there can be no doubt that a discourse on Judaism can degenerate into or become inflated with ideology.

Since the Emancipation, which I wish neither to denigrate nor to deny, which transformed us into a modern Judaism – or, more exactly, obliges or allows us to open up wide to a more fraternal humanity than before – it is through these analogies that, spontaneously, we assume this duty, or claim this right.

The modernization of Judaism, which equates with a new style of life and the reform of the ritual and ritualism, claims to preserve the spirit of the ancient religion. But the spirit preserved above all comes back to the model taught by Western humanism. This is a tendency that does not inspire only so-called liberal Judaism. The habit of justifying the Scriptures in terms of the way they harmonize with the surrounding humanism – the already philosophical concern to justify the Scriptures – was the unconscious intention, the unavowed apologetics, even of those who did not dare to touch, at least in public, the traditional institutions, the traditional forms of worship, the traditional forms of doctrine.

Can the whole of Western humanism pass for a secularization of Judaeo-Christianity? Have the rights of man and of the citizen and the new spirit that conquered in the eighteenth century not fulfilled in our minds the promises of the prophets?

Even in our day, we allow ourselves to put forward these exalting but, on many points, contestable ideas. Even if they had been entirely true, they would have lost their truth today. Our Jewish society has let go of the particular links that bind it to the prophets to the extent that its members read the sacred books in translation, like all their fellow citizens, leaving to one side the rabbinic tradition through which the prophecies reverberate with all their Jewish sonority. But they are contestable ideas. For Cicero's *De Officiis*, studied by the philosophers, explains, outside the Judaeo-Christian religious tradition of the prophets, the evolution of political and social thought in Europe. They are contestable for another reason. The notion of Judaeo-Christianity, which is on everyone's lips, certainly expresses an evolution and an ideal to be realized in synthesis inspired by the ecumenical age; but not every contradiction has yet been raised.

The respect that we have for the Christian faith, the admiration provoked by the virtues of its saints and the righteousness of its many men of goodwill and courage who, notably, revealed themselves to us during the terrible years, invites and encourages us to reach this synthesis which must first of all be practised like a friendship. Judaeo-Christian friendship: there is a phrase that embodies an absolutely proper use of this synthetic adjective. But on the level of doctrine, as regards the finality of the human, major divergences remain. And in a world that Christianity fashioned, and in which it received objective expression, the Jew has not yet overcome all the complexes of a Marrano.

It is through liberal humanism that he feels he is the equal and the brother of the Christian. This is why we do not speak lightheartedly of the Crises of humanism.

III

But this method of submitting the Jewish tradition to the norms of humanism, to the norms of its hermeneutic methods which disqualify the rabbinic exegesis, to the norms of its abstract universalism – this method explains the very crisis of Jewish education in emancipated Jewish society. This crisis seems to be enduring despite every effort made by Judaism in the name of Hitler on behalf of education, for which we must pay homage – and not because I find myself today at the Consistory – to the directors of the new Consistory.

Ladies and gentlemen, what weight could Jewish education have through these traditional forms, if Western humanism were destined to be the culmination, in all the glory of its literary, artistic, architectural, political and social presence? All that remained for us was to be proud of the precociousness of our ancestors? That was not enough to put us to the trouble of learning Hebrew and of sacrificing our free time to an 'archaic' form of thought that the whole of post-revolutionary France supposedly expressed in spirit and in truth.

It is not because the Western Jews detached themselves from Judaism that Jewish education became deprived of meaning; it is because Jewish education submitted itself in advance to the humanities that Judaism became conscious again of having certainly played a part in the birth of values which had fallen into the public domain and been embellished by European culture, but also of no longer representing anything of current affairs.

From this point on, Jewish education becomes religious instruction in which ideas, detached from the civilization that nurtured them, express, in abstract and bloodless form, the ultimate difference still separating Jews from the homogeneous society into which they had entered, thanks to the principles of humanism which were those of 1789, and which they shared with their fellow citizens.

This is an ultimate difference that many Jews no longer want because they do not want any difference and because, in the society in which religion lost its social effectiveness and its intellectual meaning, to be of a Mosaic confession was to be ruled by the uncertain, the outdated and the subjective.

This was the century in which God died – that is to say, in a very precise sense, in which a certain discourse on God became increasingly impossible. We require another with reference to the part of symbolism which is inseparable from it and to the practical meanings that support it – that is to say, basically, a discourse in the context of the Scriptures through their biblical resonances. Separated from these dimensions, this discourse astonishes and scandalizes with its rashness and impudence. One still hears it in certain assemblies where one does not hesitate when faced with phrases such as 'God wished, God chose, God ordered'; we are told about God as we might be told about someone's doctor or mother-in-law.

This is a language that must be forbidden when we do not know how to designate the appropriate place, even when addressing very young people, at the risk of making them lose everything on the day on which the literal meaning of this language will appear hollow and impossible to them. This is a day that has probably already come.

Jewish education, as a 'religious institution', detaching a few phrases from the whole context of Jewish knowledge, in the new society signifies a Judaism of pure mental reserve; while the Christian Catechism is prolonged in day-to-day social customs and habits, even in a country in which religion is separate from the State; blossoms in the landscapes and, as architecture, dominates our comings and goings.

Jewish civilization, laid down in its entirety in books that henceforth become inaccessible, allowed no resonance to emerge from the phrases taught since the Emancipation in the fusty religious instruction classes, classes which were reduced to a few hours a week in the whole life of a pupil, during which, for his *bar mitzvah*, he learned the basic elements in reading and a few quickly forgotten gestures.

IV

In order for the problem of Jewish education to be put in terms different from those of religious intruction, we therefore needed a crisis of humanism in our society. That is a sad thing to say. A crisis of humanism which began with the inhuman events of recent history.

They had profound effects on contemporary thought and, from that point on, were reflected without any restraint in social customs and habits.

Need we recall these inhumanities? The 1914 War, the Russian Revolution refuting itself in Stalinism, fascism, Hitlerism, the 1939–45 War, atomic bombings, genocide and uninterrupted war. On another level, a science that wants to embrace the world and threatens it with disintegration – a science that calculates the real without always thinking it, as if it were created on its own in the human brain, without man, who is reduced purely and simply to the fields in which the operations of numbers unfold. Or in a different atmosphere, the ambitious philosophical enterprise which charms many of us, the ambitious philosophical enterprise in aid of thought and against pure calculation, but subordinating the human to the anonymous gains of Being and, despite its 'Letters on humanism', bringing understanding to Hitlerism itself. A liberal politics and administration that suppresses neither exploitation nor war; a socialism that gets entangled in bureaucracy. The very alienation of de-alienation! A whole series of reversals, inversions and perversions of man and his humanism!

Is this the fragility of humanism in Western liberalism? Is it a basic inability to guarantee the privileges of humanity of which humanism had considered itself the repository?

We, as Jews, were the first to feel it. For us, the crisis of the human ideal, whether of Greek or Roman origin, is announced in anti-Semitism, which is in its essence hatred for a man who is other than oneself – that is to say, hatred for the other man. It is a sad privilege to be chosen in order to perceive, in the simplicity of a sensation, the collapse of a world and, in the eternal return of the Jewish question, the return of metaphysical questions! But it is also a premonition, as well as a martyrdom in the etymological sense of the term. This martyrdom attests to the fact that the meaning of humanity is not exhausted by the humanists, nor immune to a slippage that is at first imperceptible but can ultimately prove fatal. Is there a fragility to humanity in this humanism? Yes. Let us recall the progressive acclamation of the swastika by the masses. Let us recall how it became even more acclaimed because of this very acclamation. Its progressive acclamation made the intellectuals and humanists pause for 'grave reflection'! It made them reflect because in spite of all its generosity, Western humanism has never managed to doubt triumph or understand failure or conceive of a history in which the vanquished and the persecuted might have some value.

Does the political theory of the West attended to by the greatest philosophers and scholars provide a sufficient sense of equilibrium for humanity? That is the question to which the need for a Jewish education corresponds perhaps quite stupidly. Quite stupidly! A need for 'kacherout'.

In France, to offer only a few signs of this, this need was shown immediately after the First World War, when Robert Gamzon created the French Jewish Scouts movement; in 1935, when Marc Cohn founded the full-time Jewish school, the Maimonides School; before 1939, when men like the philosopher Jacob Gordin, formulating and teaching an intellectually ambitious Judaism that was most certainly open to the modern world but already measuring itself against it, were attended to and soon heard with enthusiasm. All this bears witness, not to some sort of masochism belonging to persecuted people looking for a haven for the source of their unhappiness, but to a movement towards a doctrine, better able than the surrounding humanism to give a meaning to being and life, and to keep alive (it is ultimately this which operates on the level of man's true love) the persecuted man's human essence – that is to say, to act in such a way that in his rebellion or patience, he does not himself become a persecutor and mistrusts resentment.

V

The surrounding humanism was badly shaken by the truth. The inhuman character of this century's events has determined, in the whole of our age's intelligence, what we might call – to adopt the fashionable slogan – antihumanism. From the very beginning, this mistrust is not confused with the abandonment of all human ideals and consists, above all, in putting into doubt what we described above as humanism in the narrow sense of the term.

It is a protest againt *belles-lettres* and the declamation that takes the place of necessary activities, against the decency that covers hypocrisy, the anti-violence that perpetuates abuse; but equally against the violence of the verbal indignation of revolutionaries themselves, who immediately become inverted into a cultural pastime as they turn themselves into a revolutionary literature, in which literature coats revolution and so refreshes a dulled artistic palate. It is an antihumanism that protests against all-powerful literature and finds its way even into the graffiti that call for such literature's destruction. It is an antihumanism as old as the prophecy of Ezekiel, in which the real prophetic spirit is offered as the only thing capable of putting an end to all such writing. Let me end this section, then, with this text from Ezekiel (Ezekiel 33:30–33):

> As for you, son of man, your people who talk together about you by the walls and at the doors of the houses, say to one another, each to this brother, 'Come, and hear what the word is that comes forth from the Lord.' And they come to you as people come, and they sit before you as my people, and they hear what you say but they will not do it; for with their lips they show much love, but their heart is set on their gain. And, lo, you are to them like one who sings love songs with a beautiful voice and plays well on an instrument, for they hear what you say, but they will not do it. When this comes – and come it will! – then they will know that a prophet has been among them.

This is an appeal to unhappiness. It is not certain whether in Jewish education, which we henceforth seek to offer, this antihumanism which wishes to wring the neck of eloquence has or has not a positive role to play in stripping certain commonplaces of their false foliage and putting an end to an eloquence, built on Jewish apologetics, which has become absolutely unbearable.

We should mistrust a purely rhetorical pervasion, the ideology that builds its nest in pathos. An education that takes on the child at a tender age requires elements based on sentiment and emotion. Obviously. But we must not fall into complacency. We must insist on prolonging all formality and praxis in our dealings with the Other and on the mistrust that they awake in us with regard to the apparent innocence of our natural movements before the Law.

VI

But the crisis of humanism cannot be reduced to being opposed to *belles-lettres*. Antihumanism does not confine itself to this denunciation of literature and an eloquence that disguises misery. Has not the search for frankness and truth, while unmasking the special qualities of language, laid bare in our civilization the cracks that threaten to disfigure the supposedly eternal essence of man, cracks that the cloak of eloquence hid and perhaps protected? The antihumanism in the brilliant thought and works of contemporary intellectuals (so avidly followed by the young generation who, after hearing them, is convinced that it has just left the Himalayas) has done everything to open up these cracks. Intellectuals as intellectuals, when they are real intellectuals, have the goal of extricating and measuring the possibilities released by the shift in meaning that heralds shift in land, and of revealing the presuppositions connected with a crevice, as yet invisible to the naked eye, or visible only as a crumbling at the foundations. We do not have to ask intellectuals to act as moralists to repair the structural defects they uncover, or even get their impassivity to pronounce them defects.

At best we can return to the terms within which meaning appears to them and see if, beyond the Said, within which they communicate, the responsibility for the Other [*autrui*], a commandment obeyed before it is pronounced, is not the language prior to language, signification itself. But herein lies another problem. However this may be, when faced with contemporary thought we do not have to succumb to the temptations of some 'moral order', or echo the reactions of *bien-pensants* who do not take the trouble to think and who, having carried out an inquisition on feelings that are in principle free of all constraint, finish up by saving humanity in the concentration camps. But beware of the possibilities unleashed! Antihumanism, which begins by paying better attention to the human, makes the antagonisms between Law and Freedom which we had thought resolved erupt again and, by a progressive subtraction of elements, finally announces the end of the essence of the man whose irreducibility and supremacy are the basis of the Old Testament.

Everything indisputably begins with a respect for man and a struggle for his liberation, for his autonomy, for the law he gives himself, for 'the freedom inscribed on the Tablets of stone', as our Doctors of the Law put it.

From this point on, everything comes down to a struggle for freedom from economic exploitation, which saps autonomy under the false guise of a contract between employer and employee – a contract between unequal partners – based in part on trickery. This struggle is a harsh one that demands laws, but here law seems to repress the freedom it makes possible. And beneath its rationality, beneath the rationality of law, we glimpse dark motives and secret wars. Man's freedom now no longer lies in the economic freedom which represents his privileged place. It lies in unrepressed desire and in the clear light thrown on this desire. From this point on, we can follow the sequence of consequences, the 'freedom of desire' that shakes law and obligation.

The idea of freedom 'progresses' in the following way. From economic freedom to sex education through all the degrees of this freedom; freedom as regards the obligations to which heterosexuality is still naturally attached, and even the solitary ecstasy of drugs in which we have no further need of interhuman relationships, and all responsibilities come undone! Spiritualization brought to its highest point is not solitude but the solitary ecstasy of drugs, the spirit in the cloud of opium! Opium as the religion of the people! But we can sink even lower. Everything is allowed, nothing is absolutely forbidden. Nothing, perhaps, is forbidden any longer as regards our dealings with the other man.

Our anxiety in the face of this progress, believe me, does not stem from a policeman-like concern that we no longer know whom to label the guilty party. It is not the worry of a cop, as we amiably put it these days. We believe that even the person who has not sinned does not have the right to cast the first stone at whoever is at fault, for the age of stoning is gone. He who has not sinned is less of an executioner and thinks himself more of a sinner than all the Others. But none of that is a reason why children who must become adults open to the misfortunes of others should be educated in moral confusion, with no distinction being made between good and evil – by which I mean without their knowing how to recognize the misery lurking within the illusions of happiness, and the contentment and satisfaction to be had from mere happiness.

If man's happiness and freedom demanded the suppression of law, if every law as law were repressive, if every freedom were concerned in the natural sense of arbitrary will, the West would reveal itself to be opposed to everything it had been up until then, breaking with what it had been according to the Bible and the humanities analogous to the Bible.

But Jewish values would also recover some originality and cease to be the echo of the surrounding civilization or the discharge given to it. Here Jews would audaciously be able to hesitate in the face of brilliant doctrines: an opportunity is being given to Jewish education, which for once is necessary, not because it follows the current carrying us along, but because it swims against it.

We Jews must in fact ask ourselves if the ancient divorce between love and law – which has managed to maintain itself only by recourse to the secular arm and its harsh law – or between spirit and letter, which presented itself as a biblical one, has not in fact been a concession made to the pagans rather than a method of teaching them Moses and the prophets, and if this concession has not widened the fissure which only eloquence hid until then, which allowed nothingness hidden within pagan values to ferment. From one divorce to the next, has not love without law resulted in pleasure without love, setting free the love of obligations which it still carries within it?

Once more the Jewish wisdom of the Law, the external act, is no longer simply a reflection or pronouncement of European culture, or the pride of belonging to the oriental origins of the West. Here we have the unique means to preserve the humanity and the personality of man. This agency teaches us true humanism, not in the improvisation of a few geniuses with no past but through the whole breadth of experience amassed over thousands of years, which has remained original throughout the course of history.

Judaism will certainly not be able to seduce a mature humanity, and the idea of proselytism is not part of its style: it does not assume its responsibilities only in order to suggest immediately that others share them. But men who persist in resisting dissolution cannot remain indifferent and useless to their contemporaries!

The material efforts demanded by Jewish education, the necessity of attracting teachers and training them in every way possible, echoes like an impossible demand for those who know the difficulties attached to the maintenance of what already exists. But these are efforts that are now necessary to save Man.

We have the opportunity, as present-day Jews, to retain the memory of having had Jewish ancestors, and the memory of the memory of their wisdom, which is henceforth necessary not as a supplement to education, but as a basis for education. For once, the hours of Jewish education are not doubling anything. We must be able to reply to what children and adolescents are sometimes obliged to hear in the name of freedom – not with slogans, but with a culture based on a Word which through its elevation can be called the Word of God. We must return to it for everyone. And ecumenism seems to us to be a key idea, not because it allows us to be recognized at our level by the Christian but because, when we have been brought back to the Law, we work for our Christian brothers.

VII

I can hear, ladies and gentlemen, the objection being raised in your minds. Does not turning towards Jewish education and Jewish teaching in order to save the ultimate consequences implied in the idea of freedom involve, in concrete terms, rejoining the forces of conservatism and the retrogressive morality of the family, work and the Fatherland, in which the name of freedom is not even pronounced? Can we ignore the fact that, just as for some law equals repression, for others freedom means subversion?

We must ask if Jewish education has ever raised violent people. Has it asked anyone to believe in a violence devoid of justice, the violence of a simple will to power which is now taught as though it were an example of wisdom and remains horrible, whatever embellishment and adornment we give to such a seductive notion?

The war against Amalek, a symbol with which Judaism thinks of war, draws all its power from resistance and elevation. But is it Judaism which has perpetuated the war within the war waged on war? Has its humanism been able to remain content with the peace of the conqueror? Has it ever ceased to be the humanism of patience?

Has it ever eliminated the vanquished from history? In the symbol of the suffering servant we find all the suffering that demands justice until the end of time, a justice beyond the triumph of the triumphant, and their conversion at the eleventh hour to Good is the optimism of their triumph.

It is not to the moral Order repressing freedom, veiling truth, and fleeing real reality that our present-day Judaism makes appeal. Its vocation is Jewish education, with its unique exposure of the nerve points of existence as practised by prophetism, which did shy away from scandal and loved the light, and whose questioning virtue has been perpetuated in the Talmud, the basis of all Jewish education. Has prophetism ever retreated in the face of the justice of the powerful and the reasons of State?

Has the Talmud ever disguised the sexual realities whose essence cannot all the same be reduced to the coarse information of the tract commented on by a teacher from Belfort?

Oh! I do not want to invoke the themes of sentiment and spirituality in love, nor of the platonic love that should crown love. I shall not hit you with humanism, even though we should not neglect all the dimensions raised by these themes! But I think that sexuality at the rigorously sexual level is in essence tragic and ambiguous, by which I mean enigmatic. Is knowledge, with its impassive *logos*, ever able to match a reality that, with its physiological modalities, breaks the equanimity of consciousness and overwhelms it, shattering, with this traumatism, the concepts that should enclose and illuminate it?

To speak chastely of these unchaste realities is not a problem of simple decency, and it is a discourse that remains to be found. Has not the Talmud, through the problems of Law, through the question: *What must be done?*, managed to approach this 'unheard-of' style?

Jewish education is the conviction that a limit must be imposed on the interiorization of principles of conduct, that certain inspirations must become gestures and rituals. There is no frontier in the depths of human interiority that can arrest mental reserves when one sets out to 'spiritualize'; these reserves retreat into the very abyss of nihilism.

Jewish education does not rely on the ineffective brutality of constraints imposed by the totalitarian State in order to maintain a law within freedom and guarantee freedom through law. It associates generous ideas with the discipline that is a prerequisite to ritual, the distance taken with regard to the self and nature. These are practices carried out to please God only to the extent that they allow one to safeguard the human in man. Is this a particularism? Of course. But it is not some limitation or other that is brought to bear on national allegiances, civic duty and fraternity. It is a particularism with regard to doctrines, anthropologies, axiologies and theologies. It involves no separation from men.

Yes, a particularism. Like that of Abraham. The salvation of human universality perhaps once more requires paths that do not lead to the great metropolis. Tongues are once again confused. The great confusion of language is the great inversion of concepts. The age of Abraham has returned: one must accept obedience personally [*pour son compte*] and not take account of believers [*sans compter les fidèles*]. This personal acceptance is not egoist, nor is the other mode of existence for itself [*pour soi*]: the withdrawal into itself [*en soi*] which the Jewish people achieves through the State of Israel.

VII
SIGNATURE

'The language that tries to be direct and name events fails to be straightforward. Events induce it to be prudent and make compromises. Commitment unknowingly agglomerates men into parties. Their speech is transformed into politics. The language of the committed is encoded.'

'Who can speak clearly about current events? Who can simply open his heart when speaking about men? Who shows them his face?'

'The person who uses the words "substance", "accident", "subject", "object", and other abstractions ...'
(From a conversation overheard in the Underground).

Signature

The Hebrew Bible from the childhood years in Lithuania, Pushkin and Tolstoy, the Russian Revolution of 1917 experienced at eleven years of age in the Ukraine. From 1923 on, the University of Strasbourg, where Charles Blondel, Halbwachs, Pradines, Carteron and, later, Guéroult were teaching. Friendship with Maurice Blanchot and, through the teachers who were adolescents at the time of the Dreyfus Affair, a vision, dazzling for a newcomer, of a people who equal humanity and of a nation to which one can attach oneself by spirit and heart as much as by roots. A stay in 1928–29 in Freiburg, and an apprenticeship in phenomenology begun a year earlier with Jean Hering. The Sorbonne, Léon Brunschvicg. The philosophical avant-garde at the Saturday soirées of Gabriel Marcel. The intellectual, and anti-intellectualist, refinement of Jean Wahl and his generous friendship, regained after a long captivity in Germany; regular conferences since 1947 at the Collège Philosophique which Wahl founded and inspired. Director of the one-hundred-year-old *Ecole Normale Israélite Orientale*, training teachers of French for the schools of the *Alliance Israélite Universelle du Bassin Méditerranéen*. Daily communication with Dr Henri Nerson, frequent visits to M. Chouchani, the prestigious – and merciless – teacher of exegesis and of Talmud. Annual conferences, since 1957, on Talmudic texts[1] at colloquia of the French Jewish Intellectuals. Thesis for the Doctor of Letters degree in 1961. Professorship at the University of Poitiers, from 1967 on at the University of Paris-Nanterre, and since 1973 at the Sorbonne. This disparate inventory is a biography.

It is dominated by the presentiment and the memory of the Nazi horror.

Husserl brought a method to philosophy.[2] It consists in respecting the intentions which animate the psychic and the modalities of *appearing* which conform to these intentions, modalities which characterize the diverse beings apprehended by experience. It consists in discovering the unsuspected *horizons* within which the real is apprehended by representative thought but also apprehended by concrete, pre-predicative life, beginning with the body (innocently), beginning with culture (perhaps less innocently). To hold out one's hands, to turn one's head, to speak a language, to be the 'sedimentation' of a history – all this *transcendentally* conditions contemplation and the contemplated. In showing that consciousness and represented Being emerge from a non-representative 'context', Husserl sought to contest that the place of Truth is in Representation. The 'scaffoldings' which require scientific constructions never become useless, if one is careful about the meaning of these edifices. Ideas transcending consciousness do not separate themselves from their genesis in the fundamentally temporal consciousness. In spite of his intellectualism and his conviction about the excellence of the West, Husserl has thus brought into question the Platonic privilege, until then uncontested, of a continent which believes it has the right to colonize the world.

Heidgegger used the phenomenological method to turn, beyond objectively known and technically approached entities, towards a situation that would be the condition for all others; that of the apprehension of the Being of these entities: ontology. The Being of these entities is not in turn another entity; it is neutral but it illuminates, guides and orders thought. It calls to man and almost creates him.

Is the Being of being, which is not in turn a being – phosphorescence, as Heidegger has it?

Here is the path taken by the author of this book: an analysis which feigns the disappearance of every existent – and even of the *cogito* which thinks it – is overrun by the chaotic rumbling of an anonymous 'to exist', which is an existence without existents and which no negation manages to overcome. *There is* – impersonally – like *it is raining* or *it is night*.[3] None of the generosity which the German term *'es gibt'* is said to contain revealed itself between 1933 and 1945. This must be said! Enlightenment and meaning dawn only with the existents rising up and establishing themselves in this horrible neutrality of the *there is*. They are on the path which leads from existence to the existent and from the existent to the Other, a path which delineates time itself.[4]

Time must not be seen as 'image' and approximation of an immobile eternity, as a deficient mode of ontological plenitude. It articulates a mode of existence in which everything is always revocable, in which nothing is definitive but everything is yet to come, in which even the present is not a simple coincidence with itself, but is always an imminence. This is the situation of consciousness. To have consciousness is to have time, it is to come before nature, in a certain sense not yet to have been born. Such a wrenching away is not a lesser being, but is the *manner* of the subject. This manner is the power of rupture, the refusal of neutral and impersonal principles, the refusal of Hegelian totality and of politics, the refusal of art's bewitching rhythms.[5] It is the power of speech, freedom of speech, without a sociology or a psychoanalysis establishing itself behind the spoken word, in order to seek the place of this word in a system of references and so to reduce it to something which it did not mean. From this cames the power to judge history instead of awaiting its impersonal verdict.[6]

But time, language and subjectivity do not only presuppose a being which tears itself away from totality; they also assume one which does not encompass it. Time, language and subjectivity delineate a pluralism and consequently, in the strongest sense of this term, an experience: one being's reception of an absolutely other being. In the place of ontology – of the Heideggerian comprehension of the Being of being – is substituted as primordial the relation of a being to a being, which is none the less not equivalent to a rapport between subject and object,[7] but rather to a proximity, to a relation with the Other [*Autrui*].[8]

The fundamental experience which objective experience itself presupposes is the experience of the Other. It is experience *par excellence*. As the idea of the Infinite goes beyond Cartesian thought, so is the Other out of proportion with the power and freedom of the I. The disproportion between the Other and the self is precisely moral consciousness. Moral consciousness is not an experience of values, but an access to external being: external being is, *par excellence*, the Other. Moral consciousness is thus not a modality of psychological consciousness, but its condition. At first glance it is even its inversion, since the freedom that lives through consciousness is inhibited before the Other when I really stare, with a straightforwardness devoid of trickery or evasion, into his unguarded, absolutely unprotected eyes. Moral consciousness is precisely this straightforwardness. The face of the Other puts into question the happy spontaneity of the self, this joyous *force which moves*. In a feeling of humanity stretched to the extreme, the crowd in *War and Peace* to which Count Rostropchin delivered up Vereshchagin hesitates to do violence before his face, which reddens and turns pale, while the people remain silent at the end of *Boris Godunov* in face of the crimes committed by those in power.

In *Totality and Infinity*,[9] an attempt was made to systematize these experiences by opposing them to a philosophical thought which reduces the Other [*l'Autre*] to the Same and the multiple to the totality, making of autonomy its supreme principle.

But the adaptation of the Other [*l'Autre*] to the scale of the Same in the totality is not attained without violence, War, or Bureaucracy – which alienate the Same itself. Philosophy as love of truth aspires to the Other [*l'Autre*] as such, to a being distinct from its reflection in the I. It searches for its Law, it is heteronomy itself, it is metaphysical. According to Descartes, the I who thinks possesses the idea of the infinite: the otherness of the Infinite is not deadened in the idea, as is the otherness of finite things of which, according to Descartes, I can give an account through myself. The idea of the Infinite consists in thinking more than one thinks.

This negative description assumes a positive meaning which is no longer literally Cartesian: a thought which thinks more than it thinks – what is this, if not Desire? It is a desire which differentiates itself from the poverty of need. The Desired does not fill it, but deepens it.

The phenomenology of the relation with the Other suggests this structure of Desire analysed as an idea of the Infinite. While the *object* is integrated into the identity of the Same, the Other manifests itself by the absolute resistance of its defenceless eyes. The solipsistic anxiety of consciousness, seeing itself in all its adventures as captivated by itself, ends here. The privilege of the Other in relation to the I – or moral consciousness – is the very opening to exteriority, which is also an opening to Highness.

The epiphany of that which can present itself so directly, outwardly and eminently is *face*. The expressing of the face is language. The Other is the first intelligible. But the infinite in the face does not appear as a representation. It brings into question my freedom, which is discovered to be murderous and usurpatory. But this discovery is not a derivation of *self-knowledge*. It is heteronomy through and through. In front of the face, I always demand more of myself; the more I respond to it, the more the demands grow. This movement is more fundamental than the freedom of self-representation. Ethical consciousness is not, in effect, a particularly commendable variety of consciousness.

The orientation towards the highness of the Other thus described is like a grading in being itself. The above does not indicate a turning into nothingness [*néantisation*] but a 'more than being', better than the happiness of the social relation. Its 'production' would be impossible without separation, which cannot be reduced to a dialectical counterpart of the Relation with the Other, for the dialectic of separation and union is already played out only with a totality. The principle of separation is provided not by the unhappiness solitude already turned towards the Other, but by the happiness of enjoyment. From this point on, it becomes possible to sustain a pluralism which is not reduced to a totality.

The Other, revealing itself by its face, is the first intelligible, before cultures and their alluvions and allusions. This is to affirm the independence of ethics in relation to history. Showing that the first significance arises in morality, in the quasi-abstract epiphany of the face, which is stripped of every quality – absolute – absolving itself of cultures, means tracing a limit to the comprehension of the real by history and rediscovering Platonism.

It has been possible to present, after *Totality and Infinity*, this relation with the Infinite as irreducible to 'thematization'. The Infinite always remains a 'third person' – 'He' – in spite of the 'You' whose face concerns me. The Infinite affects the I without the I's being able to dominate it, without the I's being able to 'assume' through the *arché* of the *Logos* the unbounded nature of the Infinite thus *anarchically* affecting the I, imprinting itself as a trace in the absolute passivity, prior to all freedom, showing itself as a 'Responsibility-for-the-Other' to which this affection gives rise. The ultimate sense of such a responsibility consists in thinking the I in the absolute passivity of the *Self* – like the very act of *substituting* oneself for the other [*l'Autre*], of being his *hostage*,[10] and in this substitution not only *being otherwise* but, as freed of the *conatus essendi, otherwise than being*. The ontological language which *Totality and Infinity* still uses in order to exclude the purely psychological significance of the proposed analyses is henceforth avoided. And the analyses themselves refer not to the *experience* in which a subject always thematizes what he equals, but to the *transcendence* in which he answers for that which his intentions have not encompassed.

Notes

I Beyond Pathos

Ethics and Spirit

1. André Latreille and André Siegfried, *Les forces religieuses et la vie politique. Le catholicisme et le protestantisme* (Paris, Colin, 1951).
2. Ibid., pp. 146–47.
3. The ecumenist concerns of Pope John XXIII seem to indicate a new reversal of this tendency.
4. We owe to Eric Weil's great thesis – whose philosophical importance and tenacity of logic will become crucial – the systematic and vigorous use of the term violence as the opposite of discourse (see *Logique de la philosophie* [Paris, Vrin, 1951]). We, however, give it a different meaning, as we have already shown in our article in *Revue de métaphysique et de morale*, February–March 1951, where we used the term.

A Religion for Adults

1. Talk given in 1957 at the Abbey of Tioumliline in Morocco, during several days' study on education.
2. Plotinus, Enneades, VI, 9–11, quoted in Gandillac, *La Sagesse de Plotin*.

Being a Westerner

1. Léon Brunschvicg, *De la Vraie et de la Fausse Conversion, suivi de la Querelle de l'Atheisme* (Paris, Presses Universitaires de France). [Page numbers after extracts refer to this volume.]

II Commentaries

Messianic Texts

1. In a recent article published in *Eranos*, Mr Scholem, evincing an admirable historical science and a remarkable intuition in the systematic meaning uncovered in the texts studied (an intuition that sometimes fails other historians), distinguishes between apocalyptic messiansim, which is above all popular in form, and the rationalist

messianism of the rabbis, which culminates in the famous page on the messianic eras which Maimonides gives in his Mishnah Torah at the end of the chapter relating to the laws of political power. Not everything has been said, however, as Scholem sometimes seems to think, on the subject of the rationalist nature of this messianism – as if rationalization meant only the negation of the miraculous and as if, in the realm of the spirit, we could abandon one set of values without setting other values in motion. It is this positive meaning of the messianism of the rabbis that I want to show in my commentary.

2. The suffering itself is important not for its powers of expiation, but because it is a sign of fidelity and the vigilance of consciousness (Baba Mezia, 84b).

III Polemics

Have you Reread Baruch?

1. Sylvain Zac, *Spinoza et l'interprétation de l'écriture* (Paris, Presses Universitaires de France, 1965). This book was presented in 1964 as a complementary thesis for the degree of Doctor of Letters. His principal thesis, *L'idée de vie dans la philosophie de Spinoza*, is equally a remarkable work. Let us also bring to the attention of readers interested in the history of Jewish thought the little volume by Zac on Maimonides in the Seghers collection, 'Philosophes de tous les temps'.

2. The numbers in parentheses refer to the pages of Zac's book.

3. For example: Spinoza's political ideal would have been superimposed on the Jewish State during the era of Judges; the very path of justice remains the impassable base of political life; Moses' decalogue is the Word of God, which has never been contradicted, but the prophets who make their teaching conform to the Law of Moses preach this word as the religion of the Fatherland; the patriotism of the Hebrews due to love and not the fear of God (p. 108); the books of the New Testament do not differ from the Old; Judaism as a State religion, Christianity as an individual's religion (p. 101), but Christian individualism has remained a pure pretension (p. 103). On this point, did Bergson have other teachers than Spinoza in order to forget the entire preceding point?

4. Even Spinoza's philosophy must not guide the reading of the Bible, the intelligibility of which is absolutely not of the same order as philosophy. In a very lovely final chapter, Zac shows that Spinoza could not restrain himself from offering his exegesis in the spirit of his philosophy. In the same way it is true that even the Scripture interpreted by the Scripture cannot do without philosophy. Philology is not possible without philosophy.

5. The Talmud's unbridled form does not express, as the profane who are quick to judge often think, the chaos of a disordered complication. The incessant seething mass that envelops the person who throws himself into it transcribes a way of thinking that is refractory to the always premature schematization of its object. Rabbinical commentary breaks and pulverizes what still seemed solid and stable in the first movement of the discussion. This is a sense of reason which never lapses into the virtual, a reason that runs the length and breadth of reality in multiple attitudes that retain the innumerable aspects of the world. No simple dialectical rhythm can scan this teeming plurality which plays with space and time and historical perspectives. In addition, one cannot separate these texts from the living study in which this frightening dynamism is reflected and amplified. The fact that Spinoza was not familiar with this kind of Talmud world is obvious. In our day, we need to have made the acquaintance of an exceptional teacher to divine its secret. In spite of the precision of his references to the Jewish sources and his rigour as a historian – and this is my only reservation on this point – Zac does not seem to have made this acquaintance. Taken out of the context of the talmudic discussions, the notions evoked are bloodless. A quotation from the Talmud cannot be made with the same method and aim that hold for the rest of literature (even biblical). It is as if one were quoting the Ocean.

6. The Word of God therefore opens up a dimension that is proper to the Spirit and like no other. We must not confuse it either with Philosophy or with Science or with Politics.

   Spinoza the rationalist would have seen this admirably. Philosophical systems, scientific and political doctrines can, depending on the age, bring souls to the Word. The Word remains independent while being able to attach itself to a doctrine for a while. The figure designated by such an innexion of the Word to the activities – which resound from the outset – of the intellect has been noted in a very ancient rabbinic text (Siphri, which comments on Numbers 10:8): all the sacred objects of the Tabernacle are passed on from generation to generation, except for the silver trumpets used to call together the people's assemblies and arouse the camp of Israel. These must be renewed.

   But a still young reflection confuses the Word with the cultural products of History and wants the Spirit to be gauged by their ringing and the breath that fills the wind instruments. To justify Judaism, the custodian of the Word, through psychoanalysis, Marxism or structuralism (why not through axiomatics?) is to close oneself to something that exists without beating a drum about it or blowing its own trumpet, and by not remaining attentive to the latest tune; to condemn oneself to becoming religiously deaf, and no longer hearing 'the voice of fine silence'. In Israel, you have to know how to listen. We must not forget that a gathering in turn conditions dialogues, confrontations and 'round tables'.

7. André Amar, in a remarkable article ('Les deux poles de la science contemporaine', *Science et l'enseignement des Sciences*, 36 [1965], 10–19) showed that science does not think the world (even if Amar thought to contrast such weight and calculations to the philosophy of Heidegger).

Persons or Figures

1. Paul Claudel, *Emmaüs* (Paris, Gallimard).

A Voice on Israel

1. Paul Claudel, *Une voix sur Israël* (Paris, Gallimard).

Poetry and the Impossible

1. We cannot cite them all, but let us mention in passing the contributions from C. Vigée and A. Chouraqui.

2. On the other hand, of course, for the Jew the Christian, seen as a missionary by the peoples, will remain the person who waters down and annoys Judaism; but, if he practises justice, he will also be proclaimed the *equal* of the High Priest.

The Name of a Dog

1. [*Translator's note*: *nom d'un chien* [name of a dog] is also in French a mild expletive (crikey!), and recognizably a polite version of *nom de Dieu* [in the name of God/bloody hell!].]

IV Openings

Jacob Gordin

1. An extract from this was published in *Evidences*, 21, edited by Nicolas Baudy.

Israel and Universalism

1. On a talk given by Father Daniélou on the common foundations of a Mediterranean civilization.

V Distances

From the Rise of Nihilism to the Carnal Jew

1. [*Translator's note*: literally 'in which everything was consummated'. Levinas is recalling Jesus's last words on the cross: 'it is finished', *'tout est consommé'* (John 19:30).]

Hegel and the Jews
1. Bernard Bourgeois, *Hegel à Frankfort au Judaïsme, Christianisme, Hégelianisme* (Paris, Vrin, 1970, 126 pp.).

VI Hic et Nunc

How is Judaism Possible?
1. [*Translator's note*: the days on which French school children do not go to school.]
2. [*Translator's note*: The Collins Revised Standard Version has been quoted. The French literally reads: 'Serve God with fear, and rejoice with trembling.']

Space is not One-dimensional
1. This is providing they do not close themselves to the strange things that happen in life, and do not persist in translating such experiences into a banal language – an action that can, we must admit, indicate the force of denial, and the suspicion that greets the phantasm, which we shall not treat with contempt. It is something that explains the desire for complete mimicry on the part of many French Jews, which we shall not judge, and which can have its own greatness.
2. A thought from which Mr Ikor, who does not know traditional Jewish culture, refuses to budge.
3. [*Translator's note*: Levinas is possibly recalling the closing lines of Baudelaire's poem 'Le Voyage', itself the final poem in the original 1858 edition of *Les Fleurs du Mal*.]

VII Signature

Signature
1. See *Quatre lectures talmudiques* (Paris, Editions de Minuit, 1968).
2. See *La théorie de l'intuition dans la Phénoménologie de Husserl* (Paris, Alcan, 1930 [Vrin, 1963]). Translated as *The Theory of Intuition in Husserl's Phenomenology*, by A. Orianne (Evanston, L, Northwestern University Press, 1973); *En découvrant l'existence avec Husserl et Heidegger* (Paris, Vrin, 1949 [2nd edn 1967]). Translation, in collaboration with G. Peiffer: Husserl, *Méditations cartésiennes* (Paris, Colin, 1930 [2nd edn Vrin]).
3. See *De L'Evasion* in *Recherches Philosophiques*, 1935–6; *De l'existence à l'existant*, (Paris, Fontane, 1947 [Vrin, 1973]). Translated as *Existence and Existents*, by A. Lingis (The Hague, Martinus Nijhoff, 1978).
4. See 'Time and the Other', in the *Cahiers du Collège Philosophique* (Paris, Arthaud, 1947; reissued as a book by Fata Morgana

[Montpellier, Fata Morgana, 1979]). Translated as *Time and the Other*, by R. A. Cohen (Pittsburgh, PA, Duquesne University Press, 1987); 'Maurice Blanchot et le regard du poète', *Monde nouveau*, March 1956, pp. 6–19.

5. 'La Réalité et son ombre', *Les Temps Modernes*, 38 (1948), pp. 771–89. Included in *Collected Philosophical Papers*, ed. Alphonso Lingis (Dordrecht, Martinus Nijhoff, 1987), pp. 1–13, and *The Levinas Reader*, ed. Seán Hand (Oxford, Blackwell, 1989), pp. 130–43.

6. See especially the first edition of this book, *Difficile Liberté* (Paris, Michel, 1963).

7. 'L'autre dans Proust', *Deucalion*, 2 (1947), pp. 117–23. Reprinted in *Noms propres* (Montpellier, Fata Morgana, 1976), pp. 149–56. Translated as 'The other in Proust', in *The Levinas Reader*, ed. Seán Hand (Oxford, Blackwell, 1989), pp. 160–65.
'Ethics and Spirit', pp. 3–10 in this book.
The atricles in *Revue de Métaphysique et de Morale*: (1) 'L'ontologie est-elle fondamentale?', LVI, 1, pp. 88–98; (2) 'Liberté et commandement', LVIII, 3, pp. 264–72; (3) 'Le moi et la totalité', LIX, 4, pp. 353–73; (4) 'La philosophie et l'idée de l'Infini', LXII, 3, pp. 242–53.

8. See the 2nd edn of *En découvrant l'existence avec Husserl et Heidegger*, especially the study entitled 'Langage et proximité'.

9. *Totalité et infini* (The Hague, Martinus Nijhoff, 1961; 2nd edn 1965, etc.). Translated as *Totality and Infinity. An Essay on Exteriority*, by A. Lingis (Pittsburgh, PA, Duquesne University Press, 1969).

10. See 'La trace de l'Autre' and 'Langage et proximité' in the 2nd edn of *En découvrant l'existence avec Husserl et Heidegger*, and 'La substitution', in *Revue philosophique de Louvain*, 66, no. 91, pp. 487–508, the central chapter of *Autrement qu'être ou au-delà de l'essence* (The Hague, Martinus Nijhoff, 1974), translated as *Otherwise than Being or Beyond Essence*, by A. Lingis (The Hague, Martinus Nijhoff, 1981). 'Substitution', included in *The Levinas Reader*, ed. Seán Hand (Oxford, Blackwell, 1989), pp. 88–125. See also on all these themes: *Humanisme de l'autre homme* (Montpellier, Fata Morgana, 1972), *Noms propres* (Montpellier, Fata Morgana, 1976), *Sur Maurice Blanchot* (Montpellier, Fata Morgana, 1975). See also 'Dieu et la philosophie', *Le Nouveau Commerce*, 30–31 (1975), pp. 97–128, incorporated into *De Dieu qui vient à l'idée* (Paris, Vrin, 1982), pp. 93–127. Translated as 'God and Philosophy', by R. A. Cohen and collected in *Collected Philosophical Papers*, ed. A. Lingis (Dordrecht, Martinus Nijhoff, 1987), pp. 153–73; and *The Levinas Reader*, ed. Seán Hand (Oxford, Blackwell, 1989), pp. 166–89.

Select Glossary of Names and Terms

For more detailed references, see the *Encyclopaedia Judaica*, edited by Cecil Roth (Jerusalem, Israel: Keter, 1971–2), 16 vols.

Aggadah. Those sections of the Talmud and *Midrash* devoted to ethical and moral teaching, as opposed to the legal sections of *Halakhah*.

Amalek. The first enemy Israel encountered after the crossing of the Sea of Reeds.

Amora. Speaker, interpreter. The plural, *Amoraim*, designates the rabbinic authorities responsible for the *Gemara*.

Baruch. The question 'Avez-vous relu Baruch?' refers to Baruch (or Benedictus) de Spinoza, but it also alludes to a saying of La Fontaine who, struck by the prayer of the Jews in the Book of Baruch, went about asking people: 'Have you read Baruch?' Consequently, the question is used proverbially to denote a sudden and striking discovery.

BCE. Before Common Era (or Before Christ).

Brunschvicg, Léon (1869–1944). French idealist philosopher who published the standard edition of Pascal's works.

Buber, Martin (1878–1965). Philosopher, theologian, Zionist thinker and leader. The basis of his philosophy lies in the primacy of the I–Thou relation.

CE. Common Era (or AD).

Chouraqui, André (1917–   ). Israeli author and public figure.

Claudel, Paul (1868–1955). French poet, playwright and diplomat, influenced by the Bible and the continuity of the Jewish people.

Cohen, Hermann (1842–1918). German philosopher who wrote on the 'correlation' between man and God.

Crémieux, Isaac Adolphe (1796–1880). French lawyer and statesman, whose Decree of 1870 granted the Jews of Algeria French citizenship *en bloc*.

Dreyfus, Alfred (1859–1935). Officer in the French Army, involved in a famous treason trial that had Jewish, humanitarian and political repercussions.

Espace vital. Literally, 'living space'. The term reflects the German word *Lebensraum*, often associated with Nazism, which refers to a territory believed by a people or State to be essential to its development and well-being. In using the term, Levinas restores a spiritual meaning to a biological and racist concept.

Fleg, Edmond (1874–1963). French poet, playwright and essayist, concerned with Judaism and the Jewish people.

Gemara. The traditions, discussions and rulings of the *Amoraim*.

Halakhah. The legal side of Judaism, as contrasted with *Aggadah*.

Halévy, Elie (1870–1937). French philosopher and historian. A believer in compromise, pessimistic about fascism.

Hanukkah ('Dedication'). An annual eight-day festival commencing on the 25th of Kislev (Christmas time in the Christian calendar).

Hillel (the Elder). The greatest of the sages of the Second Temple period.

Jankélévitch, Vladimir (1903–   ). French philosopher, interested in the metaphysics of time.

Kol Nidrei ('All Vows'). A declaration of annulment of vows which begins the evening service of the Day of Atonement.

Maimonides (1135–1204). The most illustrious rabbinic authority of the post-talmudic era.

Marcel, Gabriel (1889–1973). French Christian existentialist philosopher.

Marrano. Derogatory term for the New Christians of Spain and Portugal, who conformed in appearance to Christianity but retained in private their Jewish faith.

Mezuzah. Literally a 'doorpost' (Deuteronomy 6:9). A piece of parchment inscribed with the two passages Deuteronomy 6:4–8 and 11:13–21, placed in a small wooden or metal container and fixed to the upper right-hand doorpost as one enters.

Midrash. The discovery of meanings other than the literal one in the Bible.

Mishnah. Codification of Jewish law containing the basis of the oral Law traditionally given to Moses at Sinai.

Rosenzweig, Franz (1886–1929). German Jewish theologian.

Sanhedrin. The supreme political, religious and judicial body in Palestine during the Roman period.

Shalom Aleichem (1859–1916). Yiddish author and humorist.

Talmud. ('Learning'). Comprehensive term for *Mishnah* and *Gemara*.

Tannaim. Teachers of the oral Law.

Toynbee, Arnold (1889–1975). English philosopher of history, who sees in a healthy society a process of 'challenge and response'.

Wahl, Jean. French philosopher, associated with exis- tentialism.

Weil, Simone (1909–43). French philosopher, noted for the mystical strain of her writing, her social concerns and her rejection of Judaism.

Yad Vashem. The institution set up in Jerusalem to commemorate the victims of the Nazi Holocaust.

Yeshivah. Institute of talmudic learning.

Index

Difficult Freedom

Jankélévitch, V., 82, 89, 108, 162, 172, 173, 181
John XXIII, 296

Kant, I., 109, 115, 133, 191
Kierkegaard, S., 6, 118, 144, 184
Khrushchev, N. S., 205, 206
Klatzkine, J., 168

La Fontaine, J. de, 152
Latreille, A., 296
Lenin, V. I., 237
Leo XIII, 105
Lévi-Strauss, C., 201

Machiavelli, N., 147
Madaule, J., 130, 202
Maimonides, 15, 61, 111, 163, 169, 274, 297
Marcel, G., 44, 291
Marx, K., 237, 238
Mayakovsky, V. V., 185
Mendelssohn, M., 117, 274
Montesquieu, C-L. de Secondat, Baron de, 149

Nasier, A., 275
Néher, A., 163, 173
Nerson, H., 291
Newton, I., 47, 133
Nicholas of Lyra, 119
Nietzsche, F., 147, 186

Pascal, B., 44, 225, 247
Plato, 35, 109, 178, 209
Poliakov, L., 222
Pradines, M., 291
Proust, M., 301

Pushkin, A., 291

Rabelais, F., 275
Rachi, 17
Racine, J., 247
Reinach, A., 108
Renard, J., 128
Rosenzweig, F., 109, 157, 163, 181–201

Salvador, C., 109
Sartre, J-P., 212, 223, 225
Schelling, F. W. J. von, 181
Schuhl, P. M., 54
Seigfried, A., 3, 296
Simon, E., 196
Socrates, 112, 207, 233
Spinoza, B. de, 25, 106–10, 111–8, 184, 274, 297, 298
Steinberg, L., 222
Strauss, L., 111

Teresa, St., 6
Thales of Miletus, 187, 188
Thrasymachus of Chalcedon, 185
Tito, J. B., 206
Togliatti, P., 206
Tolstoy, L., 291
Toynbee, A., 54, 55

Vigée, C., 299
Voltaire, 140, 149

Wahl, J., 40, 47, 291
Weil, E., 201, 296
Weil, S., 97, 133–41, 144, 161

Zac, S., 111, 297, 298